PRINCE RUPERT
THE CAVALIER

PRINCE RUPERT IN LATER LIFE
Sir Peter Lely
National Portrait Gallery

PRINCE RUPERT
THE CAVALIER

BY

CLENNELL WILKINSON

Author of

"NELSON," ".BONNIE PRINCE CHARLIE"

ETC.

WITH

18 ILLUSTRATIONS

AND 4 MAPS

PHILADELPHIA

J. B. LIPPINCOTT COMPANY

LONDON

1935

PREFACE

THERE are in English history four or five men of action—not more—whose characteristic methods have so impressed themselves upon the public imagination that their names may be said to have 'passed into the language.' Even people who have read comparatively little about Nelson, for instance, understand perfectly well what is meant by the "Nelson touch" in naval warfare. Wellington's incomparable defensive methods—the thin red line of British infantry rising suddenly from behind the crest of the hill and blasting the head of the French column that has come gaily surging up the slope ("cheering like mad," as a British Tommy of the period put it)—are as much part of the man's character, and the English character, as his "Goddams." The name of Cœur de Lion has the same familiar ring, and the same kind of significance. But in the sense of passing into the language—becoming adjectival, so to speak—no name has acquired a more definite and popular meaning than that of Prince Rupert of the Rhine, the dashing cavalry leader of the Civil War. When our Victorian ancestors were at a loss to describe the ebullient methods of that headlong political orator the Earl of Derby they called him the "Rupert of Debate"—and every one knew at once what they meant.

One feels that there must have been real genius, and something really worth studying, in every one of these. The public is not deceived. None of these men was an advertiser in the modern sense of the word. They were outstanding types. Everything they did was in character —they could not help themselves. They became part of the English language because they typified some one part of the English character. It did not really matter that

5

some of them were foreigners. Rupert had certain qualities that have always appealed particularly to the English. He was a sportsman. He loved hunting and hawking, and nothing probably pleased him better in the course of the whole war than the graceful gesture with which the Earl of Essex, the Parliamentary general, returned to him his falcons and their falconer, which by chance had fallen into his hands.

But he was not a talker. He was as reticent as a Wellington or a Kitchener. But, unlike them, he was more than reticent—he was aloof. He was aloof not simply from the Court life in Charles II's reign (that was natural enough in a dour, saturnine old soldier, brought up to no other trade, and considerably senior in years to most of the courtiers), but he was aloof from the general life of the nation. He was a blunt soldier, and a soldier who had learned his soldiering abroad. He had been bred in the hard school of the Thirty Years War. He had it in his bones. The charge of ruthlessness, and even cruelty, so often brought against him in connexion with his famous cavalry raids rests upon a very slight foundation of fact when we come to examine it. Specific instances are few. But the point is that when he found it necessary to burn a few houses he would do it with a cold, professional thoroughness, without giving a thought to the feelings of the unfortunate English peasants who had lost their homes. It would never occur to him to apologize for any act which was a military necessity. He would no more regret it than the Germans regretted destroying the orchards and vineyards as they fell back to the Hindenburg Line in 1917. And who shall say how much the German military mentality of 1914 owed to the evil memory of the Thirty Years War? Rupert's mother was an Englishwoman, and his father would not be recognizable as a German type to-day. But in his attitude towards war Rupert was thus far German, that he had learned the business in Germany, in one of the cruellest of wars. And warfare was always the serious business of his life.

So he passes across the stage, a tall, swarthy, striking figure of a man, with his great Wellington nose and dark, flashing eyes, his curt speech and brisk, soldierly movements—not a man for making many friends, not even in his own country, and here inclined to draw into himself, eyeing rather askance the broad, open English faces of those around him, with their everlasting talk of "compromise" and "statesmanship," their dislike of any violent action, their habit of seeing both sides. He could understand caution—he showed it himself after Naseby and when he commanded at sea—but not circumlocution. In temperament he was Latin rather than German; his action was direct, logical, like his thoughts; he preferred a frontal attack to a turning movement. Such a man will inspire admiration in his colleagues, devotion in his troops; but he will also make enemies.

I am dealing with Rupert the Cavalier, as England knew him in the Civil War; not with Rupert the awkward courtier of the second half of the century, nor with Rupert the unexpectedly cautious admiral. This Rupert the Cavalier can best be understood by seeking to understand his methods as a cavalry leader. He was a soldier, and expressed his personality in soldiering, as an artist does in art, or a statesman in Acts of Parliament. That he happened also to have a natural gift for drawing is a mere accident. To emphasize it here would be as foolish as to explain Lord Balfour's politics in terms of his golf, or Disraeli's in the language of flowers. Soldiering was the form of self-expression which Rupert happened to have cultivated.

Pursuing that line of inquiry, I have found myself laying down the law on many technical points of military history, as to which I have no title to speak except an amateur's enthusiasm for the subject. It would be interesting to get a professional soldier's point of view, for instance, on Rupert's shock tactics. In the meantime I have tried to protect myself by sticking closely to the facts, as stated by the original authorities, and avoiding any kind of guessing. This was, on the whole, a well-documented war. There are the Thomason Tracts in the British Museum, a unique collection of contemporary journalism, dealing with almost every aspect of the war. There is Warburton's monumental record of *Prince Rupert and the Cavaliers*, compiled from Rupert's private papers, now unfortunately dispersed. There are the Domestic State Papers, the Clarendon State Papers, the Carte Papers, the Bromley Letters, the Lansdowne Manuscripts, and many other sources of information too numerous to mention. Clarendon's great history flourishes serenely under the withering eye of the modern microscope; and Bulstrode, Whitelocke, Walker, and others may be trusted up to a point. Among modern authors Miss Eva Scott's *Rupert, Prince Palatine* is something more than merely useful. But I have spent nearly all my time with the original authorities. As Thomas Carte says, in the introduction to his own very valuable collection of contemporary correspondence of the Civil War period,

> Letters wrote in the scene and at the time of actions and negotiations, especially when wrote by persons present at those actions and employed in those negotiations, are with reason deemed the most proper means of obtaining, and conveying down to posterity, just and authentic accounts of the transactions to which they relate.

That seems to be indisputable.

C. W.

CONTENTS

ILLUSTRATIONS

MAPS

CHAPTER I: RUPERT LE DIABLE

THERE was a scene of wild alarm in the courtyard of the royal palace at Prague. Courtiers and ladies-in-waiting, lackeys and scullions and high officials, all jostling each other as they ran, emerged from every doorway carrying armfuls of their private belongings. In the courtyard was a confusion of plunging horses, perspiring grooms, and carriages into which the refugees hurriedly climbed. There was a great shouting and cracking of whips, and that pale, tense look of fear on every face. Each vehicle, as it was got ready, was driven out upon the highroad, and the horses' heads turned northward, towards Brandenburg and safety. For this was the flight of a court—a hasty exodus of the women and children and all the men of peace, diplomatists, lawyers, masters-of-ceremonies, secretaries, and so forth, before the peremptory sword of the soldier.

It was a scene that was to become common enough before the Thirty Years War had run its course. But now, in the early stages of that mighty conflict, it affected men's nerves. It was altogether too much for Frederick, the "Winter King" of Bohemia and Elector Palatine, who had just lost the famous battle of the White Mountain outside the walls of Prague. He was prostrate—moaning over his shattered hopes. Even when the news arrived that the victorious Imperialists were at the gates, and had allowed only eight hours' grace, he could not rouse himself. It was his English wife, the daughter of James I, who had given the necessary orders for flight. And now that flight had become an undignified panic, a fittingly inglorious end to Frederick's brief three weeks of play-acting as the self-appointed champion of Protestant Germany against the Imperial power.

Nearly all the carriages were gone. Even the Queen herself had left, shedding bitter tears as she was carried jolting along the Brandenburg road. Baron d'Hona, the King's chamberlain, was to follow on horseback. He was now taking a last look round. As he passed through the royal apartments, silent and deserted, but showing on every side the signs of hasty flight, he was startled to see a baby lying on the floor. It was the young Prince Rupert, third son of the royal family, now about a year old (he was born on November 28, 1619). The child's nurse appears to have popped him down there while she went to look for something, and then to have forgotten him entirely! The horrified official snatched up the baby in his arms and dashed downstairs. He was just in time to overtake the last of the carriages as it drove out through the gates. Young Rupert was shown to his seat with singularly little ceremony; in fact, we have it on contemporary authority that the chamberlain "threw" him in. The other occupants of the vehicle never so much as noticed his presence! But the ill-used child was somehow jolted into the 'boot' at the back, and, finding himself abominably uncomfortable—probably head downward amongst the luggage—set up a lusty roar. "Whatsoever he undertakes he doth it vigorously and seriously," wrote Sir Thomas Roe long afterwards; and the sound of that stentorian voice, which in later years was to ring across a score of battlefields, seems to have brought the terrified servants to their senses. They rescued the little Prince from the 'boot,' calmed his indignation, and took the first opportunity of transferring him to the arms of his royal mother, who, we must suppose (though there is no evidence of it), was beginning to feel anxious.

She had enough troubles of her own. It was a terrible journey. As they approached the northern mountains they found the roads covered with snow, so that the carriage could not move. Queen Elizabeth was obliged to step out and mount pillion behind one of the officers, a certain Ensign Hopton. In this ignominious fashion she rode into Brandenburg, and was given a chilly enough reception by her husband's brother-in-law, George William, Elector of Brandenburg, who, though a Protestant, was a politically minded person, and by no means anxious to start a quarrel with the Emperor. But Elizabeth was not without friends. Her father, King James, sent the English Ambassador to plead for her. And, indeed, the condition of this poor queen, a stranger in a strange land, broken by misfortune, and, by all accounts, one of the most attractive women of her time, was such as might appeal to the chivalry of any man. Her apparent neglect of Rupert is partially explained when we learn that she was daily expecting to give birth to another child. George William felt that he could not decently refuse hospitality. So he bundled the refugees into his rather dismal castle of Custrin, told them that the place was theirs, and left them to look after themselves. A few days later, on January 11, 1621, the harassed Queen gave birth to a fourth son. She commanded that he should be called Maurice, after the soldier Prince of Orange, because, as she remarked bitterly, he would obviously have to work for his living, and the military profession was the only one open to bankrupt princes.

Such was the tempestuous beginning of Rupert's tempestuous career. Wild alarms in the night, the clash of steel against steel, the trampling of horses' hoofs, and the terrified screams of his nurses—this was almost the first music that assailed his infant ears. Nor was there peace even yet. Six weeks after the birth of Maurice, George William informed his guests that they must go. The baby Maurice might remain behind in charge of his wife, the Electress, but that was all he would do for them.

The rest must leave at once. So Rupert and his mother found themselves out on the road again in the winter weather, still travelling northward, this time in the direction of Holland, where they hoped for a somewhat friendlier reception from the Prince of Orange, after whom brother Maurice had been tactfully named.

And there at last they found rest. Maurice of Orange, the Stadtholder, received them with open arms. He felt a special sense of responsibility for their welfare, since he was partly to blame for their misfortune. It is necessary to glance back a little. The Thirty Years War is always reckoned to have begun in May 1618, on that fatal day when the Emperor's representatives were thrown out of the window of the palace at Prague. No one realized its importance at the time. The humble little secretary who apologized to his master, Count Martinitz, for falling on top of him never dreamed of the appalling responsibility before the whole world and before the bar of history incurred by every actor in that famous scene. For at first the war was regarded as a mere local rebellion by the Bohemian Protestants against their Catholic Emperor and King. And such a character it did in fact retain up to the date when the rebels, finding themselves hard pressed, appealed to Rupert's father, Frederick, the Elector Palatine, offering to crown him King of Bohemia if he would come to Prague, their capital, and fight their battles for them.

We have just seen the end of that particular adventure in the courtyard of that same palace at Prague. But the end of the Thirty Years War was not yet. Invader after invader, Lutheran and Calvinist, Germans, Swedes, and Danes, entered the fray, attempting to recover Frederick's lost dominions—for the Palatinate also had gone in the general collapse. And when peace was finally signed in 1648, twenty-eight years after Rupert's upset in the 'boot,' the population of Germany is believed to have been reduced by about two-thirds,[1] some of her fairest cities were in ruins, hundreds of villages had disappeared, outside the walls of the great towns there was hardly a semblance of law and order, only pestilence and famine and such a widespread desolation as Western Europe had not known for centuries and has not seen since. Such were the effects of the "Winter King's" unhappy incursion; and such was the lurid background to the early military activities of his son Prince Rupert of the Rhine.

But our concern, for the moment, is with the Dutch Stadtholder's share in the matter. At the outset of his Bohemian adventure Frederick had received singularly little support from the Protestant Princes. They had hesitated—as well they might. Some of them had condemned his usurpation on moral grounds; others had doubted whether he, a Calvinist, could secure undivided loyalty from the Bohemian Protestants, who were Lutherans. As it turned out, these doubters were right. But the Prince of Orange had advised him to go on. It was with his encouragement and moral backing that Frederick and his family had gone to Prague. Now they were back on his doorstep, defeated, exiled, penniless, craving hospitality.

Prince Maurice rose to the occasion. He sent a mounted escort to meet them at Münster and conduct them to his capital, The Hague. On the way they picked up scattered members of their *entourage*, refugees from the battle of the White Mountain, courtiers from Prague who had got away before them, and their eldest son and heir, Henry, who was waiting for them at Emerich. It was April now, and they came to The Hague in bright spring weather, with quite a following behind them, and

---

[1] In Frederick's own country, the Palatinate, the population decreased from 500,000 in 1618 to 48,000 in 1648.

their spirits considerably raised, to be received with royal honours, to be installed in a handsome mansion—with borrowed furniture, it is true, and dependent upon grants from England and Holland to pay their ordinary household bills, but still with a home of their own.

It was in this Dutch home that Rupert first became aware of himself as a sentient human being, a contestant in the battle of life. It had been very much of a battle so far. His first playmate was his eldest brother Henry, the heir to the Electorate—for the second son, Charles, and the daughter, Elizabeth, had been sent to join Maurice at Berlin. Henry was his father's favourite, a gallant, high-spirited lad, fond of horses and outdoor sports, the repository of the exiled Elector's last hopes for the restoration of the family fortunes. He was fond of his little brother Rupert, and often mentioned him in his letters to grandfather James of England and other members of the family.

It is to Henry that we owe our knowledge of the first recorded utterance of Prince Rupert, who was then nearly three years old. "Praise the Lord!" said the child, speaking in Bohemian. Taking Rupert's career as a whole, it can hardly be contended that this was a characteristic remark. But it pleased his brother Henry enormously; and, no doubt, it pleased the older members of the family, to whom Henry was quick to report it. "Praise the Lord!" There is a significance in the ejaculation. It has the authentic Puritan ring; it should be spoken through the nose. Rupert was to live to see an English Puritan named Praise-God Barebones [1] dominating the Parliament at Westminster.

Rupert's father was a strict Calvinist. When he was

[1] Barebones was said to have had two brothers, named respectively Christ-came-into-the-world-to-save Barebones and If-Christ-had-not-died-thou-hadst-been-damned Barebones (usually shortened into Damned Barebones).

PRINCE RUPERT, AGED TWELVE
Van Dyck
Photo Bruckmann, Munich

King in Prague he had destroyed the ornaments in the churches with the iconoclastic enthusiasm of a Cromwell. It had disgusted his Lutheran subjects, and was one of the chief reasons why they failed to rally to him in his hour of need. But though he desecrated the churches, he would have shot anyone who dared to spit upon his crown. That was an important difference between the Puritanism of Frederick, the Elector, and of Barebones, the Fleet Street leather-seller.

Rupert and his brother Henry were presently transferred to a new house at Leyden, given to the family by the Stadtholder; and they were joined there by their brothers and sister from Berlin, and later by still younger members of the family, born at The Hague. The family was now in comparatively comfortable circumstances, but the upbringing of the children was conducted on the severest lines. They attended divine service twice every day all through the week, and on Sundays had to write out a summary of the sermon after their return from church. They were carefully instructed in religious controversy, and were made to learn by heart the Heidelberg Catechism of the Reformers—though the youngest sister, Sophie,[1] assures us that she never understood a word of it! Their other lessons—history, geography, languages, and so forth—were numerous; but they seem to have been allowed four hours every day in which they might do as they pleased.

Their brand of Puritanism, however, was not incompatible with a considerable zest for the good things of life. They lived with some ceremony and were waited upon,

---

[1] She lived to become the Electress Sophia of Hanover, and, as such, to supply England with a new line of kings in place of the Stuarts, for whom Rupert and Maurice had fought. Some amusing translations from her memoirs, *Memoiren der Herzogin Sophie* (*Preussischen Staatsarchiven*, Bd. 4), will be found in Miss Eva Scott's *Rupert, Prince Palatine* (Constable, 1899).

and dressed to suit their station. Ready money was often so short that they were unable to pay the baker, and Sophie remarks bitterly that "there was nothing to eat at our Court but pearls and diamonds." Yet dinner was always a great occasion. The dinner hour was 11 A.M. Sophie writes:

> On entering the dining-room I found all my brothers drawn up in front, with their gentlemen and governors posted behind in the same order, side by side. I was obliged to make a very low curtsy to the princes, a slighter one to the others, another low one on placing myself opposite to them, then another slight one to my governess, who, on entering the room with her daughters, curtsied very low to me. I was obliged to curtsy again on handing my gloves over to their custody, then again on placing myself opposite my brothers, again when the gentlemen brought me a large basin in which to wash my hands, again after grace was said, and, for the ninth and last time, on seating myself at table. Everything was so arranged that we knew on each day of the week what we were to eat, as they do in convents. On Sundays and Wednesdays two divines or two professors were always invited to dine with us.

It must have been an uncomfortable situation when the baker had refused to send the bread!

Rupert, meanwhile, was developing a strongly marked character of his own. The early promise of extreme piety seems hardly to have been fulfilled: we hear of no further words of praise from his lips since that first utterance in his cradle. We do know, however, that he took to military affairs like a duck to water, quickly learning how to use pike and musket, so that "at eight years of age he handled his arms with the readiness and address of an experienced soldier."[1] In his study of the art of fortification and military architecture generally—a formidable affair in those days, governed by many strict rules—he was given the assistance of "the best masters," and made rapid

[1] Warburton, *Rupert and the Cavaliers*, vol. i, p. 449.

progress, the result, obviously, of a natural gift. He could always make a neat and convincing drawing, whether of a human figure or a counterscarp. His mind had the strictly practical bent of a born man of action. He and his eldest brother, Henry, had been entered at Leyden University; but Rupert could never be induced to exert himself in the study of the classics. "He conceived the languages of the times would be to him more useful, having to converse afterwards with divers nations." Having come to this conclusion, and having learned just enough Latin to understand a tag or a priest's blessing, he attacked modern languages with his usual fierce energy, and at the age of thirteen was able to make himself understood all over Europe. To their mother the Palatinate children appear to have talked only English; among themselves French. It was all the same to Rupert, who would have been equally at home with German, Spanish, Italian, or Dutch.

But his heart was always out of doors. Riding, fencing, and vaulting were part of his military training, and in them he soon excelled. Sometimes the young princes were allowed to go hunting, and their mother, the Queen, who had an English passion for this sport, would ride out from Rhenen, where she and her husband were now living, and join them. Warburton tells a good story (from Pyne's manuscript) of how on one such occasion Prince Rupert was found to be missing. Upon search being made, the legs of a man were seen projecting from a fox's earth. A strong pull brought to light the Prince's tutor; another, and the Prince himself appeared, considerably dishevelled; then came the Prince's favourite dog, which his Highness held firmly by the legs; and finally a snarling fox, the origin of the whole adventure. The dog had seized the fox from behind and disappeared with it into the hole; the Prince, anxious for his favourite's safety, had dived in after them; and the tutor (a Mr Billingsby), who was just in time to witness the incident, had gallantly followed. Evidently the affair attracted some notoriety in Holland, for a drawing was made of it and "copies taken and dispersed abroad."

Rupert was growing up into a tall, swarthy, handsome youth of striking appearance. His was a healthy family, and most of his brothers were tall and athletic like himself; but Rupert, according to his youngest sister, had a double share of health and strength. All his early portraits emphasize his extraordinary good looks. He had a prominent, hawk-like nose. It is the sort of feature which in later life is apt to become more impressive than beautiful—as it did in Rupert's case. But it lends a charming touch of dignity and strength to a youthful face. Van Dyck painted him at the age of twelve, Honthorst a few years later, and, unless both of them have lied, he was one of the prettiest young gipsies that ever sat to a painter, his cheeks glowing darkly with health, a slumbering fire in his brown eyes. His significant nickname in the family was Rupert le Diable.

He now stood second in the succession. His eldest brother, Henry, the father's favourite, had met his death in a disaster which was at once tragic and slightly ridiculous—like the whole career of the unfortunate "Winter King." Father and son were going to Amsterdam to claim some money due to the family. To save expense they travelled by the ordinary passenger boat—a paltry economy which might surely have been avoided in the circumstances. The boat came into collision, and all on board were thrown into the sea. Frederick managed to swim to safety, but young Henry was drowned, calling vainly upon his father for help. Thus miserably perished the hope of the house, and Frederick's last joy in life went with him.

PRINCE RUPERT AS A YOUNG MAN
Gerard van Honthorst
Photo W. F. Mansell

Yet he had sons that any man might be proud of. The next in succession, and now the heir, was Charles Louis, a pleasant, curly-headed youth, with the family good looks, a family reputation for caustic wit, and an eye to the main chance, which was lacking in his younger brothers. He wore the lovelocks of the period with a courtly grace, and knew how to make strangers like him. In his mother's affections he stood easily first. Maurice, who was to become Rupert's inseparable companion, was tall, athletic, headstrong, rather slapdash—a sort of Rupert without the steel. Of Edward, the next brother, it may at any rate be said that he had a remarkable talent for adventure. And Philip was a recklessly brave young soldier, who might have risen to high command if he had not unfortunately fallen in action at Rhetel in 1650, fighting on the French side against Spain. Then there was a charming bevy of daughters, each with a character of her own.

In fact, a brilliant family. They had brains, courage, executive ability, high social gifts. If the boys were, perhaps, a little grim, a little lacking in the saving grace of humour (though Henry had it), that deficiency was more than made up for among the girls. We hear of family jokes, friendly rivalries in amateur theatricals, and a favourite game in which they pretended that the Palatinate had been suddenly restored to them and that they were all stopping the night at an inn on their way back to take possession of the lost domains. That not one of them ever rose to real greatness must surely be ascribed to accident. Every one had ability, and most had strong character and personality. The girls were great ladies, and the boys were men of mark. It may be that in no single member of the family (and particularly in none of the boys) were combined all those special qualities, lovable and unlovable, which make for complete success in life.

But one cannot help feeling that, with just a little luck, either Henry, Charles Louis, or Rupert himself might have achieved great things and written their names firmly across the history books. If Rupert alone lives in the popular memory to-day, it is rather for what he was and what he stood for than for anything he did.

Indeed, they were an unlucky family. Frederick, after the death of his eldest son, lived quietly with his wife at Rhenen in a small house to which they had retired for reasons of economy. He was stirred into a last burst of activity by the news of the invasion of Germany by Gustavus Adolphus, King of Sweden. The new Protestant champion swept all before him. He beat Tilly at Leipzig and pressed rapidly southward, capturing town after town and slaughtering the monks and the Catholic citizens as remorselessly as the Imperialists had slaughtered the Protestants. Soon he was in the Lower Palatinate itself, and in 1631 Frederick, with beating heart, set out to join him there. At first all went well. The exile was received in the Swedish camp with royal honours, and was allowed to accompany the great Gustavus in his triumphant progress southward. When Munich itself fell he found himself installed in the Emperor's own palace, from which his enemy had but recently fled. His prospects had never been better. He wrote cheerful letters to his wife, in one of which he speaks particularly of young Rupert, then about twelve years old:

> Je suis bien aise que Rupert est en vos bonnes graces, et que Charles fait si bien; certes ils me sont fort [? chers] tretous. Dieu me fasse si heureux de pouvoir vous bientot revoir! tretous!
>
> FREDERIC

Alas! his evil genius had not deserted him. Gustavus Adolphus seems to have formed a poor opinion of his statesmanship. Perhaps, as Harte suggests,[1] he was dis-

[1] *Gustavus Adolphus*, vol. i, p. 205.

gusted by Frederick's obstinate refusal to grant toleration to the Lutherans of Heidelberg. It was the old Calvinist bigotry which had helped to lose him his Bohemian throne. At any rate, Gustavus, though he continued to treat Frederick as his honoured guest, persistently postponed the formal act of restoring him to his old position. Frederick must have felt the slight. "Would to God," he wrote wearily to his wife, "that we had a little corner of the world in which we could live quietly and contentedly together! That is all the happiness I wish for." [1] He fretted and finally fell ill.

He was taken to Mainz, and lay there a long time, suffering from a slow fever. He was only thirty-six, in the full vigour of his manhood, and there seemed no reason why he should not recover. But he had never quite got over the death of his eldest son—it was said that the boy's cries for help still haunted him—and in November of that year (1632) came the news of the fatal battle of Lützen and the death of Gustavus Adolphus at the moment of victory. It was too much for Frederick. In that same month of November the unfortunate, futile "Winter King" followed the Protestant hero to the grave.

[1] *Bromley Letters*, p. 16.

CHAPTER II: THE FIRST VISIT TO ENGLAND

To the casual eye of the visitor life at Leyden went on much as before. Rupert and Charles Louis were doing well at the university, and the last time they ever saw their father was when he paid them a farewell visit on his way to Germany, and took the opportunity of attending the examinations and congratulating his sons upon their success. But there was an undercurrent of unrest, which increased after Frederick's death. Frederick had been an affectionate, indulgent parent, and the children were united in their love for him. His sudden disappearance unsettled them. Rupert in particular was straining at the leash.

The Queen's relations with her children have of late become a matter of some controversy. It used to be considered sufficient to describe her as an adoring and devoted mother (and devoted she certainly was); but the letters of her daughter Sophie and the acrimonious correspondence between herself and Charles Louis when he became Elector put rather a different face upon it. It is clear that her treatment of these high-spirited boys and girls was, to put it mildly, unusual. (But then the whole family was unusual.) Probably she disliked children. She would not even live at Leyden, but preferred to keep her own establishment at The Hague, and afterwards at Rhenen. "Her Majesty had her whole family brought up apart from herself," writes Sophie bitterly, "greatly preferring the sight of her monkeys and dogs to that of her children." Only when her daughters were grown up would she have them to live with her, and then she quarrelled with them one after the other. She admired and liked her elder sons, making a favourite first of Charles Louis, and afterwards, when he had ill-used her,

QUEEN ELIZABETH OF BOHEMIA
Gerard van Honthorst
Photo W. F. Mansell

of Rupert. But there was a curious lack of real maternal feeling, even in her letters to them. The younger sons, Edward and Philip, who do not seem to have interested her greatly, eventually put themselves beyond the pale, the one by running away with a Roman Catholic bride, the other by killing M. d'Epinay.

And mention of M. d'Epinay reminds us that monkeys and dogs were not the children's only rivals in their mother's affections. Elizabeth Stuart was not called "Queen of Hearts" and "Pearl of England" for nothing. Her miniature court at The Hague was always crowded; her personal charm attracted hundreds of volunteers to the Protestant cause; Christian of Brunswick took arms against the Emperor for her sake; Englishmen like Lord Craven devoted their lives to her service; and that admirable correspondent and wise diplomatist Sir Thomas Roe exchanged letters with her and wrote others about her which are among the best and liveliest authorities for this period. She was still a young and beautiful woman, with the Stuart power of inspiring devotion, and we cannot be surprised if, after her husband's death, some of her younger courtiers sought to transform themselves into lovers—with what success we cannot say. But it is certain that she was furiously angry when young Prince Philip, in a street fracas, dashed aside d'Epinay's sword, which had wounded him in the ribs, and, getting to close quarters with the Frenchman, stabbed him to the heart with a hunting knife. She was still more furious when she found all the rest of her children vehemently on Philip's side. The eldest daughter, Elizabeth, felt so strongly that she left home and would not return. Philip himself fled the country. It was two years before his mother could be persuaded to pardon him and allow him to return to The Hague.

But Elizabeth's devotion to the material interests of

her children, her anxious care for their upbringing and for the planning of their careers, was as remarkable as her indifference to their companionship. Long before the incident just recorded Rupert had broken away from home. It was obvious that he could not be tied to any woman's apron-strings; nor was Elizabeth herself the woman to desire it. He was growing up into a regular little fire-eater. Not only was his personal courage a matter of comment—"what affrights others animated him"—but it was noted that he thought and spoke of nothing but war, and that the only literature which seriously interested him was military history. "That wonderful affection for war," says one of his earliest biographers, "made the whole world judge he was born for it." [1]

When, therefore, in 1633, the new Stadtholder, Prince Henry (his brother Maurice having died), approached the Queen on Rupert's behalf with a request that the boy, who was now about fourteen years old, might be allowed to serve in the Dutch army in the ensuing campaign against Spain, she consented without much difficulty. Soldiering was to be Rupert's profession in life, and the earlier he set about learning it the better. But no sooner was he gone than she began worrying about him—a human touch, which must be recorded in her favour. It was not the enemy's bullets that she feared so much as the danger to his morals. He was still very young, and some one had been telling her disturbing stories about camp life. So she whistled him back to her side, and he returned with prompt docility; but he must have spoken to the Stadtholder, for the latter came again to his rescue and had him back in camp in a few weeks. He was present at the siege of Rhynberg by the Dutch, an operation quickly brought to a successful conclusion in strict accordance with the

[1] See Lansdowne MSS., 817, ff. 157–167.

book of the rules of seventeenth-century siege warfare. Rupert saw in it an apt illustration of what he had learned. And, no doubt, the fact that his first taste of war was a victory only increased his zest for the deadly game.

The victorious campaign of 1633 was celebrated at The Hague by a tournament—not, of course, a formal affair in the medieval manner (the time was past for that), but consisting of 'running at the ring' and similar martial exercises. It warmed the heart of Prince Henry of Orange to see so many gallant cavaliers from Northern Europe assembled at his court, and he recognized, no doubt, how much the occasion owed to the presence of the beautiful Queen of Bohemia, with her little *entourage* of admirers and her athletic sons. Rupert, by general consent, was the hero of the games. "The graceful air which accompanied all his actions was such as drew the eyes and hearts of all the spectators towards him." The ladies, in particular, seem to have been greatly stirred—it is the first record of Rupert's contact with the other sex—so that they "contended among themselves which should crown him with the greatest and most welcome glories." And, of course, there was one special lady, or so our chronicler would have us believe:

But one more eminent than all the rest, both in quality and beauty, would not that her esteem should be drowned in noises, or go along in the crowd of common admirers, and let our Prince see the sense she had of his worth.[1]

We are given no clue to the lady's identity, but it is clear that this was one of Rupert's great days.

He was back with the army again in 1635, this time serving with the Life Guards of the Prince of Orange, and following the example of that prince in learning every detail of the soldier's business, from the bottom to the

[1] Lansdowne MSS., 817, ff. 157–167.

top. In alliance with the French the Dutch besieged Tirlemont, which the French sacked horribly, Schenkenseyan, which made a stout resistance, and, finally, Louvain. Rupert was always well to the fore, "always for charging the enemy," and keenly appreciative of that strange elation of being under fire. But the Dutch officers had their orders, and "care was taken of him who took none of himself." And the siege of Louvain, which was now commenced, began after a time to be a little dull, even for the most enthusiastic young soldier.

At this juncture there came a suggestion from his mother, which—though he did not know it at the time—was to mark a turning-point in his career. She had recently sent her eldest son, Charles Louis, to England, on a visit to his uncle, King Charles I. She had hesitated to accept the invitation. Charles Louis had now passed his seventeenth birthday; he was his mother's favourite, and, as we have seen, a youth not lacking in social gifts. But there was a certain angularity in all these Palatine Princes, and their mother was well aware of it. She knew, too, that the modest establishment at Leyden, or even the Stadtholder's palace at The Hague, was but a poor preparation for the stately life of St James's, then one of the most brilliant courts in Europe. However, she let him go—though she wrote in mock alarm to Sir Harry Vane: "I fear damnably how he will do with your ladies, for he is a very ill courtier; I pray you desire them not to laugh too much at him, but to be merciful to him."

And the visit, after all, had been a great success. King Charles, who was always at his best on these occasions, received his nephew "extraordinarily kindly," and passed him on to his vivacious little French Queen, who gave the shy young Palatine an impulsive kiss. He was soon on good terms with the leading men about the Court, and Sir Thomas Roe, the old family friend, wrote home ecstatically to Elizabeth: "The Prince Elector is so sweet, so obliging, so discreet, so sensible of his own affairs, and so young as was never seen, nor could be seen in the son of any other mother." As a matter of fact, the young man was perhaps just a shade too "sensible of his own affairs." He thought of little else. While appearing to join carelessly in the Court festivities, he was really up to his neck in political intrigue.

There has been preserved an entertaining letter from Charles Louis to his mother, dated "Theobalds, 23 June, 1636," in which he retails the latest news. He begins with a story about the Polish Ambassador—a Catholic, and therefore an enemy—who was rumoured to have told Queen Elizabeth that the Archbishop of Canterbury (Laud) was really a Papist. Laud publicly taxed him with it; whereupon the Ambassador "was much out of countenance," explaining that he only said, "there were many [Papists] in England." We are left wondering who can have whispered the story to Laud, unless Charles Louis himself. The young Prince goes on to report that Strafford has just come over from Ireland and

> showeth a great deal of desire to serve us, in his professions to me; but there is none of them all but doth the same; yet I will believe nothing but that I see . . . all their comfort to me is to have patience, which is very unseasonable in this conjuncture of the affairs.

There are signs of growing disillusionment and ill-temper here. He continues:

> The plague increaseth yet at London, and the town is very void of company. Sir Thomas Rhoe is yet sick of the gout. Next week I will go to see him at his house, which is hard by Hampton Court.

The Queen now proposed to send Rupert over to join his brother in England, with a view to a long stay. But this time she was genuinely apprehensive of social disaster. Rupert le Diable was a tougher proposition, as she well knew, than the suave Charles Louis, and there is no hint of mockery in her warning to Vane, "I believe he will not trouble your ladies with courting them, nor be thought a very *beau garçon*," but she "hopes he will be welcome for blood's sake." In her heart she obviously thought him a young savage.

As for Rupert, he was not the kind of boy to bother about these things. He had heard about England all his life, and had rather liked the silent Englishman who came occasionally to visit his mother and father at The Hague. He could even vaguely remember the magnificent Duke of Buckingham, who had won the heart of his eldest brother, Henry, when he came to see the exiled family, and had proposed to become Henry's father-in-law—until Felton's knife cut short all his schemes. England, he knew, had been a friend in need to his family: his uncle, Charles, had on one occasion even pawned his own jewels to send them a remittance. Now he was to visit and see for himself this foggy island in the grey North Sea, which had turned out so many gallant adventurers after his own heart and that beautiful mother whom he silently admired all his life. He accepted the offer with alacrity, and landed in England on a typical December day, of which the best that can be said is that it was probably not quite so cold as Holland, if definitely more unpleasant. He went to Court, and made his bow to the King and Queen, and stared about him rather defiantly—and suddenly found that he liked the look of Englishmen and English things.

And then the unexpected happened. England liked Rupert as much as Rupert liked England. He was a sportsman to the core, a hard-riding, hard-living, reckless kind of lad, plain and direct of speech, hearty and adventurous, totally unselfconscious—a type that England never could resist. Charles Louis suddenly disappeared from the picture. Rupert was the popular favourite everywhere. Queen Henrietta Maria adored him, and even the quiet, deliberate King regarded his impetuous career with affectionate indulgence. "His Majesty," wrote Sir Thomas Roe, "takes great pleasure in his [Rupert's] unrestfulness, for he is never idle; in his sports serious, in his conversation retired, but sharp and witty when occasion provokes him." In fact, no great talker, but with a keen edge to his tongue. Such men may make enemies in later life, but no English reader will be surprised to hear that Rupert was preferred in England to his plausible, diplomatic brother.

For Rupert a new world was opening. In August 1636 he visited Oxford with his brother, to be invested with the honorary degree of Master of Arts. The King and Queen went with them, and the two boys drove through the streets in the royal coach, listening to the cheers of the populace, and watching with eager interest the stately English ceremonial each time the coach was stopped for the King to receive some address or listen to a Latin oration. Next day, in the parish church of St Mary the Virgin, Rupert stood up before Convocation and put on his new scarlet robe; and afterwards went with his brother to St John's College, where they wrote their names in the buttery book—for they were entered at this college as a compliment to their good friend Archbishop Laud. Then a decorative play, performed by the students, with mechanical stage devices such as never had been seen before. And so back to London— and to more happy days in the sparkling society of the little French Queen and her ladies, more meetings with Laud (who was always so kind to him) and Strafford and others, more visits with the King to his wonderful picture galleries—in fact, a general widening of outlook, which was exactly what Rupert needed.

The sounds of camp life—the rattle of musketry, the screams of the civilians when the French sacked Tirlemont—must have seemed strangely far away as he walked through the royal apartments at Hampton Court or Windsor beside that diminutive little gentleman his uncle, whom he already overtopped by several inches. But there was, most certainly, both reverence and affection in his eyes as he glanced down occasionally at that comely head wherein were nearly all the higher intellectual qualities, except that kind of shrewdness which we call statesmanship. There is earlier evidence than this of Rupert's interest in art. But here, in these long galleries, where one of the finest European collections was being rapidly accumulated by the greatest of English connoisseurs, he was seized with an eager and lasting ambition, not to *talk* about art, not to be a critic or connoisseur—that was utterly unlike him—but to *do* these things himself, to develop that natural talent for drawing which the family had observed in him as a child, even perhaps to produce masterpieces. And who can tell what might have happened if his lines had fallen in more peaceful places?

This companionship between uncle and nephew is pleasant to look back upon. At first sight they had little in common, yet in essentials they were much alike. Charles probably admired Rupert's impetuosity in action —he had more than a touch of that himself. Both were rather silent, despising talk; but Charles, with his lifelong stammer, would like Rupert's trick of sudden, sharp retort, which pulled up the talker in full career. Both lacked the gift of diplomacy. Charles "did not know how to lie," says Mr Belloc in his *Charles the First*; it was "a lack in his character." Rupert never tried to learn.

King Charles I
Van Dyck
Photo Alinari

They had these inhibitions in common. And I think that the fine, athletic figure of the younger man, and the easy grace with which he excelled in every outdoor sport, must have appealed to one who was more or less a cripple in his youth, and had only very painfully acquired his single manly accomplishment of horsemanship. To Rupert, on the other hand, Charles must have seemed a very mirror of European culture, the first man who had ever interested the boy in the arts of peace. Anyhow, the evidence is indisputable: Charles grew to like his nephew Rupert better every day. They hunted together in the royal parks, Rupert sat for his portrait to Van Dyck, heard the latest sayings of old Ben Jonson, and knew all about Inigo Jones's scheme for the rebuilding of Whitehall.

But Rupert's mother, Queen Elizabeth, called it "idling." She never seems to have trusted Rupert an inch farther than she could see him; and her elder son, Charles Louis, had been writing ill-natured, gossiping letters, in which he described his younger brother, whose success he obviously envied, as being entirely under the influence of the English Queen and her Papist friends, and hinted that he was in danger of losing his faith. Sir Thomas Roe to some extent shared these apprehensions. None of them understood Rupert's point of view in such matters—that he was not religiously minded, nor ever could be interested in theological dispute, but at the same time had enough of the artist in him to be profoundly affected by the beauty of the old ceremonial. He is said to have declared afterwards that another fortnight in the Queen's society would have converted him to Rome. That was probably just one of his sharp retorts.

Elizabeth had other causes for anxiety. Rupert's English friend Endymion Porter, the "patron of poets" and man-about-town, was quite unfairly represented to her as an undesirable companion. She got an impression that Rupert's way of life was "giddy." Nor was the more worldly-wise Charles Louis entirely beyond reproach. When Elizabeth sent an Englishwoman, a certain Mrs Crofts, to visit the young men in London and report upon their doings—in fact, to spy—they were both of them openly hostile. Charles Louis excused his behaviour by saying that he had, at any rate, talked more to the lady than he ever did when he knew her at his mother's house in Holland; and Rupert, appealed to by his brother as a witness, answered that he could hardly be expected to put himself out for Mrs Crofts, since she cut him dead when they met!

All this was very upsetting. And then came the mad proposal that Rupert should lead an English naval expedition to the Indian Ocean, conquer the island of Madagascar for Charles I, and establish himself there as the local Governor. Elizabeth's deep-seated common sense was outraged by this fantastic suggestion. When she heard that her brother, King Charles, was apparently considering it quite seriously, and that Rupert, in his boyish enthusiasm, was already beginning to study ship-building (he was to take twelve warships with him, and twenty-four merchantmen) and the problems of arming and victualling fleets at sea, her indignation knew no bounds. No sons of hers, she wrote emphatically, should "go for knight errants." But Rupert, when she sent some one to expostulate with him, answered not a word. Charles Louis tried to sound him, but found him "very shy." [1]

The combined perils of Rome and Madagascar determined Rupert's mother to get him back to Holland as soon as she could. Knowing that Charles would not

[1] Rupert was probably annoyed by his brother's further advice: "I bid him take heed he do not meddle with points of religion among them, for fear some priest or other, that is too hard for him, may form an ill opinion in him." (Charles Louis to Elizabeth, *Bromley Letters*, p. 86.)

easily consent to let him go, she appealed to Archbishop Laud. She must have known that the stories of Laud's secret conversion to Roman Catholicism were mere nonsense—in fact, almost the reverse of the truth, for he became more obstinately Anglican every day. But she put her appeal on other than religious grounds. The innumerable schemes for the recovery of the Palatinate were at last beginning to ripen. Charles I, having tried in vain to help his sister by diplomatic means, had at last come down with a small lump sum, and had allowed a subscription list to be opened in England for the financing of a military expedition, which Charles Louis was to lead. "I think," wrote the Queen to Laud, "that he [Rupert] will spend his summer better in an army than idly in England; for though it be a great honour and happiness to him to wait upon his uncle, yet, his youth considered, he will be better employed to see the war." Laud agreed. "You do exceedingly well to put him into action."

They underestimated Rupert's spirit. There is no evidence that he hesitated for a moment when he heard that the old family cause of the Palatinate was once more at stake. His heart was in England—it would remain there all his life—but he never doubted where his duty lay. Even the King could not refuse him, and it was arranged that the brothers should embark for the Continent in June 1637. They had been in England about two years, and the parting was a wrench for both of them. It moved Rupert more than anything that had happened since his father's death. Garrard, the chaplain, wrote to Strafford:

> Both the brothers went away unwillingly, but Prince Rupert expressed it most, for, being a-hunting that morning with the King, he wished that he might break his neck, so he might leave his bones in England.[1]

[1] *Strafford Letters*, vol. ii, p. 85.

No doubt he meant it. A homeless, landless boy, of mixed nationality and cosmopolitan upbringing, he had found at last the country that he loved, and the country that was home to him. And now, almost at a moment's notice, he must leave it, with no apparent prospect of return.

But there was plenty of excitement where they were going. Leaving Charles Louis to organize the family expedition against the Palatinate with the aid of King Charles's guineas, Rupert himself hastened to join the Dutch army at the siege of Breda in the more congenial company of his younger brother, Maurice. The two princes enjoyed every moment of that siege. Their most resounding exploit was when they set out together one night, crawling on their stomachs across No Man's Land, until they got so close to the enemy's lines that they were able to hear the Spanish soldiers talking, and brought back valuable information of an impending sally by the besieged. Rupert found many English officers serving in the Dutch army. The Earl of Northampton, Lord Grandison, and Sir Jacob Astley held important commands. Goring was there, and Wilmot, whom he was to know so well (and like so little) in later years, and the famous Monk, the history-maker, commanded a stand of pikes. It is interesting to glance through the list of names of these English volunteers, both now and at somewhat earlier dates—Philip Skippon, Thomas Culpepper, Lord Warwick, Sir Faithful Fortescue, a Slingsby, a Luttrell, a Cromwell (not Oliver), a Fleetwood, a Lambert—and to note how they seem to have divided themselves about evenly between the two sides in our own Civil War.

To return to Breda. It was while acting temporarily under Monk's command that Rupert took part in a desperate assault upon one of the enemy's outworks—though he was well aware that the Prince of Orange had expressly forbidden him to be present. Happily the assault was successful. The outwork in question was technically known as a 'hornwork,' because, on the side nearest the besiegers, it thrust out two pointed corners like the horns of a bull. It was a strongly fortified earthwork, standing up, isolated, in the midst of the open ditch (ditches were then thirty to fifty yards wide) which ran all round the city, and well in front of the curtain wall and bastions which formed the main line of defence. The muzzles of its guns were, of course, a little lower than those on the bastions behind it, but were still high enough to command the parapet over which the besiegers must scramble before jumping into the ditch to advance against the walls; at the same time it could bring enfilading fire to bear along the ditch on either side. It fulfilled, in fact, the same function as the triangular ravelins which were so popular with Vauban and his school half a century later. But at the time we are writing of Vauban was still in his cradle; his ingenious methods of attacking a town with parallels and zigzag communication trenches had not been perfected; and the defence, with its bastions and outworks, and wide, exposed, open ditch, had still a tremendous advantage over the assailants. The importance of capturing the hornwork before attempting to advance in force across the ditch is obvious.

The assault upon this particular hornwork had been entrusted by the Prince of Orange to the French and English volunteers who were serving in his army, the French to attack on the right, the English on the left. Each party had driven a mine under the projecting corner of the hornwork opposite to it, and these mines were timed to go off simultaneously, when the volunteers, taking advantage of the ensuing confusion, would rush in and carry the place. But the mines, as often happened in those days (and is not unknown to-day), chose to go off separately. First the French mine exploded, and did hardly any damage. There was then an awkward pause, while the volunteers, pouring over the parapet, and no doubt losing heavily from hostile artillery, hesitated to attack; for it was known that the hornwork was strongly held by Imperialist pikemen. Then came the loud roar of the English mine, and it was seen that this time a large breach had been made in the side of the work.

Immediately Monk's volunteers swarmed into the ditch and assailed the hornwork on its right front. But the hero of the occasion was Sir Jacob Astley, who led a party of twenty-four musketeers right across the ditch to the curtain wall, where they turned to the right and ran along under the wall, until they came against the hornwork from behind. A volley fired into the backs of the defending pikemen completely demoralized the defence, and in a few minutes the English were in the hornwork and, after a fierce *mêlée*, had captured or killed every one of its defenders. The English had thus gained their objective and fairly earned their general's thanks. But it appeared that beyond the hornwork there was another small post, called a 'cutting-off,' and this the volunteers also attacked, beating out the enemy and establishing themselves there.

On the whole, it was a smart piece of work; but it had not been accomplished without heavy losses. There were many slain, and Goring and Wilmot were among the wounded. Rupert, as usual, was untouched. When the hand-to-hand fighting was finished he and a few English officers lay panting on the grass, close to a heap of slain, most of whom had already been stripped of their clothing. Suddenly a half-naked figure sprang up from among the corpses. "Messieurs," he inquired in cultured accents, "est-il point de quartier ici?" It was a Burgundian officer who had been lying 'doggo'! He was greeted with a roar of laughter, and one of the Englishmen christened him "Jack Falstaff," a nickname which is said to have clung to him to his dying day.

Bright little affairs like this enlivened the siege operations, otherwise so foreign to Rupert's temperament, and in due course Breda—that town of many sieges—surrendered to the Dutch. Maurice went reluctantly back to school in France, and Rupert joined Charles Louis for the invasion of the Palatinate. He was made colonel of a regiment of horse—his first command.

CHAPTER III: THE EMPEROR'S PRISONER

RUPERT's characteristic qualities as a soldier had now begun to manifest themselves—those qualities which, for good or ill, have ever since been associated with his name, and have, indeed, added it to the English language. At the time of the invasion of the Palatinate he was not yet nineteen years of age, but he was already an experienced soldier. He had been many times under fire, and had seen his comrades fall dead beside him, and had fought hand to hand in the narrow trenches with pistol and sword. He knew well that feeling of mad excitement which comes upon every young soldier when he first looks death in the face. He was now almost a veteran, but he never lost the joy of battle. He never lost it all his life. It was often observed in the Great War that the familiar picture of the hard-bitten veteran with iron nerves, who had become so accustomed to the sound of hostile bullets that he noticed them no more than flies buzzing round his ears, was seldom recognizable in real life. It was noticed that the more a man was shot at the less he liked it; that the strongest nerves eventually became frayed; and that the first to duck his head when a *Minenwerfer* came over was not, usually, the young soldier fresh from England, but the veteran who had almost reached the limit of his endurance.

These were amateur soldiers, of course, and Rupert had chosen his profession while still a boy. But the point is that he never ceased to enjoy it with the zest of a boy. He rode into every fresh encounter with eager anticipation of military glory to come, and headed each cavalry charge as though it had been his first. He had studied his profession soberly: he knew all about the technical side of soldiering: his strategical ideas had even a touch of genius, and might have altered the course of the English Civil War if they had been adopted. He was always for striking direct at the enemy's heart—what was later called the "Nelson touch." But on the field of battle itself this instinct became uncontrollable, so that all other considerations were forgotten, and he could think of nothing but the opposing regiments immediately opposite to him. And his desire to get at them was unchecked by any sense of fear—there was apparently no such word in his vocabulary.

It would be the greatest mistake in the world for the modern critic, with memories of the wholesale slaughter in Flanders and France, to belittle the dangers of a seventeenth-century battlefield—when every volley, to be effective, must be fired at very close range, when the line of retreat was frequently closed in the early stages of the encounter, when the heavy cavalry were always waiting to ride down the fleeing infantry, and when victory was too often followed by massacre. Contemporary estimates of casualties compared with the total numbers engaged are eloquent on this point. And it is certain that commanding officers stood in greater personal danger than they do to-day. Yet in all his engagements Rupert was never seriously wounded—only twice touched. He seemed to bear a charmed life—his enemies, at any rate, believed it—and he may have had some feeling of that himself. More likely, he never bothered his head about it. He needed no such assurance. He was swept forward by a fierce exultation in battle which is part of the natural equipment of every male creature, but which in Rupert burned so brightly that it inspired not only himself but every trooper who rode behind him. To the end of the Civil War he never grew tired or faint—he never lost that boyish delight in danger which he showed in the trenches at Breda. He was not, perhaps, a great general in the highest sense of the word—though it must be remembered that he never had a great opportunity. And he was certainly not always the wisest of counsellors. But he was a first-class fighting man.

Now this invasion of the Lower Palatinate, financed by King Charles I of England and led by the two boy generals, his nephews, was possibly the very maddest exploit in the whole history of the Thirty Years War. Rupert, if he had been but a little older, would certainly have refused to have anything to do with it; for his impetuosity in action, of which we have just been speaking, was never allied to recklessness in the planning of a campaign. War was to him a serious business, not a gamble. But in the autumn of 1638 he was a mere boy, and his brother Charles Louis, who was to grow up into such a cool and calculating man, was little more. They had chosen a moment when hostilities had temporarily ceased elsewhere in Germany, so that the Emperor was for once in a position to turn his whole strength against any new assailant. They had made no arrangements with any of the other Protestant Princes to distract the attention of the Emperor's generals by threatening their flanks. They had not even made sure of the co-operation of the Swedes who lay at Münster in considerable force under the command of General Baner, one of the successors of Gustavus Adolphus. For six years, since the death of their great leader at Lützen, the Swedes had kept the war alive and maintained their position in Germany; but they did little or nothing to help the young Palatines. And the total force with which Charles Louis proposed single-handed to rescue his ancestral domains from the grip of the Empire amounted to four thousand men!

There were three regiments of horse, of which Rupert commanded the first, and two troops of dragoons, who may be described roughly as mounted infantry. Count Ferentz and Count Königsmark, a faithful friend of the Palatine family, shared the chief command, and there were many English volunteers present, of whom Captain Armstrong and Sir Richard Crane are mentioned. Another staunch friend, Lord Craven, led the guards. This loyal little Englishman had suffered much at the hands of the younger Palatines, who were apt to laugh at him and his devotion to their handsome mother. Acting on Elizabeth's instructions, he had done his best, with indifferent success, to bear-lead Rupert and Charles Louis during their stay in England, and no doubt she was relying upon him to watch over their safety on this occasion. He was quite unequal to that task, but he never lacked courage and meant to do his best. It may be added here that he had put a large sum of money into this mad expedition, and that he continued to pour out his private fortune at Elizabeth's feet up to the day when the victorious English Parliament confiscated his estates.

The little army set out in October 1638, directing its march towards the Lower Palatinate, where Charles Louis could, at any rate, be sure of a certain amount of moral support from the civilian population. On the way they were joined by the Swedish general King (he was a Scot by birth), who had been sent from Münster to assist them. He brought with him much advice, but few soldiers. The army had now three commanders-in-chief, not counting the young Elector. Rupert, with his cavalry, rode in the van, and as the broad fields of Westphalia opened out before him his spirits rose amazingly. The official objective was the rich town of Lemgo, which it was proposed to take by storm; but it was highly characteristic of this expedition that, "having a curiosity in their passage to take a view of the town of Rhennius

[Rheine?]," where there was an Imperialist garrison, part of the cavalry were deflected in that direction, Charles Louis riding with them. On reaching the place they found three troops of Imperialist horse drawn up in the plain outside the gates; whereupon the young Elector, who had about eight hundred men with him, immediately sent forward three troops of his own to drive them back into the town. This was the sort of occasion that had often figured in Rupert's young dreams. He got permission to ride in advance with the forlorn hope, and, with his few companions, crossed swords with the enemy well ahead of the main body. The three troops of Palatine cavalry, advancing with great spirit, drove their opponents back through the gates, and nearly succeeded in following them into the town. After which gesture of defiance they turned their horses and rode away, in high fettle, to rejoin their own army.

This was Rupert's first cavalry charge. It was marked by an incident which seems to have made some impression upon his contemporaries. It must be remembered that a cavalry charge in those days was a very different affair from the headlong gallop of medieval chivalry or, again, of modern mounted troops. There was no idea of shock tactics; it was a crab-like advance, frequently interrupted by halts for the purpose of pouring in volleys at close range. Even when the horsemen mingled hand to hand they relied upon their firearms at least as much as upon cold steel. During this particular skirmish, probably just before the opposing lines met, one of the Imperialists raised his carbine and took deliberate aim at the young Prince at a range of less than ten yards. Rupert could do nothing to protect himself, for, though no doubt he wore the usual helmet and breastplate of the period, they would offer no resistance to the passage of a bullet. But the weapon misfired. It was not the last time in Rupert's career that his life was to be saved unexpectedly in this way.

The absurd little army continued its march, until it reached Lemgo and solemnly sat down before the town. But almost immediately came news that Hatzfeldt, the Imperialist general, with a force many times larger than their own, was moving in their rear towards the Weser, with the evident intention of cutting off their retreat. The siege of Lemgo was promptly abandoned, and it was decided to make for the nearest large town in possession of the Swedes. Of these the most suitable was Minden, about twenty miles north; but between Minden and Lemgo lay Hatzfeldt's army, and it became a matter of vital consequence to choose some route which would evade him. There was the road through Rinteln to the west, and there was the road through Vlotho to the east. It was known, apparently, that Hatzfeldt was watching the Vlotho road; but that was the more direct route, and the one which lay nearer to the Dutch frontier and home, and Charles Louis, on the advice of the Swedish general King, chose it. By doing so he walked "into Hatzfeldt's very mouth." [1] Count Hatzfeldt, indeed, seems to have anticipated their decision; for the very next morning, when the Palatine army moved out from before Lemgo, the cavalry, who formed the advance-guard, had ridden only about half a mile northward when they bumped into eight regiments of cuirassiers and a regiment of Irish dragoons. Behind these were the Imperialist foot.

The Palatine cavalry drew rein, and there was a hurried consultation among their several leaders. The opposing horsemen outnumbered them by more than two to one. General King, with a party of horse, galloped to the top

[1] From the contemporary description of this campaign, quoted by Warburton from the Benett MSS. (Warburton, vol. i, p. 453).

of a neighbouring hill, and, after taking a look at the
enemy, gave it as his opinion that they might best be
resisted upon the raised ground; and there he posted his
few Swedish auxiliaries, with the horse. He then hastened
to the rear to bring up the main body of the infantry and
the guns. No sooner was he gone than the cavalry commanders, Königsmark, Ferentz, and the two young
Palatine Princes, began to dislike their position. They
could see the Imperialist horse advancing in a solid mass,
and they felt that on this exposed hillock they must
quickly be surrounded and submerged. Königsmark was
the senior colonel among them, and, with Rupert's
consent, he now led the cavalry down into the lower
ground, apparently a deep valley or defile, where he
drew them up in three ranks, Colonel Loe's regiment in
front, Ferentz's next, and Rupert's in the rear. Königsmark himself was in reserve.

Hardly had they taken this position when the Imperialist cavalry came in on them like a torrent, riding
over Loe's regiment, and then over that of Ferentz, and
sending the survivors headlong down the valley on both
flanks of Rupert's men, who, however, continued to
stand firm. Rupert counter-charged and beat the enemy
back. He received no support whatever from Königsmark (who, in fact, had taken to flight), but Lord Craven
coming up with the guards, these two advanced again
and temporarily cleared the defile. They were hopelessly
outnumbered. Eight hundred Imperialist horse had
ridden over the hills and got into the valley behind them.
There was no support forthcoming from their own side.
(Charles Louis had ridden off the field with General King,
and had narrowly escaped by swimming his horse across
the river Weser. The horse was drowned, but the young
Elector got to land by clinging to the branches of a willow.)
Rupert, charging with his usual impetuosity, suddenly

found himself in the midst of the enemy, far ahead of his own men. As he took a firm grip on his sword, preparing to sell his life dearly, he noticed that the hostile horsemen were taking not the slightest notice of him, but were pressing past towards the scene of action, as though he were one of their own side. And from every headdress flowed a crest of white ribbons (for such had been Hatzfeldt's orders), so that they looked like a mountain stream in spate dashing down the defile. Then Rupert remembered that he himself, only a few hours previously—in boyish imitation, perhaps, of the Protestant hero Henry of Navarre at Ivry—had "bound a snow-white plume upon his gallant crest" and bidden his men follow it into the thickest carnage. He realized that he was now being mistaken for an Imperialist, and, wheeling round, he joined the stream of horsemen, hoping to make his escape.

He had not ridden far when he saw one of his brother's cornets of horse, entirely surrounded by the enemy, fighting desperately to save the flag. Without stopping to think, Rupert rushed in to his assistance, and succeeded in getting him off; but he himself was now identified as one of the Palatine army, and was soon the centre of a vigorous cavalry *mêlée*, Ferentz, Craven, and others having come to his assistance. An Imperialist seized his bridle, but Rupert slashed at the man's fingers, spurred his horse, and again got clear. There was a stone wall in front of him, and for a moment it seemed that he might escape. But his tired horse refused the jump, and, after a little more sword-play, he was overborne and thrown heavily to the ground. They stood all round him, and one of them pushed up the visor of his helmet and demanded to know his rank. "I am a colonel," said Rupert, proud of his first command. "Sacrament!" exclaimed the veteran Von Lippe, staring at him, "you are a very young one."

That night Prince Rupert, his identity now established, was honourably lodged in a house near the battlefield, in company with his fellow-prisoners Ferentz and Craven, the latter of whom was wounded in the hand and thigh. Rupert had two bullet-holes through his cloak. The Elector's army, they heard, had dispersed in panic, but it does not appear that they allowed these ill tidings to interfere with their sleep. They owned, perhaps, the three clearest consciences in the whole of that ill-fated little force. The officer in whose charge they had been placed to convey them to their first prison at Warrendorf was sufficiently famous in his own way to deserve a word of notice here. He was no less a person than Colonel Devereux, the murderer of the great Wallenstein. Rupert must have heard of that lurid midnight scene in February 1634, when the conspirators burst into Wallenstein's bedroom, and Gordon, the Scotsman, held a torch aloft, while some one drove a halberd through the General's breast and Devereux shouted abuse into his dying ears. Devereux did well out of that crime when the Emperor heard of it; and he did well for the Protestant Princes too, since no great Imperialist leader ever arose to take Wallenstein's place. But Rupert knew he had a traitor to deal with, and he probably estimated Devereux fairly when he offered him the five pieces, which were all the money he had in his pocket, to help him to escape. Nothing came of it—nor of the offer of a kind-hearted woman who, at a halt on the way to Warrendorf, was so much affected by Rupert's youth and good looks that she approached him secretly and offered to do anything to help him to get away. But some rumour must have reached the ears of Hatzfeldt, the Imperialist general, for their escort was changed.

At Warrendorf there was a halt of some weeks, while Craven's wounds were attended to. Rupert seized the opportunity to obtain permission for another fellow-prisoner, Sir Richard Crane, to return to England with the news that all the members of his party had survived. This concession on the part of the officer commanding at Warrendorf—one Veale—was marred by his refusal to allow pens or ink to his prisoners; but Rupert scribbled a pencil note on a scrap of paper, and entrusted it to Crane for delivery to his uncle, King Charles. Most of his time was occupied in making plans for his escape—rather to the embarrassment of the other prisoners, who, not being of royal blood, might have expected to be allowed to buy their liberty by ransom in the ordinary way. Before any plans of escape could be put into execution they were all moved on to Dillenburg, and thence, in a south-easterly direction, to Bamberg. Here Rupert was separated from his companions in misfortune Ferentz and Craven, both of whom had arranged to be ransomed. It cost Craven twenty thousand pounds, and he offered to pay a further sum if they would allow him to remain with Rupert and keep him company; but the Emperor refused.

So Rupert went on alone, under escort, to Ratisbon, and finally to Linz, in Austria, where he was to endure a long period of imprisonment under the mild rule of the Governor, Count Kufstein. The castle of Linz, in which he now found himself, was a fine old building, which, in happier circumstances, might have appealed to his artistic taste. But for two and a half out of the three years which he spent there he was given hardly any liberty, except to walk about the castle grounds and dine occasionally with the Governor. He was allowed one or two servants to look after him, but no male companion of his own age or condition—no one to talk to. Perhaps he grumbled too loudly. At any rate, Count Kufstein became colder in his manner and stricter in his surveillance, so that "twelve musketeers and two halberds attended the Prince in all his motions"—just the kind of thing that would drive Rupert mad.

Yet there were compensations. Count Kufstein had a daughter. She was a beautiful child of about sixteen— and Rupert himself was not yet twenty! Her name was Susanne Marie, and she is confidently asserted to have been as wise and witty as she was fair. The sight of this handsome, dejected young Prince, mooning about the battlements, now glancing idly down at the bold sweep of the river Danube which flowed beneath the walls, now gazing eagerly northward under his cupped hand, looking for the rescue party [1] which never came—here was something to touch a maiden's tender heart. Soon they became friends; and soon her pretty pleadings with her father began to take effect. Rupert was treated as a friend of the family; he was continually in and out of the Governor's house; visitors were introduced to him; and he was allowed to take exercise at tennis.

It was in Susanne's company, no doubt, that he began to revive his interest in drawing and painting. His natural gift developed rapidly, and, having little else to do, he fell into the pleasant habit of sketching heads and human figures on any chance piece of paper, such as the back of a letter. Some examples of this casual scribbling of his, done in later life, have happily been preserved, and may be seen to-day at the British Museum. They are more remarkable for vigour of execution than for subtlety or characterization; but they are in no sense grotesque or caricatures. On the contrary, they indicate a genial view of one's fellow-men, with, perhaps, a little more interest in their costumes than in their faces. And they are

[1] After all, the nearest Swedish garrisons were not far away, there was always the possibility of a rising by the local Protestants, and only fourteen years before this date a crowd of discontented peasants had attacked Linz and burned its suburbs to the ground.

RUPERT'S SKETCHES ON AN ENVELOPE
British Museum

wonderfully intimate memorials of Rupert—more so than anything he ever wrote or said.

But the scientific bent of his mind became apparent even in this new hobby. Dürer had invented an instrument for getting a correct perspective in drawing without

A Sketch by Prince Rupert

continually taking measurements; but he had not carried the matter far enough for his invention to be of any practical use to the working artist. Rupert, the nineteen-year-old soldier, was strongly attracted by the idea, and spent many weeks of his captivity in working it out; until he produced a really serviceable instrument, which, in later life, he presented to the Royal Society in London. It was the first, but by no means the last, of his contributions

to the technique of art and science. In the meantime,
with his pencils and paper and his new instrument, and
with sweet Susanne by his side, the days began to slip
by quite pleasantly at Linz.

There is not the slightest excuse for weaving a romantic
love story round this pretty friendship of a boy and a girl
three hundred years ago. If, as his biographer puts it,
Rupert "was for a second time happy in the favour of one
of the brightest beauties of her age"[1] he is to be congratulated. He knew nothing of the arts of love. He was
as innocent in such matters as an athletic undergraduate
of our own day—though he may have pretended, as
undergraduates do, to a cynical worldly wisdom. But of
marriage proposals he was not without experience. As
long ago as 1636 it had been proposed to match him with
Marguerite de Rohan, daughter of the wealthy Huguenot
duke. The idea commended itself both to his mother and
to his elder brother. "I think it is no absurd proposition,"
wrote Charles Louis from England, where he then was,
"for she is great both in means and birth and of the
Religion."[2]

Rupert, who would be about seventeen at the time,
displayed no interest. But Mlle de Rohan, when
approached by the English Ambassador in Paris, "gave
me a smile and a blush, which I took for a sufficient
reply."[3] Her family also were favourable. Even when
Rupert was taken prisoner and incarcerated at Linz they
held to their side of the bargain, and the little *mademoi-
selle* went out of her way to declare that "it would be a
lâcheté to forsake one because of his misfortunes." But
there was still no response from Rupert. It was not until
1643, in the midst of the English Civil War, that it

---

[1] Lansdowne MSS., 817, f. 162.   [2] *Bromley Letters*, p. 56.
[3] Letter from Lord Leicester, July 22, 1638 (*Collins Sydney Papers*,
vol. ii, pp. 560–561).

became known that Mlle de Rohan was definitely tired of waiting. Charles I then made an awkward attempt to induce young Prince Maurice to propose to her, and so "take your brother handsomely off." But Maurice was as obdurate as Rupert, and in 1645 Marguerite married M. Henri Chabot, who made her an excellent husband.

As for Susanne, she was married three times. But Rupert "never named her after in his life without demonstrations of the highest admiration." Undoubtedly she made a profound impression upon him, in spite of—or perhaps because of—her youth. He may have dreamed of marrying her, but the difficulties were obvious. Her father was a converted Lutheran, who had risen in the service of the Emperor by reason of his change of faith. Neither in blood nor in wealth was the family equal to that of the Rohans. But we may surely thank Susanne for cherishing that softer side of Rupert's character which always prevented him from becoming a mere man of war.

Two years and more passed by at Linz. It was a period of marking time in Rupert's tempestuous youth—or, perhaps, a kind of doze, with half-awake dreams of art and love, during which his natural impatience seems entirely to have deserted him. In the careers of most men of action we find these intervals of rest, of whole-hearted abandonment to the pleasure of doing nothing. It is their temptation. In Rupert's case it was brought to an abrupt termination by the arrival from Vienna of official proposals for his release. Three proposals in all were made to him, each emanating from the Emperor himself.

It was first suggested that he should change his religion and become a Roman Catholic. This he instantly rejected as an "affront"—a word which very well sums up his attitude in these matters. He had written to assure his mother that "neither good usage nor ill could make him change his religion or party." It shows an extraordinary misunderstanding of his character that Elizabeth should have required such an assurance. But she never trusted him. When she heard of his capture, "I confess in my passion I did rather wish him killed," she exclaimed. And she added, "I pray God I may not have more cause to wish it before he be gotten out"—a plain indication of her fear for the safety of his soul.[1] She would have been still more alarmed if she had known that Count Kufstein, by the Emperor's orders, was sending Jesuit missionaries to visit Rupert in prison and endeavour to shake him in his faith. They might as usefully have argued with Praise-God Barebones.

The second proposal was that he should ask the Emperor's pardon for having taken part in his brother's invasion of Germany. That also he refused. The third—which seems to show a distinct weakening in the Imperial attitude—was that he should accept a command under the Emperor against the armies of Sweden or France. This must surely have tempted him; but he refused as before. His obstinacy had the usual unpleasant consequences. His guards were strengthened, his liberty was restricted, and it was about this time that the twelve musketeers and two halberdiers, referred to above, were detailed to accompany him wherever he went. There was also a further and better reason for this severity. The Swedes were moving. Their garrisons had suddenly sprung to life; raiding parties were abroad; and there was even a Swedish army in the field, with Rupert's younger brother, Prince Maurice, serving in its ranks. It seemed not unlikely that Linz might be their objective.

The Archduke Leopold, the Emperor's brother, came hurrying northward. His instructions were to beat up

---

[1] In the very same letter (addressed to Sir Thomas Roe) she refers to Rupert's elder brother, Charles Louis, as "him I love best."

the Swedish quarters and test their strength. But at Linz he rested a few days, and—very happily for Rupert—took the occasion to visit his brother's prisoner. He found a desperately bored and miserable young man. The two princes were of about the same age, and there arose an immediate and rather unexpected sympathy between them—unexpected because, as Miss Scott has pointed out,[1] they were at the first glance utterly unlike in character. Leopold, who was slightly the older of the two, was a gentle, charming youth, whose piety had won him the nickname of "the Angel"; whereas Rupert, as we have seen, was known in his own family as "the Devil." But Leopold pitied Rupert; Rupert was pining for a male friend of his own age; and it soon appeared that "the Devil" and "the Angel" had much in common after all. They became fast friends.

When Leopold had disposed of the Swedish peril he returned to Vienna, and there eloquently pleaded Rupert's cause. The Duke of Bavaria, hereditary enemy of the Palatines, had been assiduous in warning Ferdinand of the evil consequences that might result if another, and the most warlike, member of this pernicious family were allowed to go free. But Leopold's eloquence completely turned the scale. The Emperor Ferdinand was persuaded that whereas an imprisoned Rupert must always be at best a nuisance and at worst a menace, a grateful Rupert, set at liberty with memories of an easy captivity, would surely find some other use for his sword than to turn it against the Emperor and the Emperor's brother, who was now his devoted friend. With a little well-timed flattery and caressing he might even be turned into a good Catholic and a possible ally. The Duchess of Bavaria threw herself at the Emperor's feet and urged him to reconsider; but the Empress, perhaps annoyed by

[1] *Rupert, Prince Palatine*, p. 46.

this gesture, took Rupert's side; and he had another powerful friend in a Colonel Leslie, who had known him in England and was now one of the Emperor's advisers. Sir Thomas Roe was having a word to say on behalf of the King of England. So it was settled that Rupert should be put on parole, that all his old liberties should be restored to him, and that he should be allowed to leave Linz for as much as three days at a time when he so desired.

Rupert, when the news arrived, was moping in the castle grounds. He was almost without companions, but Lord Arundel had presented him with a powerful white dog, of good breeding and tried courage, and this famous animal—it was to become an historic figure in the English Civil War—was with him day and night. He called it Boy, and lavished upon it a devotion which he was slow to give to human beings. He had also acquired a 'hare' (possibly of the Belgian variety), and, being at desperate shifts for something to do, had practised upon this unlikely animal, until it would follow him about like a dog and obey his every word. But as soon as he knew that he could leave Linz at will the dog and the hare were thrust into the background, and Rupert began a series of visits to the leading families of the neighbourhood.

Events now crowded upon each other fast. There was a letter from King Charles I of England, inviting him to come over to the country of his adoption, where the shadow of civil war was now plain for all men to see. And there was an offer from the Emperor to give him his liberty on the mere promise not to bear arms against the Imperialists. To this Rupert could safely agree, since he now saw a career for himself elsewhere. But when they asked for a written agreement he replied so unpleasantly that Leslie dropped the subject. It was arranged that he should meet the Emperor at a boar hunt, as if by accident, and should kiss the Imperial hand, as a sign of reconciliation and dismissal. Rupert kept the appointment, and characteristically dashed in in front of the other hunters and slew the boar with his own spear. Ferdinand was delighted with him. He was invited to visit Vienna before his departure for the north, and was there fêted like a hero, the courtiers, male and female, vying among themselves to do him honour.

It was a strange experience for a wild, rather uncouth young soldier, fresh from nearly three years in prison. Evidently a serious attempt was being made to bring Rupert over to the Imperial side, both in politics and religion. The Emperor showered so many civilities upon him "that the modesty of the Prince could not receive them without some confusion," [1] says his biographer. The extraordinary kindness of the Viennese ladies made him blush even more. But either he still thought of little Susanne; or he remembered his uncle in England, now asking for his help; or he realized all the time that these Viennese Delilahs were merely trying to detain him for political purposes of their own. Anyhow, he "wanted not prudence to break through such soft obstructions" and get clear away, without losing even his popularity. Rupert was no Puritan, of course, and there was something—it is not clear what—in his conduct which seems to have brought upon him the censure of Sir Thomas Roe; for we find him writing apologetically to the latter from Linz in September 1641:

> SIR,
>
> I must give you a greate dele of thankes for the reale frendshipp you shewed in remembering me of my faults, whiche I confesse, and strive, and shalle the more heereafter, to mend. But I doubt not, according to the manner of some people heere, they have added and said more than the thinge itselfe is. I beseech you not to hearken to them, but assure yourselfe that

[1] Lansdowne MSS., 817, f. 164.

it has been only from an evill costum, which I hope in short time to mend. Desiring you to continue this your frendshippe in leting me knowe my faults, that I mai have to mend them,

I rest,

Your Lordshippe's most affectionat frend,

RUPERT

Whatever this mysterious fault can have been, it was certainly not drunkenness, the prevailing vice of Germany. For when Rupert was at last allowed to leave Vienna for home he went first on a brief visit to Prague, his birth-place, and then into Saxony; and it was here that he astonished the Elector and the Saxon nobles by his temperance. They had prepared a great feast for him, but he left in the middle, before the wine had fairly begun to circulate. "What shall we do with him," cried the Elector, "if he won't drink?"

From Saxony Rupert went direct to Holland, and embraced his mother after an absence of three years. She found him "not altered, only leaner, and grown." Nor was she altered herself, for when he informed her of his intention to go to England she poured out the usual lament to Roe: "Here he would live but idly, in England no better; for I know the Queen [Henrietta Maria] will use all possible means to gain him, to the prejudice of the Prince Elector, and of his religion." As usual, she completely underestimated this tall, dark son of hers, standing before her "lean and weary," as the English Ambassador described him on his arrival. Rupert's bare word was good enough for his enemies at Vienna, but never for his mother. And note that it was not even for his own sake, or for the good of his own soul, that she dreaded his apostasy, but lest it should operate "to the prejudice of the Prince Elector."

CHAPTER IV: RUPERT'S HORSEMEN

RUPERT came to England in February 1642. It was not mere chance that brought him, but, as Professor Gardiner [1] puts it, "the true instinct of a soldier." He had even secured his mother's approval. There were strong rumours of an English civil war, and it had always been Elizabeth's idea of him that, though he could not be trusted in the affairs of everyday life and might change his religion at any moment, he had been trained as a soldier to earn his living that way, and a soldier he must be. England seemed at the moment the most suitable field for the exercise of his profession.

But when Rupert reached Dover he found the King and Queen of England there, an anxious, worried couple, very different from the royal pair he had known in 1638. With his precocious experience of public affairs, he must have realized at once that war was in the air. The Queen was about to cross to the Continent, and it required little perception to see that there were other matters on her mind than the marriage of her daughter Mary (who accompanied her) to the Prince of Orange. In fact, she was being sent overseas to collect money and munitions for the impending war. At Charles's request, which could hardly be refused, Rupert turned back and escorted his aunt to Holland. And there, at The Hague, he remained throughout the spring of that eventful year, keeping himself as quiet as possible—that he might not give a handle to the King's enemies in England—but watching eagerly for news from across the water. It was clear beyond argument now where his destiny lay. England was the land of opportunity.

In August he heard that the King had left London for

---

[1] *History of the Great Civil War*, vol. i, p. 2.

the North, and had been refused admission to Hull. In the meantime Henrietta Maria had passed on to him the King's promise, by letter, to make him general of the Royal horse. There seemed no reason for any further delay, and in August he set sail on the *Lyon* (the same English ship by which he had brought the Queen over to Holland), intending to make for Scarborough—since London was now openly hostile to the Royal cause. But the wind was adverse, and the commander of the *Lyon*, Captain Fox, put Rupert ashore at the mouth of the Texel, and then quietly slipped away; for his sympathies were on the side of the Parliament, and he could hardly mistake the young Prince's intentions. But Rupert borrowed a ship from the Prince of Orange and put to sea again. He was seasick, groaning in his bunk—and obviously altogether out of sorts. Off Flamborough Head an English ship, the *London*, came out and challenged them, demanding the right to search; but the Dutch captain crowded on sail and got into Tynemouth, which was then held for the King, and where there were several Royalist ships to support him. The *London* thereupon gave up the chase and stood out to sea. Rupert, who had come on deck wearing a rough mariner's cap and feeling horribly ill, was taken ashore in a rowing-boat, and ought, of course, to have gone to bed. But his eagerness was such that he set out that same day for Nottingham, where the King was to raise his standard, riding hard, in company with his young brother, Maurice, and a few other officers.

The English climate, as uncertain as ever, provided a hard frost on that August night, and as Rupert, more than half-asleep, rode southward at the head of his little party over those execrable seventeenth-century roads, for which England was deservedly notorious, his horse suddenly stumbled and fell, bringing him heavily to the ground. His shoulder was dislocated, so that it was impossible to move him. But a bone-setter lived only half a mile away, and this gentleman, who was fortunately a staunch Royalist, came promptly at the first summons and set the Prince's shoulder, refusing to accept more than half the fee offered to him. Within three hours of the accident they were galloping southward again, waving farewell to the loyal bone-setter. So they came to Nottingham, where Rupert was at last persuaded to take to his bed.

But the King was not there. He had gone south, and was said to be at Coventry, demanding the surrender of that town. Rupert prepared to follow as soon as he could sit a horse. In the meantime he got a curious insight into the state of the King's army and the kind of men he was presently to meet at the council table. The Governor of Nottingham, Lord Digby, came to see him. He explained that he had received an order from the King for two petards out of the arsenal. But neither he nor, apparently, any officer on his staff would recognize a petard if he saw it! Would Rupert mind coming to the arsenal and pointing them out? Rupert rose from bed and went with him. But there were no petards in the Royal arsenal. As he turned away impatiently from this egregious governor (who was afterwards one of his bitterest enemies) there entered a young officer, Major Will Legge, who, as it happened, was to become his closest friend. Legge at once volunteered to manufacture a practicable petard from two apothecaries' mortars. Rupert left him to it, and, with a sigh of relief, went back to bed. How many later war-time friendships (and dislikes) have begun in just this kind of way!

Then to horse again, and another fifty miles or more southward—only to miss the King a second time, for Charles had found the gates of Coventry closed against him as firmly as were those of Hull, and, after vainly demanding surrender, had drawn off his forces towards Leicester. The triumphant Roundheads, following up, came into contact with some of Wilmot's horse at the village of Southam, near Coventry. It was the first skirmish of the war. Neither side behaved with much resolution. But after they had shot at each other for some time the Royalists, who were inferior in artillery, made an untidy retreat; and the Roundheads, hurrying after them, were elated to find a dead drummer and several other dead or dying Cavaliers scattered about the fields. There was some rumour at the time that Prince Rupert himself, accompanied by his uncle, the King, had witnessed this skirmish, both disguised as civilian spectators. It seems unlikely. If it is true Rupert must have been unfavourably impressed by the behaviour of the Royalist horse, of which he was presently to take command. They had never so much as attempted a charge.

But we may take it that uncle and nephew met at Leicester for the first time. Here Charles invested Rupert with his new and independent command as General of the Horse. And it was through the narrow streets of that ancient city, where he was afterwards to give and receive so many hard knocks in this quarrel, that Rupert rode one August morning to the first parade of the Royalist cavalry. He cannot have expected much—he who had served against the veteran Imperialist horse in Germany. But he would not be deterred by that. On the contrary, with characteristic concentration of purpose, he was pouring all his ardent spirits into the task before him. It was his firm intention to create the most formidable cavalry in Europe—men who would follow him anywhere, riding like the Palatine cavalry did at Rhennius (but not at the Vlotho!), as though the devil were behind them. He would make them do it, he thought. Nothing should stop them. Give him a few weeks to lick them into shape and he would inspire every man jack of them with his own youthful *élan*.

Here was the raw material before him. He rode slowly down the lines, studying them carefully, noting their honest, homely English faces, their fine physique, and the ease with which most of them seemed to sit their horses. (The animals, though small to modern eyes, were strongly built and in good condition.[1]) There were great possibilities here. The senior officers riding with him told him something of the men and their origin. Here were gentlemen volunteers serving in the ranks, with perhaps one or two servants; stout yeomen farmers, each with a few followers; and larger groups of mounted men, sometimes several hundred strong, equipped and led by the Royalist squires and noblemen who had answered the King's call to arms. Sometimes there was a uniformity of dress, or a wearing of livery, to distinguish some big man's command; more often they were dressed as they pleased. They had one point in common—the large majority were obviously good horsemen, accustomed to the saddle. Above all, there were no pressed men among them. Neither the King nor the Parliament, at this early stage, had been driven to the expedient of recruiting their ranks by force. The nearest to conscripts on either side were the London trained bands, now drilling at Finsbury Fields.

On the other hand, they were quite without any sense of military discipline. Many of them had never heard the ordinary words of command. Some, who had arrived without proper supplies, or had been left without pay by the Royalist noblemen or landowners who had raised

---

[1] When we consider the seventeenth-century trooper's equipment it is clear that they must have been expected to carry twenty to twenty-five stone.

them for the service, were already falling into the evil habit of robbing the neighbouring hen-roosts to supply their deficiencies. When the thieves were arrested their comrades mutinied and released them by force. The junior officers, with the exception of those who had served in the wars in Germany and the Low Countries, had hardly more idea of discipline than their men.

Sorted out, under Rupert's eye, they numbered at first only eight or ten troops. (A troop consisted of about fifty men.) But new recruits were constantly arriving, and at every daily parade the line lengthened out, until there were eighteen troops in all. Parliament at this time had seventy-five troops of horse and five troops of dragoons. But, as Fortescue has pointed out,[1] the numbers mattered little, for, except on paper, these were not armies at all. Neither side felt any immediate lack of man-power. Parliament had, of course, a great and increasing advantage here; partly because they held London and its neighbourhood, all East Anglia, and, presently, the South —in fact, the most thickly populated parts of England— and partly because they had the rich merchants and the monied interest behind them, and were always in a position to pay their troops. But in August and September 1642 the leaders on either side found their time fully occupied in training the raw recruits already collected, without asking for more. It was, at this early stage, a haphazard, amateur, rather half-hearted war. Most people, indeed, expected it to finish on the first battlefield[2]—a common mistake in every age. But it was obvious to all that the side which could first create an effective mounted force would start with a great advantage—just as the side which first created a real army would win the war.

The equipment of Rupert's horsemen left much to be

---

[1] *A History of the British Army*, vol. i, p. 199.
[2] Gardiner, *History of the Great Civil War*, vol. i, p. 40.

desired. The Parliament, having money to spend, had lavishly encumbered its cavalry with the body armour popular at that period. One Roundhead regiment—Hazelrigg's—was so well protected by helmet, cuirass, and so forth that it earned the nickname, among its opponents, of "the Lobsters." (No doubt it wore no ordinary pot-helmet, but the heavy burgonet, with bars across the face and the 'lobster-tail,' as it was called, down the back of the neck.) With the Cavaliers, on the other hand, any kind of helmet or breastplate was hard to come by, and many of the young gentlemen fighting on that side had been reduced to bringing out ancient suits of armour from the family halls to equip themselves or their sergeants.

But far the worst defect of the Royalist cavalry in the eyes of most professional soldiers was its lack of firearms. Some of the men carried pistols, and a few muskets might be seen here and there in the ranks. But the majority were armed only with their swords. And to Rupert's contemporaries, without exception, the idea of a cavalryman going into action relying solely upon his sword would have seemed a ridiculous and suicidal heresy. It may even be argued that Rupert himself only adopted the contrary opinion *malgré lui*, because firearms were not available. But if he made a virtue of necessity—and I cannot believe that—he did it so effectually as to revolutionize cavalry tactics and establish them on a new basis, which endured, essentially unaltered, from his day until quite recent times.

And since this was Rupert's greatest achievement as a soldier and his most important contribution to military history, let us see what it really amounted to.

We must begin by forgetting all our modern notions of a cavalry charge, along with all memories of the avalanche of mail-clad knights in the great days of chivalry. Richard

Cœur de Lion is as far removed from the seventeenth century in this respect as the 21st Lancers at Omdurman, the Light Brigade at Balaclava, or Murat galloping into action at Austerlitz with his cavalry thundering behind him, rank after rank, their horses "stretched out like greyhounds." We must forget all that if we are to get any mental picture of the horse-soldiers of Rupert's and Cromwell's day. Shock tactics were a thing of the past. Gunpowder and small arms had scared them off the field. The seventeenth-century trooper was a clumsy, lumbering figure, in a stout buff coat, with breastplates, a heavy iron helmet with bars across his face, and further encumbered with pistols or (in the case of the dragoon) a weighty and unhandy musket, advancing at a slow trot towards his enemies (with frequent halts to fire volleys at them), and finally coming in among them, sword in hand, at a speed that can never have amounted even to a canter —until Rupert took him in hand and revived the old glory of the charge.

It was not Gustavus Adolphus who restored shock tactics, though one still hears that claim made. It was Rupert. The Swedish King was a great military reformer. What he did for the cavalry was to give them increased *mobility*. He saw that without mobility the cavalry lost their tactical *raison d'être*. He took away all their armour, except helmet and breastplate; he reduced their ranks to four, which greatly increased their speed; he advanced them on a much wider front; and he insisted that it was their duty to get to close quarters with the enemy. He always led them himself, and he made them a much more dangerous weapon than before.

But he still thought of them as mounted infantry. He failed to grasp the principle that, since a horse has four legs and a man two, the evolutions of horse and foot must

68

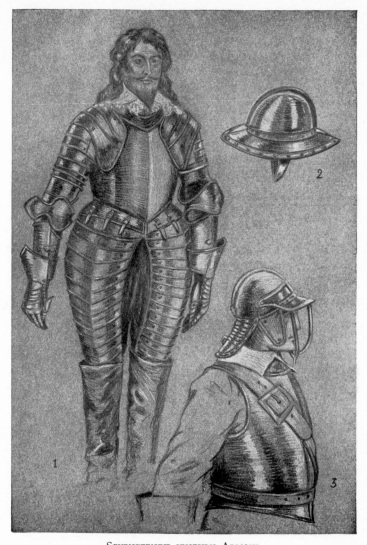

SEVENTEENTH-CENTURY ARMOUR
1. Three-quarter suit of armour. 2. Pikeman's pot helmet. 3. Trooper with buff coat,
cuirass, and triple-barred helmet or lobster-tailed burgonet

be fundamentally different.[1] He interspersed his cavalry front with platoons of musketeers, who advanced on foot with the cavalry, firing volleys, till they got to close range. That range was so close that the cavalry, when at last they charged with their drawn swords, cannot have had *space* to gather impetus for a gallop. Gustavus, to get them moving, had ordered that the first volley must not be fired till they could see the whites of their opponents' eyes. By the time the last volley was discharged—and bearing in mind the short range of seventeenth-century small arms—they must have been so almost comically close to the opposing ranks, according to all modern ideas, that no horse could get into its stride. They arrived in the midst of their enemy at the trot. A cavalry 'charge' in Gustavus's army was, in fact, a trot.

Rupert revived the charge. He did away with the musketeers on foot, and—what is much more important —he did away with all those preliminary volleys which had so fatally checked the speed of a cavalry attack. At Edgehill, the first battle of the Civil War, he specifically instructed the Royalist horse that they were not to use their firearms at all, until they had broken through the opposing ranks—in fact, they were to use them only in pursuit. This order, given at Edgehill, marks a new epoch in cavalry tactics. But it is ridiculous to suppose that Rupert never thought of it until he arrived on that battlefield. He must have trained his raw recruits at Leicester along these lines. He cannot have allowed it to come upon them as a complete surprise at Edgehill that they should be expected to ride across hundreds of yards of open country, with only their naked swords in their fists, without pausing, in the time-honoured manner, to reply to the volleys of the enemy which were thinning their ranks. Few of them had ever been under fire before, and the fine

[1] Fortescue, *A History of the British Army*, vol. i, p. 183.

spirit with which they carried out this new and apparently dangerous order surely precludes the idea that it was sprung upon them on that occasion for the first time.

Rupert, then, revived the charge. One would like to assert out of hand that he always brought his men in at the gallop, himself well in advance, with his famous scarlet cloak across his shoulders, his black hair streaming in the wind. Unfortunately, there is little contemporary evidence on this point of speed. They used the word 'charge' quite vaguely, to indicate an advance upon the enemy. Cromwell, describing his victory at Gainsborough, speaks of "charging fiercely upon them," but goes on to add that the pace was "a pretty round trot"! Yet it is obvious from a glance through the military manuals and other writings of the period that the cavalry trooper was trained to put his horse into a gallop as quickly as possible, and it was certainly intended by his instructors that he should break into the opposing ranks at the gallop. All the illustrations show him doing so.[1] But he had to steady himself, according to the book, at the end of every *carière* (120 to 160 yards) to fire a volley, and we can well believe that, in such circumstances, the final 'charge,' across the last hundred yards or so, hardly ever rose, in practice, above a trot.

But there was no doubt at all about the *intention*. In the case of lancers (though lancers were out of fashion then) it is specifically laid down that their charge must be made at the gallop.[2] And I find a significant instruction

[1] For instance, Hermannus Hugo, *History of the Cavalry*, pp. 262, 266, 267, 268 (1630).

[2] It may be noted, in passing, that Rupert did not revive the lance, the ideal weapon for shock tactics. If he had he would have been nearly a hundred years ahead of his time. Yet that shrewd military critic Sir James Turner, writing in 1670, is puzzled at the unpopularity of the lance, especially as the gradual disappearance of defensive armour laid men's breasts more open to its thrust. "I shall not doubt that there are strong reasons," he remarks caustically, "though I know them not" (*Military Essays*, pp. 171–172).

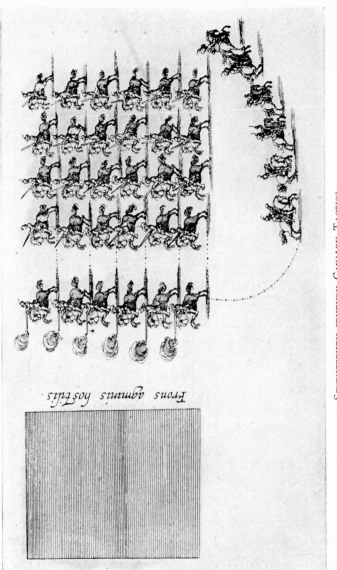

Frons agminis hostilis

SEVENTEENTH-CENTURY CAVALRY TACTICS

An example of the 'interrupted charge,' much practised by Cromwell, but never by Rupert.
From *De Militia Equestri*, by Hermannus Hugo

published just before the outbreak of the rebellion, to
the effect that when enemy horse are retiring before you
and it is desired to charge them in the rear, it must be
done "upon a full trot or gallop." [1] This is one of the
very few cases in which the word 'gallop' is used in laying
down instructions for the cavalry charge. The reason is
obvious. When the enemy have turned their backs in
retreat, even the seventeenth-century instructor recog-
nizes that speed has become the most important factor,
if they are to be engaged at all. For the moment he forgets
his beloved volleys. But he still never thinks of shock
action as a method of making them turn their backs. His
emphasis is always on the small-arms fire, not on the
charge. It was Rupert who reversed this process.
Whether he did so merely because he was short of
muskets, or because—as seems much more likely—the
idea of shock tactics naturally appealed to his fiery
temperament, and was, in fact, his own original notion,
is a point that need not detain us. What we can plainly
see is that he hurled his cavalry over such a wide stretch
of ground, without ever allowing them to pause in their
stride, that they must inevitably have gathered speed to
the extent of making contact with their enemy at the
gallop. Speed, indeed, was their only hope, for they
were being shot at all the time. And the speed and
shock of their impetuous charge was the explanation of
their long series of successes, unbroken down to the date
of Marston Moor. It was the beginning of modern shock
tactics.

Just one more technical point. Rupert, improving
upon Gustavus Adolphus, still further reduced the ranks
of his cavalry to three. (Cromwell later got it down to
two.) Rupert was thus enabled to widen his front—an

---

[1] Robert Ward, *Animadversions of Warre*, p. 320 (1639). See also
Gervase Markham's *The Souldier's Accidence*, pp. 41 and 52.

important consideration in his case, since the Cavaliers were nearly always outnumbered. It also added greatly to the speed of his charge. But, as Fortescue has pointed out, a charge of horsemen, riding only three deep over a wide front, could never be carried out successfully except by well-drilled troops. And that brings us back to Leicester, and that first parade of the eight hundred or so Royalist cavalry, when Rupert, their twenty-three-year-old commander, took their training in hand.

We can see now that it must have been a *tour de force* of concentrated drill-instruction. It is not just a question of the many famous charges that they made. Their patrol work also was excellent. Their fury on the battlefield was equalled by the coolness with which they would extricate themselves from some skirmish in which they had become entangled with a superior force. Yet their period of training was only a few weeks. Late in August 1642 they were, as we have seen, a mere rabble of mounted ploughboys, lackeys, and gentlemen volunteers, whose indiscipline was becoming a scandal to the countryside. A month later they won their first victory in the field. Rupert, it is obvious, must have been a far better organizer and trainer of troops than is commonly supposed. The praise of historians, as so often happens, has gone all to the great man on the winning side. But Sir Philip Warwick was not alone among contemporaries in his astonishment that Rupert had "so soon raised and disciplined this small body of men" [1] as to make them an effective striking force. With a little luck—and a little more courage in the council-chamber—the marked superiority of the Royalist cavalry in the early stages of the war might have been decisive.

No man could have done it unaided. Rupert had many capable and zealous officers under him—men whom he

[1] *Memoirs*, p. 226.

had known in the Continental wars. Right up to the outbreak of our Civil War—it is a fact too often forgotten —there existed close at hand those two great schools of soldiering, Germany and the Low Countries. That was where Roundheads and Cavaliers alike got their drill-instructors. But no instructor and no regimental officer can effect anything unless there is inspiration in the higher command. Rupert was the driving force. "He put that spirit into the King's army," wrote Sir Philip Warwick, "that all men seemed resolved." "Of so great virtue," he goes on to remark, "is the personall courage and example of one great Commander." And it may be added here that Cromwell contributed, in a very peculiar degree, precisely those qualities which Rupert lacked; so that by the end of the Civil War the English cavalry— speaking now of both sides—were undoubtedly the best in Europe. It was the only contribution to military science made by a war which was otherwise a mere provincial 'side-show,' in the military sense, like our earlier Wars of the Roses.

So much for Rupert's horsemen, who are the real heroes of this book. We get a few intimate glimpses of them during their absurdly short period of training. After that first parade at Leicester Rupert had ridden north, in obedience to orders, and rejoined his uncle at Nottingham for the setting up of the Royal Standard on August 22. It was a rather dismal ceremony, performed in the pouring rain. But the King kept his cavalry pushed southward towards Leicester, and Rupert was back with them there within forty-eight hours, and was instantly up to his neck in the difficult business of turning plough-boys into troopers. He established his headquarters at the village of Queenborough.

Being a soldier himself, it never occurred to him that any deficiencies in his commissariat department should not be made up by levies upon the houses of leading Roundheads in the neighbourhood. In spite of the loud outcries of the London pamphleteers, who labelled him "Prince Robber," "Ravenous Vulture," "Bloody Prince," and so forth, the thing seems to have been carried out, on the whole, quite decorously. Hearing that Roundhead military stores were hidden at Bradgate, he sent five troops of horse, who carried them off without difficulty. In Warwick Castle, which was then held for the Parliament against the King, one of the leading officers of the garrison was a certain Colonel Purefoy. Now Colonel Purefoy's estate was within easy reach of Queenborough. One day Rupert arrived with a body of horse and surrounded the house. Mrs Purefoy, assisted by her son-in-law, a Mr Abbott, and three or four serving-men, put up such a stout resistance that the Cavaliers, who had no artillery with them, lost several officers and men before they broke in the doors. As Rupert stood on the threshold Mrs Purefoy threw herself, weeping, at his feet. But he raised her up, consoled her, and declared that he so admired the heroic resistance of her little garrison that not one of the defenders should be hurt, nor should anything be taken from the house by his men.

About that time the Roundhead cavalry, who had already desecrated Canterbury Cathedral and sacked the houses of the Royalist nobility and gentry all over East Anglia and the South, were disporting themselves in Worcester and Hereford and the districts south and west of Rupert's command. A Roundhead subaltern of cavalry [1] has described for us with quiet satisfaction how at Coventry they seized upon an aged clergyman, rector of an adjoining parish, Sowe, [2] who was suspected of

[1] Nehemiah Wharton, *Letters from a Subaltern Officer* (*Archæologia*, vol. xxxv, pp. 318 *et seq.*).
[2] Now called Walsgrave-on-Sowe.

Royalist sympathies, and "led him ridiculously about the city." Drunken soldiers swaggered through the streets wearing surplices stolen from the churches. At Worcester Essex promised that the churches and private houses should be respected, but his orders were ignored. At Hereford, which they captured by a stratagem, and where the feeling of the populace was entirely against them, they all attended church service at the cathedral, and "some of our soldiers could not forbear dancing in the holy choir" while the service was going on—"whereat the Baallists were sore displeased."

They smashed up family pictures, furniture, and plate from sheer love of destruction; and "all the venison belonging to Malignants in the country is destroyed." They fought among themselves, cavalry *versus* infantry, or cavalry *versus* cavalry. Our Roundhead subaltern had his sword stolen by a brother officer, and only recovered it after a violent scene. In fact, it is impossible to glance through the literature of the period without realizing that their discipline was worse than that of Rupert's men. But they all referred to Rupert as "Prince Robber," and turned up their eyes in horror at the London-made stories of his evil deeds.

Rupert, when he heard of this, must have smiled sardonically. Things were going well with him. He could feel his cavalry growing under his hand: the elation of the creative artist was upon him. The crowd of undisciplined iconoclasts on the other side, who obeyed orders when they felt inclined, had no terrors for him. In the meantime he sent a cool note to the Mayor of Leicester, demanding two thousand pounds on behalf of his Majesty King Charles I. The demand was outrageously tactless and ill-timed; for, while most of the leading citizens of Leicester were for the Parliament, there was a strong party for the King, and the Mayor himself was wobbling. Rupert's action showed, not only his youth, but his essential 'foreignness.' It seemed perfectly natural to him to lift this money from the sleek civilians, if he could. And the best of it was that the terrified Mayor handed over five hundred pounds to keep him quiet before sending off a galloper to Nottingham to the King, who promptly repudiated, in rather severe terms, the action of "my said nephew."

The fact is that Rupert knew nothing of English politics. To the day of his death he never understood the hesitations which accompanied the outbreak of the English Civil War. He never realized the attitude of the English people—that nobody really wanted to fight, except the small group of stalwarts on the Parliamentary side, and that his uncle, the King, was among the most reluctant. He could not share the horror of Falkland and all the more moderate Cavaliers at the prospect of fighting against Englishmen,[1] because he himself was not an Englishman. He was a foreigner. He was a professional soldier. And he was only twenty-three.

While Rupert was training his cavalry at Leicester Charles had made his famous offer to take down his standard—to strike his flag—if the Parliament would agree to withdraw their charges of treason against his followers, he to do the same for theirs. Negotiations might then begin afresh—and he had privately intimated that he would make concessions, especially in religious matters. But the answer of Pym and his well-disciplined majority at Westminster was to insist that every penny they had raised for the purpose of making war against their King must be repaid from the confiscated estates of the Royalists and "other malignant persons." They

[1] And the moderate Roundhead General Waller wrote to the Cavalier Hopton: "The Great God, Who is the searcher of my heart, knows with what reluctance I go upon this service and with what perfect hatred I look upon a war without an enemy."

would treat on no other terms. It amounted to a sentence of confiscation suspended over the heads of all who had resisted the pretensions of Parliament.[1] And, considering that Parliament at that time consisted of not more than two-thirds of the Commons (the rest being with the King) and a mere remnant of the Lords, it is not surprising that this answer aroused resentment on the other side.

At Nottingham and Leicester it produced union out of disunion. Every man in the Royalist camp, from the typical, roistering Cavalier whom the Roundhead pamphleteers have immortalized, down to a pious Puritan like Sir Edmund Verney, who hated bishops, but had "eaten the King's bread and served him near thirty years, and would not do so base a thing as to forsake him" —or Spencer, who only remained at Nottingham because, as he wrote to his wife, "unless a man were resolved to fight on the Parliament side, which, for my part, I had rather be hanged, it will be said without doubt that a man is afraid to fight." [2] Every man, from the rich landowner, who saw his estates in danger, to the yeoman farmer, who began to fear for his six acres and a cow; from the play-actor, who had noted the new Bill just passed by Parliament prohibiting stage plays, to the ordinary Englishman, who dimly realized that something worse than our modern D.O.R.A. was upon him—all these now began to see that they were in the same boat and might as well pull together. There would be no mercy for "delinquents" or "malignants" of any kind if the Westminster fanatics got the upper hand. Royalist recruits came pouring in, and the King's motley host of volunteers rose rapidly from about two thousand men to nearer twenty. Even its leaders forgot their personal quarrels and returned hastily to their drill. Falkland and Spencer, who had

[1] Gardiner, *History of the Great Civil War*, vol. i, p. 61.
[2] *Sydney Papers*, vol. ii, p. 667.

striven to the last for an accommodation, gave up their task in despair.

Otherwise news was bad. Goring had surrendered Portsmouth, almost without a blow (September 7). He was drinking heavily, and even his loyalty was in doubt. From King's Lynn to Portsmouth the whole coastline was held by the rebels, together with the ports of Hull and Plymouth and Bristol; so that the King was now without any big port through which he could draw his supplies. Moreover, the Duke of Northumberland had betrayed the Navy into the hands of the enemy, and the Parliamentary Admiral Lord Warwick swept the seas. On September 9 Lord Essex, the Parliamentary Commander-in-Chief, moved out from London to Northampton, travelling in much state, accompanied by many members of Parliament.[1] But the King broke up from Nottingham and marched, first, due west to Shrewsbury, and then southward towards Worcester and Oxford, where he knew he would find support. Whereupon Essex moved west in the same direction, with a superior force, to intercept him. Meantime Sir John Byron had been compelled to abandon Oxford to the Roundheads, who were amusing themselves by throwing stones through the stained-glass windows of the colleges and shooting at the images of the Virgin and Child over the gates of St Mary's and All Souls. Byron retreated to Worcester, carrying with him a considerable treasure-chest.

Rupert cared little for all this. He disliked Goring almost as much as he disliked Wilmot and Digby—with whom he had already had words. He expected nothing from any of them. On the other hand, he had parted from his uncle on the best possible terms. He had seen the King at Stafford during the march west from Nottingham, and it is recorded that, as they stood talking in the church-

---

[1] Whitelocke, *Memorials*, p. 63.

yard of St Mary's, Rupert, upon a challenge by some one present, drew his pistol and put a bullet through the tail of the weathercock on the steeple. The King laughed, and declared that such marksmanship must owe something to luck. Whereupon Rupert shot again, with the same result.

They parted in high spirits, and the Prince rode south, with instructions to lead a strong party of horse to Worcester and bring off Byron and his treasure-chest. The mission suited him exactly. All he asked was the earliest possible opportunity of "blooding" his new cavalry. It was not to be withheld.

CHAPTER V: POWICK BRIDGE AND EDGEHILL

O N the afternoon of September 23, 1642, Rupert and a group of Royalist officers were in a field just outside the grey crumbling walls of the city of Worcester. Rupert's brother Prince Maurice was there, with Digby, Wilmot, Northampton, and the faithful Charles Lucas. It had been clear at the first glance that the walls of Worcester—like those of Shrewsbury, Hereford, and many other towns at this time—were too far decayed to be defended. So Byron, with his treasure, was already hurrying along the northern road to join the King. Rupert would follow presently. But he knew that a party of Roundheads had been at the gates of Worcester that very morning, and that the advance-guard of Essex's big army, rolling slowly westward, must soon be close at hand. He thought he would ride out south a little way and try to get a glimpse of them.

It was a warm afternoon, and the officers had dismounted and thrown themselves upon the grass to rest. None of them wore any armour—for this was only a reconnaissance—and but few had their pistols with them, nor any weapon but their swords. Behind them a body of Rupert's newly trained cavalry—it is impossible to give the exact numbers; probably two hundred at the most—were taking their ease.

The officers talked among themselves about the movements of their enemies. They do not appear to have pushed out a single patrol. If they had done so they must have become aware that in the field opposite, just beyond the trees and the little stream which they could see glistening from where they sat, Colonel Sandys, with Nathaniel Fiennes and at least five hundred Parliamentary horse, was riding slowly down towards the stream, to cross

Powick Bridge, and so up the narrow, leafy lane which terminated only a few hundred yards from where the Cavalier officers sat.[1] Sandys, for his part, was equally oblivious of danger. Though his own advance party had reported that same morning (quite wrongly) that Worcester was strongly held, here he was ambling up to the very walls with his horsemen, as though upon a picnic party! The scouting seems to have been weak on both sides.

Suddenly the alarm was given. Rupert sprang to his feet. The sinking sun was behind him, and he could now plainly see the hostile horsemen, buff-coated, steel-helmeted, emerging from the narrow lane, and deploying in the field below him, almost within pistol-shot. Even as he looked the last of them rode out into the field. Taking in the situation at a glance, he shouted an order for every one to mount and follow him; and himself, springing into the saddle, gave his horse the spur and galloped headlong down the slope, sword in hand, accompanied by all the gaily dressed officers, who thus came to form the decorative spearhead of the first Royalist charge in the Civil War. What they thought of this impetuous order we cannot tell. But Rupert's instinct was right. The Roundheads were completely surprised, and smitten hip and thigh.

It is stated by most historians, I cannot tell why, that Sandys and his men were still extricating themselves from the lane, still trying to deploy, when the Cavalier whirlwind descended upon them. That might excuse their defeat. But it is untrue. We have a clear account of the charge, written by Sir Richard Bulstrode,[2] who was in it

---

[1] See Webb, *Civil War in Herefordshire*, vol. i, p. 146, f.n. Up till only seventy years ago, says this author, the scene of the skirmish on Powick Bridge remained untouched. It is now hidden from sight beneath a flood of dingy architecture; even the old bridge is gone.

[2] *Memoirs of the Reign of King Charles I*, p. 74 (London, 1721).

himself, and his evidence must be accepted in preference to second-hand versions. Bulstrode makes it clear that Sandys had "passed the bridge" and "passed the defiles," and had drawn up his troops in proper order in the field (which the Prince "gave him time to do," whether intentionally or not) before his enemies reached him.

The result was the same. The Cavalier officers, in their slashed doublets, their wide-brimmed hats and plumes, crashed in among the heavily armed and visored Roundheads with an impetus that hurled them back into the lane, and, as the next wave of assailants came, through the lane and over the bridge, in hopeless confusion, jostling and trampling each other in their flight. Young Bulstrode, in the first fine frenzy of that charge, found himself far ahead of his comrades, among the flying Roundheads on the bridge. But they never noticed him in their panic, as they struggled to reach the other side. Many fell into the stream and were drowned. Sandys himself and a few stalwarts made a gallant stand before the bridge, but he and Fiennes were both cut down and taken prisoners. His troopers (who had found it so easy to overcome the poor old parson of Sowe) had already seen enough of these new opponents. All who survived galloped hard from the field, leaving forty or fifty dead behind them. And so along the road to London, nine miles or more, in a shameful panic, spreading wild stories of the Robber Prince and his terrible men behind them.

But Rupert's small party had been in the saddle for many hours, and their horses were in no condition for pursuit. Their casualties, though numerically slight, included almost every officer except Rupert himself, who, as usual, had come off untouched. Wilmot got a sword thrust in the side, Sir Louis Dyves a slash across the shoulder, and Prince Maurice a scalp wound, which led to a report that he was killed. (All this because they wore no body armour.) But their little victory was beautifully complete, and they knew it. Sandys, their gallant opponent, died of his wounds at Worcester, and the story went round the Royalist camp-fires that night that he had called upon God with his last breath to forgive him for his unnatural rebellion against an anointed king. They had easily beaten an enemy twice their size (Clarendon puts the Roundheads at five hundred; Ludlow, their own historian, at a thousand), and the moral effect was considerable, upon both sides. It was Rupert's first encounter with a vainglorious foe, and its result, as we can easily believe, acted upon his troopers like a tonic.

A day or two later a letter was delivered to the Lord-General, Essex. It was in Rupert's handwriting, but had been written before the affair of Powick Bridge. It contained a boyish challenge to a set combat between the two armies on Dunsmore Heath on a fixed date, or, alternatively—and, no doubt, preferably—a "single duel" between the two commanders. And any more that need be said, concluded Rupert with a flourish, "shall be delivered in a larger field than a small sheet of paper, and that by my sword and not by my pen." He signed himself: "Your friend, till I meet you next—Rupert." Essex had known Rupert's reputation on the Continent. He now wrote a stiff reply, gravely declining to engage in any such contest. Humour was never a strong point with the Lord-General.

The King, meantime, on his western march, had reached Shrewsbury. Just before he entered the town one of Prince Rupert's secretaries, a Mr Crane, rode up to him with the joyful news of Powick Bridge, and presented to him the colours captured from the enemy in that encounter. It was the first serious engagement of the war, and the news of it sent a thrill through the army. They entered Shrewsbury like conquerors; and it is just possible that if the King had been in a position to march at once against his rebellious capital—for we know from Roundhead accounts what a panic fear of Rupert's horsemen had been spread all along the London road—he might have crushed the rebellion at a blow. But his troops were still a mere mob, many of them not even divided into regiments. They needed weeks of training before they could be put through the simplest evolutions on a battlefield. At Edgehill, the first big battle of the war, the deficiencies of the Royalist infantry, both in drill and equipment, were still painfully apparent. And between Shrewsbury and Edgehill there was yet an interval of a whole month.

The only trained troops in the Royal army were Rupert's cavalry, the victors of Powick Bridge. They had now fallen back through Worcester upon Ludlow (on the way to Shrewsbury), still covering Byron's retreat. Legends were already beginning to spring up round the personality of their young commander. Rupert was nothing if not vivid. To adopt modern phraseology, he was the first commander on either side in the Civil War to catch the public eye and provide 'copy' for the journalists. It was said that he had made Captain Wingate, one of the prisoners taken at Powick Bridge, ride stark naked on horseback up the northern road; and, contrariwise, that he had used Sandys and Fiennes with extraordinary courtesy, never treating them as prisoners, but leaving them behind at Worcester with their friends.

It was also alleged that he would ride among his enemies in disguise, to pick up news—though how that swarthy countenance, with its hawk-like nose, could remain unrecognized passes comprehension. Perhaps those amateur theatricals at Leyden helped him. Dressed as a civilian, he came to a humble cottage near Worcester, and asked the old woman who lived there for a dish of collops and eggs. While he ate she apologized for having no drink in the house but small beer. She was a poor widow, she explained, and her son, her only child, was away from home.

He asked her where her son was. She told him, "Gone to Worcester, to hear what news of the Cavaliers"; for she heard say (thank God for it!) that his Excellency [Essex] had made them fly the city: a company of rude knaves they were! He asked her what she thought of Prince Rupert. "A plague choke Prince Rupert!" said she. "He might have kept himself where he was born; this kingdom has been the worse ever since he landed." "There's three pieces for that word," said the disguised Prince; "for I'm of thy mind." [1]

She took the money gratefully, wondering at his sardonic laughter. On another occasion, riding as near to Essex's army as he dared, he overtook a countryman driving a horse with a load of apples.

He asked the fellow what he had got there, who told him "he was about to sell his ware to his Excellency's soldiers." "Why dost thou not go to the King's army?" inquired the Prince. "I hear they are generous sparks, and will pay double!" "Oh," said the fellow, "they are Cavaliers, and have a mad Prince among them; and the devil a penny could I get in the whole army." The Prince asked him what he would take for the load, and the fellow answering ten shillings, "Hold thy hand," said the Prince; "there is a piece for thee: now hold my horse, change habit with me, and stay here while I sell thy apples— only for a merry humour that I have—and at my coming back I'll give thee a piece more." The fellow willingly lent him his long coat and hat, and away went the Prince, selling the apples through the army at any rate; viewing their strength and in what kind they lay; and, returning to the fellow, gave him another piece, with this charge: "Go to the army, and ask the commanders how they liked the fruit Prince Rupert, in his own person, did but this morning sell them." [2]

These stories may be apocryphal, but they illustrate

[1] *Prince Robert's Disguises* (London, November 16, 1642; Thomason Tracts, E. 127 (18)).　　　　　　　[2] *Ibid.*

Rupert's early hold on the popular imagination. He was the first officer in either army to get his troops into fighting trim. For that reason alone he was bound to be in the news. But there was more in it than that. The public instinct, seldom at fault in these matters, had already recognized one of the outstanding personalities of the Civil War.

At the end of September 1642 the strategical position was as follows. The King was at Shrewsbury. He had paid a visit to Chester, and, while there, had called out the loyal gentry of Lancashire, among whom were many Catholics, whose whole future was bound up with his cause. At Chester also he had taken possession of the wagons and stores which had been assembled there by Parliament with a view to an invasion of Ireland. But he was still desperately short of money. It seems clear that, in default of pay, Rupert's cavalry were compelled, in the modern phrase, to 'live on the country'—a circumstance which did nothing to diminish the growing terror of their name. As for the infantry, they were a heterogeneous collection, so ill-armed that some of them, according to Clarendon, "marched without any weapon but a cudgel." The latest addition to the Royal ranks consisted of "1200 poor Welsh vermin" on foot, "the offscourings of the nation," armed only with scythes and pitchforks, and dressed just as when they left their ploughs. But their numbers were always growing, and their spirits were high. It was their confident expectation that at the first general engagement half the rebel army would go over to the King. And, whatever their other defects as soldiers, they could at any rate march.

So the King left Shrewsbury on October 12 with his whole force, and headed direct for London, where he hoped to make an end of the war at a stroke.

Essex was at Worcester. He was superior in numbers

still, and his troops, as we have seen, were better armed than their opponents. But their discipline was, if anything, even worse. They had more opportunities, perhaps, of misbehaving themselves—certainly more incitement, for the very articles of their faith, and the fervid harangues of the preachers attached to every regiment, seemed to encourage vandalism. Arthur Trevor, writing to Lord Ormonde a few weeks after this date, describes the appalling condition of Worcester Cathedral after the Roundhead army had left—all the glass and wood-carving smashed, stone images disfigured, and all over the church "the droppings of those unclean birds." An aged verger, with tears in his eyes, told Trevor how he had witnessed the deliberate defiling of the altar and the font, amid the laughter of the onlookers, and jokes about "naming the child" and "signing it with the sign of the Cross." The officers could do nothing to prevent this beastliness. As Trevor shrewdly remarks, "They have raised a spirit that they cannot tell how to lay again." [1]

But they also could march, and when Essex heard of the King's advance towards London he broke up from Worcester and followed him. London, as he knew, was in no condition to resist attack. The trained bands had been called out, on the alarm of the King's approach, and money voted for raising another army of sixteen thousand men. But at present this army existed only on paper. And in the City a strong Royalist minority looked forward eagerly to the arrival of their king. It was of the utmost importance, from Essex's point of view, that Charles should be overtaken and brought to action before he could get there.

Rupert was covering the King's advance. He was well pleased with the course of events, for he heartily approved

[1] Carte's *Letters*, vol. i, p. 15.

this march on London. It was always his opinion, as he had already told the King, that the proper strategy to pursue was to strike at the hostile capital, the heart of the rebellion. Meantime his cavalry patrols, which were daily becoming more expert at this work, were thrown out westward, feeling for Essex's advance-guard. The King had marched south-east, by Coventry and Warwick, leaving Worcester away to the right. He was marching light, taking with him few wagons and fewer tents (Clarendon even asserts that he had none!). Yet it is obvious that Essex, if he had started quickly, could have cut across his path and stood between him and London. But, with his usual sluggishness, Essex moved too late, and Charles was now just ahead of him on the London road. Neither of them knew it yet.

On October 22 a party of Rupert's horse, operating on the right flank of the Royal army, rode into a village near Kineton looking for billets. They were surprised to find some Parliamentary cavalry there, but after a brisk skirmish drove them out, taking several prisoners. Brought before Rupert, these prisoners acknowledged that Essex with his main body was at Kineton, only four miles away. Rupert's messenger, galloping hard, came to Charles's headquarters at Edgcott that same night and found him sleeping. Rupert seems to have followed up the message personally. No doubt he arrived hot and excited, and it may be, as Warburton suggests,[1] that it was on this occasion that he had that regrettable exchange of words with Falkland which Clarendon reports.[2] Charles, roused from his bed, sent Falkland out "to direct Prince Rupert what he should do"; but Rupert, as always, insisted violently that he would take orders from no one but the King. The incident is of no import-

[1] Vol. ii, p. 11.
[2] *History of the Rebellion*, vol. ii, p. 33.

ance except to show that, even at this early date, the quarrels in the Royalist camp had already begun. Rupert always despised men like Falkland and Hyde and the "politicians"—and he had as little use for some of the soldiers.

On this occasion the point to be decided was a simple one. The King, as we have said, was travelling light, and he might succeed in outdistancing Essex and getting to London first. But Essex was in superior numbers and was uncomfortably close. The Royalists had marched far, their billets were scattered, and they needed a few hours' rest. Rupert's inclination, as the wording of his first message shows, was to stand and fight. He now further advised that the King should lead his army, early on the Sunday morning, to the top of the rising ground called Edgehill, and there turn and wait for the arrival of the enemy. A few hours later Rupert, back at his cavalry headquarters—if indeed he ever left them—received the following brief note:

NEPHEW,

I have given order as you have desired; so I doubt not but all the foot and cannon will be at Edgehill betimes this morning, where you will also find

Your loving uncle and faithful friend,

CHARLES R.

4 o'clock this Sunday morning.

And on this same Sunday morning, which seemed so big with fate, the Parliamentary army moved out from Kineton to continue its eastward march. No report had come in from the Roundhead cavalry of last night's skirmish. The leaders were totally unaware of the near proximity of their foe. But they had marched not more than two or three miles from Kineton when they saw before them the gently rising ground called Edgehill, and plainly perceived, at the top of the slope, "a fair body of

89

horse." They realized, as Clarendon puts it, that their march that day would be a short one.

Essex decided to halt. Hampden, with two regiments of foot, one regiment of horse, most of the artillery, and the ammunition train, was a day's march behind him, so that, although he had ten thousand men with him, he was for the moment slightly inferior to the King in numbers. To advance to the slope of Edgehill was to invite attack. He therefore stood where he was, and drew up his men in line of battle, the infantry in the centre, the cavalry, as was customary, on both wings.

It is important to get some idea of the appearance of the English countryside in those days. The hedgerows, which we think of as typically English, were much fewer; the country, in general, was not parcelled out into small fields divided by bushes, hedges, and trees, but was much more open than anything we are accustomed to; and this stretch of country between Kineton and Edgehill is particularly described by Clarendon as "a fair [or open] campaigne." But Essex's right flank was to some extent protected by a few enclosures and hedges, and here, therefore, he posted a strong force of musketeers under cover, with only two regiments of horse; while the bulk of his cavalry, under the Scottish general Ramsay, covered his exposed left wing. There was a strong reserve of horse under another Scot, Sir William Balfour. So he stood, looking at the mounted Cavaliers on the opposite slope.

They were Rupert's men. The King, for all his efforts, could not assemble the infantry in time. This was not due to lack of discipline. All things considered, he had his men well in hand. (On the long march from Shrewsbury there had been only one case of pillaging—at the Puritan town of Birmingham—and even in that instance the offenders had been caught and hanged.) But their

ROBERT DEVEREUX, THIRD EARL OF ESSEX
Robert Walker
Photo E.N.A.

billets were scattered now, so that some of them had to march seven miles to the rendezvous at Edgehill. And many were hungry, for the country people in these parts had been so plied with Roundhead propaganda about the barbarity of the Cavaliers that they were afraid to bring provisions for sale. Thus it was that Rupert with his horsemen, making a brave display on the skyline, held the position almost unsupported until nearly one o'clock in the afternoon, when the foot were got into line, the cannon planted on the top of the hill, and the cavalry disposed upon either wing.

Nothing happened. Essex, very sensibly, stayed where he was, a little drawn back from the foot of the hill, at a point where the ground rose again slightly in his favour. It was not for him to make the first move. He was waiting for Hampden and his reserves. When they came he might consider the advisability of attempting a frontal attack up the slope of Edgehill—not before. The day wore on. By three o'clock it was apparent to the King and his advisers that if they were to force an action before nightfall they must do it now. Hampden was coming up fast, and in an hour or less their temporary superiority in numbers would be lost.

There was a consultation among the leaders. The Earl of Lindsey, the Commander-in-Chief, had resigned his position when he realized that Rupert would take no orders from him and that the King turned always to his nephew for advice. (That old friendship between the delicate, diminutive monarch and the tall, fiery young Prince was having unexpected effects.) Lindsey decided to fight in the centre with the King, as colonel of his own Lincolnshire regiment of foot; and his son, Lord Willoughby, who commanded a troop of horse under Rupert, dismounted, and went and stood at his father's side. The King gave Lindsey's post to the Scottish veteran Lord Forth, who had been strongly of Rupert's opinion on every point of strategy. Rupert, as General of the Horse, commanded the right wing, Wilmot the left.

These officers, and others, stood on the brow of the hill, considering what to do next; and as they talked they must often have glanced at the stolid, immovable line of the Roundheads on the opposite slope. They were looking for some movement indicating that wholesale desertion to the King's side which every Royalist had confidently expected. The King, in particular, gazed long and earnestly through his glasses. "I never saw the rebels in a body before," he said quietly, as he put the glasses down.[1] However, there was only one thing to be done in the circumstances, and about three o'clock Charles gave the order to attack. The Royalist army, horse and foot, moved slowly down the slope towards its enemies. As it did so, that gallant soldier and loyal gentleman Sir Jacob Astley fell upon his knees in the grass and offered up his famous prayer: "O Lord, Thou knowest how busy I must be this day: if I forget Thee, do not Thou forget me." Then, rising hastily to his feet, "March on, boys!"

It was a bright, keen October afternoon, and the northerly wind, blowing up the slope, set the Cavaliers' plumes fluttering as they moved down to engage in the first great battle of that fratricidal war. In spite of the popularity of the buff coat and steel helmet, there was a variegated display of colour on both sides. To a combatant it must have been desperately confusing. Among the Parliamentarians might be distinguished regiments of redcoats (but the King's guard also wore red), Lord Brooke's men in purple, Lord Say's and Lord Mandeville's in blue (but the Royalist "blue guard" died heroically at Naseby), and other infantry in grey or green.

[1] Warburton, vol. ii, p. 13.

Hampden's eagerly awaited reinforcements also wore green; but there were greencoats, under Lord Northampton, on the Royalist side, and only a few weeks before this, at the Southam skirmish, Rupert's friend Will Legge had suffered his first imprisonment through riding in among a group of green-clad Roundheads, supposing them to be his own men. We shall later meet Newcastle's whitecoats and Rupert's redcoats, and find white and green as the Royalist colours at Bristol. Red eventually became the Parliamentary colour, and Cromwell's New Model, in scarlet, set the fashion for British uniforms to this day. In the meantime it was a maddening kaleidoscope. The Welsh ploughboys, now in reserve behind the King's centre, wore anything they liked.

But as the Royalist line drew nearer and nearer, and just before the cavalry were unleashed, one colour came out, clear and predominating, all along the opposing line. Orange was the colour of the Devereux family, and Lord Essex's officers, in compliment to him, had adopted it as their distinguishing badge, tying "orange-tawny scarfs" across their breastplates.[1] Many of the common soldiers followed suit, so that there was the appearance of a long ribbon of orange across the field on their side.

This was Rupert's moment—the moment of which he and his horsemen had been dreaming all through those weeks of training. There were Ramsay's troopers inertly awaiting him. It remained only to give the signal to charge. But one order must come first. Our old acquaintance Bulstrode, who was serving with the cavalry of the right wing, in the Prince of Wales's regiment, has told us what happened. "Prince Rupert," he says, "passed from one wing to the other, giving positive orders to the horse" —apparently of Wilmot's wing as well as his own—to ride "as close as possible," to "keep their ranks with

[1] Clarendon, *History of the Rebellion*, vol. ii, p. 38.

sword in hand," and "to receive the enemy's shot without firing either carbine or pistol, till we broke in amongst the enemy, and then to make use of our firearms as need should require." In other words, modern shock tactics.

When that order was given Rupert sounded the charge, and the mounted Cavaliers on both wings, setting spurs to their horses, swept down upon their enemies, gathering speed with every stride. From the orange-tawny line opposite a group of horsemen were seen to detach themselves and ride rapidly to meet the advancing Cavaliers. As they did so they fired their pistols into the ground. They were Sir Faithful Fortescue and his men, who, having come over from Ireland on the King's service, and been forced into the Parliamentary ranks, were taking this first opportunity of returning to their allegiance. As the Cavaliers thundered past them they turned their horses and joined in the charge. It was the first and only desertion of that day, but it had its moral effect.

The orange-tawny line still held. They fired at least one volley with their small arms. But when they saw how little effect was produced they began to waver. They were not accustomed to these new tactics. They had heard terrible stories of Rupert's horsemen; and here they were close upon them, roaring like furies, with the black-avised young Palatine raging devilishly at their head. Those in the front rank tried to back into the rank behind. Before the shock came they were already beaten men. And then, in a minute, their line was swept away, men and horses tumbled head over heels, and those who remained galloping disgracefully, head down, towards Kineton and safety, with the Royalist sword-points at their backs.

It may be that Rupert went mad. If he did it would be quite in character. But the more reasonable explanation of what followed—and it is supported by contemporary authority—seems to be that neither he nor any of his officers could restrain those maddened horsemen, who had come through that deadly charge, and now found their enemies flying before them. They "had the execution of them above two miles." Through the village of Kineton, plundering the rich Parliamentary baggage, out into the fields beyond—there was no holding them. The very impetuosity of this new kind of charge made it the harder to restrain. Only when they saw the steady ranks of Hampden's greencoats approaching, with Hollis's foot, the London redcoats, and other Parliamentary reinforcements behind, did they seek to return, in scattered parties, to the battlefield.

Lieutenant Bulstrode was trying to find his way back to the main battle as quickly as possible, when he was "wounded in the head by a person"—presumably a Parliamentary foot-soldier in flight—"who turned upon me and struck me with his pole-axe, and was seconding his blow when, Sir Thomas Byron being near, he shot him dead with his pistol." Historians should be grateful to Sir Thomas Byron for that shot. (He was colonel of Bulstrode's regiment.) The incident aptly illustrates the confusion of the battlefield at this point. Greencoats, redcoats, and Rupert's Cavaliers were all mixed up together, and it is recorded that many of Sir Faithful Fortescue's men, having forgotten to discard their orange scarves, were slain by mistake. Rupert, as he reined in his horse and glanced anxiously round, could see that the cavalry reserve of the right wing, which had been posted immediately behind him under Sir John Byron, had followed him off the battlefield, and was now mingling with his own men in the outskirts of Kineton. Even the King's own mounted bodyguard, annoyed, perhaps, by some scoffing references to the "show troop"—for they were all gentlemen, serving as private soldiers—had, with

Byron's permission, galloped clean off the field in the tide of that glorious charge.

On the left wing Wilmot had been equally successful. He was incommoded at first by the fire of the musketeers hidden behind the hedges on his left. But Sir Arthur Aston, commanding the Royalist dragoons, or mounted infantry, dealt with these people in the approved Swedish style, riding steadily towards them, and halting at intervals to fire volleys, until he had driven them from their cover. Then Wilmot pressed his charge home. The two or three regiments of horse opposed to him, seeing what was happening at the other side of the field, never waited to feel his steel. He chased them right away behind, as Rupert had chased Ramsay. And Digby, commanding the reserve, followed blindly at his heels, as John Byron had followed Rupert. The King's two victorious wings of horsemen had disappeared from the scene in a cloud of dust!

That was bad enough. But they made in addition a fatal oversight. As they converged, from right and left, upon the Kineton road, behind Lord Essex's line, they failed to notice the reserve of Parliamentary horse, under Sir William Balfour, which was immediately behind the centre, and was therefore somewhat out of their reach. At any rate, they made no attempt to engage it. And Balfour, that wily Scot, did nothing to draw attention to himself. On the contrary, he is said to have ordered his men to throw away their orange scarves and shout for the King, as though they were Royalist horsemen. Only when the last of the mounted Cavaliers had disappeared behind him did Balfour reveal himself, and set about doing what he could to restore the fortunes of the day. The opposing lines of infantry in the centre of the field were exchanging volleys at about a hundred yards range, and in one or two places had come to thrust of pike. The

Roundheads were the better armed, but the Cavaliers for the moment had the moral advantage, and felt that victory was declaring itself for their side.

Suddenly Balfour, choosing his moment, made a charge. It would appear that his men rode in column or wedge formation, for, though he broke right through the Royalist ranks and came out on the other side, they were able to form again behind him. He cannot, therefore, have covered a wide front. But he shook them badly. The Earl of Lindsey fell, shot through the thigh, and was carried off prisoner by Balfour's men. His son, Lord Willoughby, attempting a rescue, was taken with him. Many other officers and men were ridden down and slain. Sir Edmund Verney, carrying the Royal Standard, was killed, and the standard taken. But a certain Ensign Smith rode after the Roundheads, and, taking a leaf out of their own book, pushed his way through their ranks as though he were one of them, coolly wrested the flag from the hands of its captor, and galloped back with it to his own lines before he could be stopped. The King knighted him on the field.

Accounts of this part of the battle are extraordinarily confusing. It would seem that two regiments of infantry on the Roundhead left had been carried away by Rupert's onset. But the rest now came on bravely. And Balfour, having cut the traces of the King's cannon, turned and charged the Royalist footguards from behind. Colonel Stapleton was with him, and a certain Captain Oliver Cromwell, who commanded a troop of East Anglian horse. The guards were broken. The "poor Welsh vermin," who formed the reserve, had already faded away —and who can blame them? But the Royalist main body, assailed on both sides, still hung together round the standard. Charles himself was among them, fighting gallantly. Essex, with a pike in his hand, led on the opposing foot. If Balfour and Stapleton had used their cavalry more efficiently, and pressed home the attack, it seems highly probable, as Clarendon suggests, that they might have swept the Royalist infantry from the field, and captured the King himself. They missed their chance of making history.

Rupert rode back on to the field just before darkness fell. His horsemen were coming in behind him in small and scattered parties, flushed with the joy of battle, most of them fondly imagining that they had made an end of the rebellion there and then. At the same time Essex's tired infantry felt the presence of Hampden's reinforcements in their rear, and, though their last attack had been repulsed with loss, were inspired to stand firm. There was an atmosphere of stalemate. If either side could produce the energy for another attack a decision might yet be won. The initiative was with the Royalists; for the lower slopes below Edgehill were once again flooded with their cavalry, and the Parliamentarians on foot could do no more than stand and wait to be charged. In the failing light, staff officers galloped from group to group of the returning horsemen, urging yet one more effort. It was useless. They were too widely scattered, their horses too tired after the long ride. Only Wilmot's men were still in their ranks, still comparatively fresh. But Wilmot, when appealed to by Lord Falkland, to make another charge for the King, answered crudely, "My Lord, we have got the day; let us live to enjoy the fruits thereof." If that was the spirit of the officers it is hardly surprising that it was impossible to rouse the men. Wilmot's remark was widely reported. Rupert never had a good word for him afterwards. But, in truth, the Royalist horse seem to have been exhausted. Nothing could be done.

Night fell, and with it a bitter frost. The sufferings of the wounded were terrible—though it is said that in many cases the extreme cold stopped the flow of blood. The Earl of Lindsey died that night, for want of a surgeon's attention, in a cottage to which the Roundheads had carried him. Essex sent Balfour and other officers to see how he did ; but he raised himself upon his elbow and heaped reproaches on them for their rebellion, until they left him. Lesser men lay out in the field. There were five or six thousand of them, killed and wounded, in the proportion of about two Parliamentarians to one Cavalier. Most of them lay along the grassy slope between the two lines of bivouac fires. All night they could be heard—Englishmen crying to Englishmen for help, and getting none. Instead there came the usual prowlers, who stripped many of them of their clothing, leaving them naked to freeze.

In the course of the following day Essex drew off his army through Kineton to Warwick. The King was free to pursue his march upon London unmolested.

CHAPTER VI: THE THRUST AT LONDON

THERE was disappointment on both sides at the indecisive result of Edgehill. King Charles, in his address to his troops immediately before the engagement, had plainly indicated that he expected the dispute between himself and his rebellious Commons to be settled, once and for all, on that day. Rupert's and Wilmot's horsemen, returning from their victorious pursuit, fully supposed that they had settled it. Their failure to produce another charge was due not to lack of courage, but to the fact that they had ridden their horses to a standstill. On the following morning (October 24) they were rested, and eager to be at it again. They looked upon themselves as victors, and they chafed as the day wore on, and the infantry on both sides licked their wounds, and the King sent over futile flags of truce, offering free pardons to any in the Parliamentary army who would join his side. Essex, of course, took good care that no such messages reached his men.

It was not till the 25th that it was known that Essex was evacuating Kineton. Then Rupert and his horsemen went after him like hounds unleashed. They entered Kineton close on his heels. They surrounded and made prisoners of his rearguard; they captured his plate and private baggage and all his papers. And, by a curious stroke of irony, one of the first discoveries they made among these papers was a series of letters to Lord Essex from Rupert's own private secretary, giving valuable information to the enemy in return for cash!

But if either side could claim the victory—and both of them did—it was obvious that the King had the better title of the two. He now turned his back, almost contemptuously, on the Parliamentary army, and continued his southern march, receiving the surrender of Banbury, and entering the loyal city of Oxford like a conqueror, on October 29, acclaimed with equal enthusiasm by town and gown. There he established his general headquarters, and, having set his affairs in order—and hanged Rupert's erring secretary—he prepared for the final stage of his march upon London, which could no longer be prevented.

In London there was, at first, something like panic. The City Fathers and the Puritan preachers, by the very success of their propaganda, had so filled the minds of the common people with fantastic stories of the wickedness of the "Malignants," and especially of that "debauched Cavalier" and "Robber Prince" who led their cavalry, that every apprentice trembled in his shoes at the mere rumour of their approach. It was forgotten that the King's soldiers were plain honest Englishmen, of precisely the same stuff of which the London trained bands were made. They were "the ungodly," "the sons of Belial," "the worshippers of Baal," alien monsters, more foreign than any foreigner. Such miracles can assiduous pulpit propaganda achieve. The thought of these heathen hooligans in their midst set the Londoners eagerly digging trenches in Lincoln's Inn Fields and throwing up stout barricades across the streets leading to the City. Such Royalists among them as were not already locked up— there cannot have been many—watched these proceedings with amusement, and began to sing among themselves in their favourite taverns a topical comic song called *Cuckolds, Come Dig*, which, according to Warburton, did more to embitter party feeling than a dozen battles. But, apart from the taverns, most of the shops were shut, and there was a general air of apprehension, as of a city already besieged. The arrival of emissaries from Essex's camp with vainglorious accounts of a victory at Edgehill did little to dispel the gloom; for there was no denying the fact that the Royalists now lay between Lord Essex and London, and that communications with the Parliamentary army were becoming more difficult every day.

But the King delayed his advance—unaccountably, as it must have seemed. There were the usual dissensions among his advisers. Rupert, it need hardly be said, was for an immediate dash at London, and many of the younger officers supported him. Bulstrode, for instance, thought that "in all probability" it would have succeeded and "made an end of the war." What, after all, did Banbury and Oxford matter? Within forty-eight hours of the battle of Edgehill the King might have been sleeping in his own palace at Whitehall, leaving these other towns to be dealt with later. Rupert, according to his diary,

> offered to push on [immediately after Edgehill] with the horse
> and three thousand foot; to seize Westminster and the rebel
> part of the Parliament, and occupy the palace of Whitehall
> until the King should come up with the remainder of the
> army.[1]

He might have succeeded. In the light of subsequent events we can see that it would have been worth trying at any rate. But the more cautious among the soldiers were against him, and Hyde and the politicians opposed him tooth and nail. They had already entangled the King in diplomatic negotiations with the Parliament. They hoped for a peaceful settlement. As Englishmen they did not even *want* a victory by force of arms—certainly not one of the kind that Rupert visualized. The old Earl of Bristol put the objection very frankly at the counciltable—if Rupert got into the City, he said, he would probably set it on fire!

Charles listened. He thought Rupert the best soldier of them all; but in matters of statecraft—and especially if there were any hope of peace—his sympathies were with

---

[1] Quoted by Warburton, vol. ii, pp. 37–38.

the other side. If Edgehill had been a victory . . . but it was only a drawn fight, though undoubtedly in his favour. He kept hoping that the Westminster irreconcilables would presently come to terms. He must give them a little time to see reason. He delayed at Banbury, and afterwards at Oxford. He even allowed the sluggish Essex to march past him on the north and get to London first. So the military effort of Edgehill was thrown away! We can see now that Rupert's fighting instinct was right —that this was probably one of the fatal decisions of the Civil War.

Baulked of his London adventure, Rupert got rid of much superfluous energy by raiding the Home Counties for supplies. The King was in need of provender for men and horses, and his troops, as a whole, were still wretchedly armed. Rupert's horsemen, with the Prince in his scarlet cloak at their head, were soon clattering out of the streets of Oxford (where a pretty little court was already beginning to form round the King) and down the London road towards Abingdon, which Rupert had pitched upon as his headquarters. From Abingdon he organized a series of forays through the surrounding counties. By this means he did much to relieve the King's necessities, but nothing to improve his own popularity as a neighbour. It must be remembered that the English countryside still bore the aspect of peace. Law and order were maintained, and the judges, with their marshals, still rode in state on their circuits, displaying flags of truce as they passed through districts held by the oppos-ing armies. Throughout the Civil War, indeed, as Nugent justly boasts,[1] there was no serious instance of popular disorder or massacre on a large scale, though the whole of England was divided into two hostile camps. Into such a peaceful scene the arrival of parties of Cavalier

---

[1] *Memorials of Hampden*, vol. ii, p. 401.

horsemen, requisitioning right and left, and paying for what they took in tokens (which the King hoped one day to honour) was a disturbing and distasteful irruption.

Rupert cared little for popularity. His mind was set on winning the war, and he was well aware of the military value of the terror which his name was beginning to inspire. If he could, he would have subsidized the London pamphleteers who were making him into a bogy-man. What probably disturbed him more was the discovery of the limitations of cavalry action unsupported by infantry or guns. After Powick Bridge and Edgehill he seems to have been inflated with the idea that he could gallop his gallant horsemen over any obstacle, from gun-fire to castle walls. But the results of one or two skirmishes about this time brought him down to earth.

He was at Aylesbury on All Saints' Day, November 1, resting his men after several days of hard work collecting cattle and supplies for the Royal army, when he heard that a Parliamentary force was marching against him from Stony Stratford, commanded by Sir William Balfour— the same who had spoiled his victory at Edgehill. Riding out of the town, he found the Roundheads, consisting of both horse and foot, waiting for him on the other side of a stream. Rupert instantly charged, and his mounted Cavaliers, splashing across the stream, broke through the first two lines of infantry and into the midst of Balfour's horse. They could get no farther, though Sir Louis Dyves, with the reserve, also charged across to their support. According to a Roundhead version of the affair,[1] Dyves, on reaching the scene of action, dismounted his men, and poured in a volley which did considerable execution. But the Parliamentarians, as usual, were much better supplied with firearms than their opponents, and

---

[1] Thomason Tracts, E. 125 (9). This account does not mention the stream.

Balfour's horsemen were using their pistols with great effect in the *mêlée*. Rupert, in spite of his "fiery soul" and "native courage," was gradually forced back across the stream; and even the intervention of Wilmot with further reserves only temporarily restored the situation. For as Rupert was rallying his men for another charge the Roundhead infantry on the other side of the stream opened a brisk fire of small arms, and emptied so many saddles that he was compelled to draw off. In the retreat some foot-soldiers who were attached to his party were roughly handled by the pursuing cavalry.

But the morale of Rupert's horsemen was unimpaired. No doubt they realized that, in this patrol work, an occasional retreat was nothing to be ashamed of. Only six days after the affair at Aylesbury we find them attempting to surprise Windsor Castle. A single charge gave them the town, sending Roundhead sympathizers scurrying for safety to the castle. Rupert had four or five guns with him, and with these he opened fire from the grounds of Eton College, hoping to distract the attention of the defenders of the castle while his men began to dig trenches as close as they dared to its walls. But they were discovered, and their trenches soon knocked to bits. It was unnatural work for cavalry. Some of them are said to have protested openly that "they would willingly attend Prince Rupert to fight against men, but not against stone walls." [1]

Rupert's main object was to intercept the river traffic to London from the West. Having failed at Windsor, therefore, he moved cautiously towards Kingston—an equally good position for his purpose—sending out spies to endeavour to ascertain the enemy's strength. A certain "Master Cary," "Keeper of Mary-bone Parke," and "a strong Malignant," volunteered for this service, being

[1] Thomason Tracts, E. 127 (10) and E. 126 (42).

well acquainted with the countryside. Having disguised himself as an ordinary miller, with a miller's cape over his clothes, Cary set out on foot along the Kingston road. At first all went well, but, says the Roundhead chronicler,

> when he was within a mile of the town some of our horse met him, and, not suspecting him by his habit, let him pass, till one that came behind, knowing him, made a stop of him, and, bellowing in the rest of his fellows, they carried him to Kingston and there put him in safe custody.[1]

The trained bands of Berkshire and Surrey were all in Kingston at this time, as it happened, with a detachment from Essex's army. Their leaders prepared to give Rupert a warm reception.

Rupert, on his part, hearing nothing from Cary, chose, as usual, the bold course and advanced against the town. Almost before he knew what was happening he found himself confronted by a force of at least 3500 men. The Cavaliers might have turned their horses' heads and ridden off without much difficulty. They preferred to charge. It was this stubborn preference of theirs—not their harryings and burnings—that gave terror to their name. Whitelocke, the Roundhead lawyer, has given us a lively picture of the skirmish:

> The Cavaliers came on with undaunted courage, their forces in the form of a crescent: Prince Rupert, to the right wing, came on with great fury: in they went pell-mell into the heart of our soldiers, but they were surrounded, and with great difficulty cut their way through and made their way across to Maidenhead, where they had their quarters.[2]

But this is only a shorter version of a description in a contemporary pamphlet already quoted.[3] From this it would appear that the terrain was not easy for cavalry action, being broken up by hedgerows, behind which the

[1] Thomason Tracts, E. 127 (10).   [2] *Memorials*, p. 64.
[3] Thomason Tracts, E. 27 (10).

106

Roundheads had posted their musketeers, who fired into the charging Cavaliers as they passed. These flanking troops were continually reinforced; until Rupert, finding more enemies behind him than in front, turned and broke out that way, and so got clear to Maidenhead. He took off nearly all his cavalry, but a small force of infantry attached to his command again suffered heavily. It was a gallant and successful charge, and, if the Cavaliers had been half as skilful as their enemies in the arts of propaganda, would no doubt have been commemorated as it deserved. The Royalist horsemen, on the testimony of their opponents, fought "like blood-thirsty Tygers." As at Edgehill, Rupert seems to have relied entirely upon shock tactics.

In the first days of November the King left Oxford and began feeling his way towards London, Rupert's cavalry acting as his fingertips. It was foggy, uncertain weather, and intelligence difficult to obtain. At Reading he was met by envoys from the Parliament, proposing peace negotiations; but Essex had got into London before him with the remnants of the Edgehill army, the defences of the City were now almost complete, and they had six thousand men under arms there—so that there was some justification for believing that these negotiators were merely playing for time. The King pushed on. Rupert's men were seeking comfortable quarters wherever they could find them, choosing for preference the mansions of the wealthier Roundheads—the City merchants and lawyers and that large class of new-rich landlords, the Hampdens, Says, Hutchinsons, Cromwells, and the rest, who were the backbone of the rebellion, and some of whom had the misfortune to live on the Oxford-London road.

Whitelocke has described with bitterness how they treated his handsome residence at Fawley Court. "The brutish fellows," he says, "had their whores with them" (a practice almost universal in seventeenth-century armies); they stole the linen and the feather beds, and lit their tobacco pipes with papers from the library. Some of the books they threw about the floor, others they took away with them. They broke down the fences in the park and killed most of the deer. They requisitioned the carriage horses (another universal practice in time of war), and they frightened the servants out of their wits, though they do not seem to have touched them. In fact, they behaved much as soldiers always did, and do, in such circumstances.

There were two Roundhead merchants who were captured by the Cavalier outposts about this time, and they have left us a vivid little description of their experiences.[1] After being escorted for many miles through dirty country lanes they were at last brought before Prince Rupert, whom they found in bed with all his clothes on. (This habit of Rupert's gave birth to the Roundhead legend that he had taken a solemn oath "not to undress nor shift himself till he had brought King Charles to Whitehall"; a much more likely explanation is that he never had time to undress.) He now rose from his couch to examine the prisoners. While he was doing so his eye fell on a bunch of ribbons stuck jauntily in one of their hats. He picked it up and ran his fingers through the colours. "There is none of the King's favours here," he remarked sourly. "No," replied the Roundhead, "they are my mistress's favour." Rupert instantly relaxed, and there was a broad smile on his dark countenance as he returned both hat and ribbons to their owner. These merchants were made prisoners at Hounslow, and it was near there that they saw the dead body of a civilian, dressed in scarlet, hanging from the bough of a tree.

[1] Thomason Tracts, E. 242 (21).

They were told that he had been executed for speaking against the King, and that no man durst cut the corpse down.

But the slowness of the advance against London was telling on Rupert's temper. On the day following his interview with the two Roundhead merchants these observant gentlemen saw him in conversation with King Charles on Hounslow Heath, and noticed that, while the talk went on, the Prince "often scratched his head and tore his hair, as if in some grave discontent." It was partly, perhaps, the effect of Rupert's entreaties, partly the advice of others around him who thought that London might still be frightened into surrender—whatever the cause, the King suddenly decided upon a daring move. The Parliamentary forces assembled for the defence of London must by this time have outnumbered his own army by more than two to one. There was a danger of being surrounded, if he advanced any farther. Yet he now boldly ordered Rupert to make a dash forward and seize Brentford. No order was ever more joyfully received.

We have said that it was foggy weather. The mist lay so thick along the Thames Valley on this November 12, 1642, that it was impossible to see more than a few hundred yards. The side with the better cavalry had an obvious advantage, and Rupert was not the man to miss his chance of a dramatic *coup*. With the Prince of Wales's regiment of horse (in which our old friend Bulstrode was serving) he appeared suddenly out of the mist in the very streets of Brentford itself, driving the Roundhead outposts before him. The town was garrisoned by a single regiment—Hollis's redcoats, who had distinguished themselves at Edgehill. They were taken by surprise. But the streets were commanded by the Parliamentary artillery, and stout barricades had been erected. From behind

these the startled redcoats, when they had recovered
from their first bewilderment, opened a well-directed fire.
At once it was seen that the cavalry could do no more.
Well-built barricades were as impregnable against their
charge as castle walls. (If only every battle could be
fought in an open field!)

Rupert ordered his horsemen to take cover, and
hastened back to meet the Royalist infantry who were
coming up in his support. The leading regiment was
Colonel Salisbury's Welshmen, those much-maligned
"vermin" and "offscourings" whom we met at Edgehill. Rupert placed himself at their head, and led them
against the barricades. The Welshmen, anxious, no
doubt, to rehabilitate their reputation as fighting-men,
made a fierce attack. As they pushed desperately forward
they could hear the cheers of other Royalist regiments
coming in behind, and the now familiar battle-cry,
"For God and the King!"[1]

Hollis's gallant redcoats, outnumbered and without
supports, were pushed back from street to street, losing
heavily. As they left the shelter of the barricades
Rupert's horsemen charged them repeatedly. They seem
to have been driven out into the suburbs, before the
survivors descried the purple uniforms of Lord Brooke,
with Hampden's greencoats behind, advancing belatedly
through the mist to their assistance. It was too late to
save the day for the Parliament. The three regiments of
infantry were forced out of Brentford and along the
London road towards Turnham Green. Scattered parties
of them were chased into the river; cavalry charges took
toll of their ranks; but they would not break, and made,
on the whole, a very creditable retreat.

---

[1] The battle-cry of the Roundheads at this time (see contemporary
pamphlets) was "For King and Parliament"; which was a little tepid
by comparison and suffered from being too obviously untrue.

The Royal army followed them out of Brentford that same evening. By the capture of this town Charles had acquired a useful base for the last stage of his advance. He had also taken some hundreds of prisoners and fifteen pieces of artillery. But in return he had presented the hostile pamphleteers of London with ammunition of another kind. Since peace negotiations—of a sort—were still going on it was possible to accuse him of treachery in making this sudden advance. The Roundhead propagandists leaped at the opportunity. Furthermore, Charles's "Welsh vermin," elated by their victory, had unfortunately been making whoopee in the streets of Brentford, breaking into the houses and taking what they willed. Roundhead writers, describing their atrocities, seem to find it no excuse that—with a deplorable ignorance of English political distinctions—they robbed Cavaliers and Parliament men alike. Their name, indeed, began to stink in all English nostrils: officers serving in the Royalist army complained bitterly of their thieving ways.[1]

A glimpse of the other side. While Lord Essex was concentrating his troops (including those of Hampden and Brooke) upon Turnham Green, to oppose another and final barrier to the King's advance, the City of London, behind him, was making its first great effort of the war. Roused by the common peril, recruits came pouring in. The trained bands had been assembled at Chelsea, and all through that Saturday night of November 12 they might be seen streaming down the western road to Hammersmith, and on again to Turnham Green, regiment after regiment in column of route, going to meet their King. The round, boyish faces of the young apprentices, who formed the rank and file, glowed with enthusiasm for their cause—the cause of a Parliament

[1] John Wiat's letter, Thomason Tracts, E. 128 (34).

which, they had been taught to believe (though not one of them had a vote), would henceforth devote itself entirely to their interests. The goodwives of the City had risen to the occasion. Probably no better-provisioned army ever set out to fight. Carts laden with foodstuffs and barrels of wine lumbered westward with the troops, and at every halt the citizen soldiers refreshed themselves "merrily," drinking prosperity to the comfortable homes they had left behind, and confusion to "Prince Robert"—or "Robeart," or "Robber"—and his malignant Cavaliers.

Their officers stood to watch them pass, and from all accounts were well satisfied. The propaganda had worked: here was a united London effort at last. They shouted words of encouragement to the brave lads as they marched. Old Colonel Skippon, the veteran of the German wars, with the ramrod back and the far-away fanatic stare in his eyes, walked up and down the road, greeting each regiment in turn. For every company he had some happy word. "Come, my Boys, my brave Boys, let us pray heartily and fight heartily!" You might hear his rough, masculine voice, now far down the road, now close at hand. "Your wives and children!" . . . "Remember the cause is for God!" . . . "Come, my honest, brave Boys, pray heartily and fight heartily, and God will bless us!" [1] They greeted him with cheers and laughter. They seemed to like his talk much better than the "set orations" of their preachers. Then there would be another brief halt and more refreshments—by the side of that Hammersmith road where the tram-lines run to-day. Modern soldiers would have called it a picnic.

On the following (Sunday) morning the tired apprentices could still keep up some of the holiday atmosphere

[1] Whitelocke, *Memorials*, p. 65.

They knew that they outnumbered their enemies by two to one. The fog had lifted. The rival armies, Cavaliers and Roundheads, stood looking at each other from opposite sides of Turnham Green. Essex, with a retinue of Members of Parliament and grim, high-hatted Puritan divines, rode along the Parliamentary ranks. The apprentices had always liked "his Excellency," as he was called. "Hey, for old Robin!" they shouted, throwing up their caps. There was some desultory skirmishing, with Rupert, as usual, well to the fore. According to a Roundhead authority, he made several charges and "did lay about him like a fury." He was shot at, at close range, "a thousand times," but never touched. When the Parliamentary guns opened fire he spread out his troops of horse with wide spaces between them, so that little harm was done—an early instance of the use of artillery formation, which even the hostile chronicler admits to have been "cunning."[1]

But the King's small army was thrust like a spearhead deep into the heart of a peaceful countryside, which felt its presence like a wound. Hungry invaders from the West and North were no more welcome in these peaceful Middlesex towns in 1642 than they were in 1461 and 1745. Essex felt that public opinion was coming over to his side. He had a vast superiority in numbers, and even his sluggish spirit was stirred to an attempt to march round behind the King and cut him off from his retreat to Oxford. He went so far as to detach a column for this purpose, under the command of Hampden, with instructions to encircle the Royalist left wing—but recalled them almost as soon as they had started! It would probably have been too late in any case. For by this time the King and all his advisers could see that they were wasting their time. There was no hope of serious negotiations, nor

[1] Thomason Tracts, E. 127 (15).

of wholesale desertions from the rebel ranks. Rather was London hardening against them. The bold gesture of Turnham Green had failed, and Charles wisely decided to draw off while there was yet time.

He fell back on Reading, while Essex forced Rupert out of Brentford. And so to Oxford, where that winter Charles kept his court.

CHAPTER VII: THE "ROBBER PRINCE"

WE have reached the end of the brief opening episode of the most enduring quarrel in English history. It was of ancient origin, no doubt, having the character of universality; but never before, in England or anywhere else, had it been so clearly marked and defined. It divided England into two camps, and those two camps remain divided to this day. It is still a favourite subject with debating societies—not simply because it affords ample material for debate, but because the secretary knows in advance that every one of his members who was taught any history at school will be strongly Roundhead or Cavalier. It is not a question of argument, but of temperament. It is a permanent division of mankind.

There were peasants and apprentices in 1642 who never understood what was happening to them or what were the principles at stake; who took the field, at the behest of some local landowner or wealthy City merchant, much as they might have done in the Wars of the Roses, quite oblivious of the issues involved. There are agricultural labourers and artisans to-day who could not tell you off-hand whether their sympathies would have been with King Charles or 'King' Pym. But talk to them for five minutes, show them a picture or two, put some simple text-book in their hand, and they will declare their side with surprising emphasis and enthusiasm. There were, and are, moderate men in both camps (just as there were soldiers of fortune in 1642 who would fight for pay on either side). The ordinary Englishman neither talked through his nose nor bellowed and blustered at the top of his voice. The ruffianly Cavalier of the London pamphleteers and the canting, Puritanical humbug whom

Butler immortalized a generation later were mere caricatures. But, speaking quite generally, there was a difference between the typical Cavalier and the typical Roundhead which could be distinguished at a glance in each individual case, which went much deeper than seventeenth-century politics, which has persisted in the English nation ever since. It was plain to see in their literature—plainer still in their dress and manners.

How, then, are we to get a close-up view of them? In the matter of personal appearance we get little help from contemporary portraits, for men of good social position—men who could afford to have their portraits painted—continued to dress much alike. Hampden and Cromwell wore their hair long. Hutchinson, the regicide, was particularly proud of his "very fine thickset head of hair," and always "kept it clean and handsome, so that it was a great ornament to him." But he got into trouble over it with his "godly" neighbours, who, when he joined their side in the war, "would not allow him to be religious because his hair was not in their cut, nor his words in their phrase, nor such little formalities altogether fitted to their humour."

His widow, who is our authority here,[1] adds some interesting notes about the "affectations of habit, looks, and words" which distinguished the Puritanical party; as also of the origin of the word 'Roundhead,' which, she admits, was very well applied to the Parliamentary side in the early stages of the war—though not so much later. With unconcealed contempt this typical English lady of her time remarks that "few of the Puritans wore their hair long enough to cover their ears," which was "something ridiculous to behold." Essex's soldiers, marching to war, looked "as if they had been only sent out till their hair was grown." Hence the "scorned term" 'Roundhead.'

[1] *Memoirs of Colonel Hutchinson*, p. 99.

Now Rupert, it will be remembered, had a dog. He was fond of animals—men of his disposition often are. For one thing, animals could not talk. He loved horses and falcons. During his long imprisonment at Linz, as we saw in Chapter III, he amused himself by teaching a hare to perform tricks. But the great solace of that captivity was his dog, Boy. This Boy was white in colour, powerfully built, swift in the chase. We can only guess at his breed. But we know that he must have been a dog of distinction, the kind of dog a man might be proud to have known. There are such dogs. Rupert, when he came to England, brought Boy with him, and the animal was his inseparable companion, on the march and in billets. He must have been present at that interview with the two London merchants—asserting himself, no doubt, by hostile noises from behind the bed, for he would surely know the smell of a Roundhead! On the field of action the small, white figure of Boy became a sight as familiar to friends and foes alike as the Prince's famous scarlet cloak. Indeed, Rupert would often discard the cloak, before making a charge, for a less conspicuous grey one; but the dog, if we can believe the pamphleteers, was always there.

Yet it is to the Roundheads that Boy owes his fame. They made him one of the principal objects of their propaganda. Rupert, they asserted, would have a place laid for him at the dinner-table, and he and the other roistering Cavaliers would often drink the dog's health— a scene of horrible indecency to the Puritan mind. The "dogge" was bewitched, they declared, the Prince's "familiar," invulnerable to bullets, like his master. He met his death, in the end, like a gentleman, on the stricken field of Marston Moor; but long before that date he had become a traditional figure with the Roundhead pamphleteers. He, with a mythical "she-monkey," which Rupert was alleged to possess, became a Fleet Street obsession. The printing presses round St Paul's Church-yard were busy turning out imaginary conversations in which Boy was made to take part as representing the Cavaliers—and holding them up to ridicule, of course. I quote from one of these pamphlets,[1] not for anything that it tells us about poor Boy, but for the vivid light which it throws upon the difference between the two parties—their thought and speech and dress—as a Roundhead scribbler saw it in 1643. (The stories about the she-monkey are too obscene to quote.)

Here are Prince Rupert's dog and the Roundhead dog, and they meet in the street. Their greeting is as follows:

> *Prince Rupert's dog.* What yelping, whindling puppy dog art thou?
> *The Roundhead dog.* What bawling, shag-haired Cavalier's dog art thou?

In the same rather personal strain the Roundhead dog observes, "If you be a Cavalier you must wear long hair." And the Cavalier: "Thou art a round-headed puppy . . . with thy ignorant spirit and prick-ears." There we have the popular idea, which has so well served our modern novelists, and was evidently true enough at the time. The Roundheads whined through their noses and had exposed, protruding ears; the Cavaliers were bawling and shag-haired. Later the Roundhead dog, to clinch the argument, threatens to send for "a regiment of redcoats and a troop of horse" to help him. The Cavalier replies, "I care not for your leather troops of horse, nor for your red-cotton soldiers." There is an implication here of the superiority of Roundhead uniforms. In another dialogue the Roundhead animal proclaims, "I will have no out-landish cur domineer in our land"—a remark of some significance for Rupert's biographer. For, of course, the

---

[1] Thomason Tracts, E. 246 (23).

whole pamphlet is aimed at Rupert, though the dog, when asked outright whether he be "Prince Rupert's white Boy," replies, "My name is Puddle"—presumably poodle. (But there is another story behind that remark which need not concern us here.)

The value of these absurd pamphlets consists entirely in the fact that they were contemporary, anonymous,

CAVALIERS AND ROUNDHEADS

From a contemporary pamphlet.

irresponsible, outspoken. When dealing with the opposing side the unnamed London author said what he liked, drew what he liked, and, with a little tact, he could even put into the mouth of some imaginary Cavalier a not very kindly caricature of the extremists on his own side. The illustration (reproduced above) on the title-page of the particular pamphlet from which I have been quoting shows the two quarrelsome dogs held back by opposing groups of Cavaliers and Roundheads, whose dress and general appearance is so carefully drawn and differentiated —yet without any gross exaggerations—that we may take it as a fair representation of what a typical Cavalier and

119

a typical Roundhead looked like to an unbiased journalist of the time.

Rupert was a dandy. He had an instinct for bright colours, set off against a sombre background of dark velvet. He was not dandified in the sense of being fashionable. He never grew a Vandyck beard, like Digby and Hyde and all the men of fashion (and most of the "politicians") on the Royalist side. He does not seem to have affected the light, "gay" colours of the Cavaliers, as opposed to the "sad" hues of the Puritan dress. He may have looked a little "foreign"—with his dark hair, hawk-like features, and long, lean body. But he was a dashing and distinctive figure in the council-chamber or on the battlefield, and we know that many young English officers strove earnestly to imitate his style.

Was he foreign in other respects? In particular was he foreign—and German—in his methods of waging war? Is there any truth in the accusations of ruthless cruelty and barbarity continually brought against him? Was he another Tilly? Is it true that his soldiers were distinguished above those of the other side by their savagery? We know that they were "sons of Belial"; we may accept that familiar description for what it is worth. But were they also "inhuman Catterpillers," "unbridled Rorers," who dwelled habitually in "a wilderness of Tobacko," surrounded by "Legions of Whores," and whose "wickedness is so great that words cannot express it."[1] And did they behave in this way with the approval and encouragement of their "Robber Prince"?

To take the last charge first, it may be observed that the two accusations commonly brought against Rupert— that his men were utterly undisciplined, and that he was personally responsible for their alleged atrocities—cancel each other out. The King was always short of money;

[1] Thomason Tracts, E. 126 (36).

the pay of the Cavaliers was frequently in arrears; to live at all they had often to 'live on the country.' It would be no great credit to the Parliament if their well-fed, well-clad troops were better behaved. Yet it is impossible for their stoutest modern partisan to deny that they committed just as many atrocities as their opponents. This is an unprofitable controversy. The truth is that in this English Civil War both sides behaved, in the circumstances, extremely well. The worst things done were the destruction of the churches, the slaughter of the women after Naseby, and the later massacres in Ireland. In all these cases the perpetrators were the Parliamentarians.

But the Roundhead pamphlets on this subject are worth studying for their own sake. For instance, on the subject of the notorious "blasphemy" and "swearing" of the Cavaliers the modern historian of bad language—should one ever arise—will doubtless take note that every age swears by the things it holds sacred, and will offer appropriate comments upon the fact that, whereas the bad language of the common people in the seventeenth century was chiefly concerned with religion, ours more often refers to sex. He will observe that oaths which in those days sent a shudder through the land would mean little or nothing to the men (or even the women) of to-day.

When the Cavaliers were in Leicester it is alleged against them that they swaggered through the streets shouting, "Damme and sink me if we do not kill all the Puritans and Roundheads in the town." They were heard by one Jane White, an aged woman of the Puritan persuasion, who, aghast at their language, began to reprove them publicly, in the manner of her kind. But the story—it is frequently repeated in the pamphlets—had a tragic ending; for a drunken ruffian among the Cavaliers took a shot at the old woman with his musket, and unfortunately hit her in the back, with fatal results.[1] Apart from this, the accusations of misbehaviour in Leicester are of the usual vague kind: many houses are said to have been burned and robbed, but only one or two names are given. The truth is that almost anything was believed against them. Another pamphlet of about the same date is entitled:

> A Wonderful and Strange Miracle: or God's Just Vengeance against the Cavaliers. Declaring how Mr Andrew Stonesby, a Cavalier . . . dranke a health to the Devill, daring him to come and pledge him, with many blasphemous imprecations. Also how the Devill appeared to him at that instant, so that he was distracted and died raving and blaspheming, to the terror and amazement of all the beholders. [The names of Roundhead witnesses are given.] [2]

It is alleged that Rupert's officers were such enthusiastic connoisseurs of swearing that they "offered sums of money" to those who could invent bright new "blasphemies" or "execrations against the Roundheads." The author of this story is a certain Andrews, who was a prisoner with the Royalist army in December 1642.[2] Another Roundhead authority gives, as an example of the hideous blasphemy of the Cavaliers, their oft-repeated statement that "they would rather be in hell with their comrades than in heaven with the Roundheads." Surely, exclaims this author, they were "worse than the heathenish Turk or cannibals." [3] And these examples of Cavalier language are not quoted here for their absurdity; but because they are typical of the worst that the pamphleteers could find to say!

Some of the charges, it need hardly be said, were more serious than this. The gravest of them, up to the date at which we have now arrived in this history, concern the brief occupation of Brentford by Rupert's troops,

---

[1] Thomason Tracts, E. 242 (33).
[2] Ibid., E. 126 (36).   [3] Ibid., E. 242 (33).

recorded in the last chapter. We have already seen that Salisbury's Welshmen were accused of setting fire to the houses and robbing the citizens impartially. But it is further alleged that Rupert's horsemen bound their prisoners hand and foot and threw them into the pound, and some of them into the local slaughter-house, and that these latter prisoners included respectable Roundhead citizens of advanced years, who suffered terribly in such a "nasty and noisome place." They stole beef and wine and feather beds, and when they found that they had more wine than they could carry they let it run out in the gutters, and ripped up many of the feather beds and "scattered the feathers abroad in the fields and streets." They stole so many candles that their whole line of march down the road from Brentford to Turnham Green must have looked like an illuminated procession.

A graver charge is that when some of Hollis's flying redcoats took to the river the mounted Cavaliers rode along the banks, shooting at them and treating it as a sport. And this charge is repeated so often that one feels that something of the kind must have happened and that Rupert's officers were greatly to blame. Indeed, the Brentford stories seem better authenticated and have more of the air of truth about them than the vague accusations of wholesale massacres at Leicester and Birmingham, where hundreds of unnamed "men, women, and children," and "even the very dogs," are said to have been done to death. Brentford cannot be brushed aside.

But what had all this to do with Rupert personally? It is implied by his enemies that, if he was not actually present at these scenes, he approved them, instigated them, liked to hear of them. He is specifically accused of "unnatural, inhuman and strange cruelties," [1] as though he were a sadist. But everything we know of his char-

[1] Thomason Tracts, E. 128 (17).

acter flatly contradicts this assumption. He was a normal, healthy-minded man. He "abhorred the debauchery of the age," and the excesses that were common in Germany in his youth.[1] His private life compared well with the lives of most of his contemporaries—and particularly with that of the Roundhead Lord Wharton, who was the originator of many of these stories against him. According to Campbell,[2] the people of Berkshire, where Rupert spent some of his declining years, still remembered him a hundred years later as an excellent landlord and neighbour, "so just, so beneficent, so courteous." He was a hard-headed, practical soldier, and he did not believe in waging war with kid gloves. But he did believe in 1642—and this is the real origin and gravamen of the charges against him—that the best way to finish the war was to strike direct at London. That was why the London pamphleteers hated him. "The Commons of England will remember thee, thou flap-dragon, thou butter-box!" exclaimed one of them.[3] And so they did.

Rupert himself was aware of and resented the hostility of London. He knew that even members of his own party had taken it for granted that, if he once got into the City, he would sack the place. In that fine piece of nervous prose which was the only answer to his accusers that he ever troubled to publish he roundly declares:

I think there is none that take me for a coward, for sure I fear not the face of any man alive; yet I shall repute it the greatest victory in the world to see his Majesty enter London in peace, without shedding one drop of blood; where I dare say (God and his Majesty are witnesses that I lie not) no citizen should be plundered of one penny or farthing, whereby that ancient and famous City would manifestly perceive how desperately it hath been abused by most strange, false, and bottomless untruths,

[1] Lansdowne MSS., 817, f. 158.
[2] *Lives of the British Admirals*, p. 250 (1779).
[3] *A Nest of Vipers* (London, 1644).

Dauentny

Brimidgham

CARICATURE OF PRINCE RUPERT AND BOY
From a contemporary Roundhead pamphlet entitled *The Bloody Prince*
British Museum

for which somebody (without repentance) must be ashamed at the day of judgment, if they escape a condign legal punishment in this world.[1]

As to the alleged atrocities,

I take that man to be no soldier or gentleman that will strike (much less kill) a woman or child, if it be in his power to do the contrary; and I openly dare the most valiant and quick-sighted of that lying faction to name the time, the person, or the house where any child or woman lost so much as a hair from their head by me or any of our soldiers.

He goes on to give a long list of Roundhead outrages, and to comment upon the manner in which they "have stuffed all the prisons in London with earls, lords, bishops, judges, and knights, masters of colleges, lawyers, and gentlemen of all conditions and counties . . . only because they are suspected to love their King." As to the insinuation that he was a Papist in disguise, who would "rather hear Mass at Oxford than come to private prayers or a sermon," he answers triumphantly that "the world knows how deeply I have smarted and what perils I have undergone for the Protestant cause"—referring, of course, to his captivity at Linz. In reply to the familiar accusation—which was also perfectly true—that "when the King's council are persuading his Majesty to an accommodation with his Parliament, thou, being an enemy to peace and all the Parliament's good purposes, com'st in, and presently they speak of blood and war, and the destruction of London," he answers, in effect, that his only purpose was to win the war for God and King Charles, "a cause my conscience tells me is full of piety and justice."

In fact, a fine, slashing reply, quite in the manner of a cavalry charge. It surprised his opponents. But Rupert sourly remarked: "It will seem strange, no doubt, to see

[1] Thomason Tracts, E. 242 (32).

me in print, my known disposition being so contrary to this scribbling age." And he never did it again.

At Oxford, meantime, amid those dreaming spires, in that home of causes not yet lost and beliefs still passionately held to be possible, the dignified little King was holding court and eagerly awaiting the arrival of his vivid French Queen. The King lived at Christ Church; Parliament assembled there; Tom Quad can never have looked so gay. There was a spirit of optimism in the air, which seems to be enshrined in stone in that gay façade at Oriel. The first campaign of the Civil War had not gone badly for the King. Wales and the North had rallied to his side; there was good news from the South-west; London trembled at the mention of his nephew's name. The time had arrived to relax a little and talk things over. Negotiations were begun with the Parliament, and dragged on interminably, each side putting forward proposals which the other was certain to refuse. The fact that Hollis, at Westminster, was leading a peace party against Pym deluded the "politicians" at Oxford with false hopes.

There was something in Rupert's temperament that must have responded immediately to the charm of Oxford. He had an artist's eye; he was intellectually wideawake; he could, on occasions, loll at his ease as shamelessly as any man. He had done it at Linz. He enjoyed doing it now. But, as Sir Philip Warwick says—and it is the real secret of Rupert's character—"il estoit tousjours soldat."[1] Even resting at Oxford he showed, as usual, "a great and exemplary temperance," which so well "fitted him to undergo the fatigues of a war," and was born of his unquenchable "eagerness to fight." Except during the last few weeks of 1642, the citizens of Oxford more often saw him riding out with his cavalry than lounging in the college quadrangles.

[1] *Memoirs*, pp. 227–231.

CHAPTER VIII: THE ROYALIST PLAN OF 1642-43

THE military position was interesting. The King had a plan. It was a bold, strategical conception, which has justly won the admiration of military critics. Its invention has been variously attributed to the Prince of Orange (who was in frequent communication with Oxford at this time), to King, the Swedish general, whom we have met before at the Vlotho, to Ruthven, the Commander-in-Chief, to Charles himself, and to Rupert. It seems hardly likely that it should have come all the way from Holland, where local conditions in England were little understood; the same applies emphatically to General King; and Ruthven, though an intelligent general, lacked the personality to force so bold a scheme upon his colleagues. Charles was a much better soldier than is commonly supposed. Two years later, in 1644, he was to show his ability in the field by outgeneralling Waller and Essex. In fact, the royal art-connoisseur was becoming interested in the art of war. He never grew to be as sure of himself as he was in the purchase of pictures, but he soon understood enough of the technique of this picturesque, bloody business to form strategical ideas of his own. It is only just that the lion's share of the credit for the great plan of 1642-43 should go to him. On the other hand, it is well known that in military matters he was apt to turn his back on his council and go direct to Rupert for advice. Moreover, this plan seems to have Rupert's signature scrawled right across it.

The scheme was this. The Royal forces lay strung out across the map of England from north to south, facing towards London and the east. The King, at Oxford, was in the centre of the line. He had the loyal West behind him. He was strong enough to maintain a bold front and to hold Essex with the main Parliamentary army in check. His presence was a continual threat to the rebellious capital, only some thirty miles distant from his advance posts. On the other hand, the failure at Turnham Green had proved conclusively that he was not strong enough, and had no immediate prospect of being strong enough, to advance against London alone. But far away, to the left and to the right, in Yorkshire and in Cornwall and Devon, his commanders were making rapid progress, and their numbers were increasing every day. Sir Ralph Hopton, in the South, had begun a series of victories which was to establish him as the most successful commander on the Royalist side. The Duke of Newcastle, in the North, though less skilful as a soldier, was steadily increasing the area which owned allegiance to the King.

It was proposed to press these two extreme points of the Royalist line, inward, like pincers, Newcastle moving south-east into Essex, and Hopton north-east into Kent. Eventually they were to meet on the banks of the Thames, *below* London, and, by seizing the bridges, cut off the river traffic from the sea. Meantime the King, keeping up a steady, holding pressure from Oxford, would cut the inland river traffic at Kingston or some other suitable spot. London would be starved into surrender. It was a daring plan, and it sounds very much like Rupert's. He had always been so clear that London was the real objective—that nothing else mattered. He had taken every opportunity of urging a dash at London; and only when that failed, chiefly through delay, had he concurred in the retreat to Oxford. The frontal attack having been called off, he cordially welcomed this alternative plan— if he did not actually originate it.

In the meantime it was his duty to keep Essex occupied. The King, in the centre, had garrisons at Banbury, to the north, and at Abingdon, Wallingford, and Reading, on

MAP TO ILLUSTRATE THE ROYALIST PLAN OF 1642-43

the way to London. Essex watched him warily from Windsor. Rupert determined to extend this circle of Royal garrisons so as to secure the position at Oxford. First he made up his mind to drive the Roundheads out of the northern parts of Gloucestershire which were still in their hands, and which lay almost immediately behind the King, cutting off direct communications with Hopton and threatening those with Wales. He pitched upon Cirencester for a beginning—the stronger town of Gloucester must wait.

The cavalry were concentrating at Abingdon for the expedition into Gloucestershire. Rupert's own regiment was already there, and Sir Louis Dyves, who was now Commissary-General, wrote that he was doing his best to protect their quarters against the later arrivals, who were veritable "caterpillars," and had already knocked the quartermaster on the head and stolen a whole week's provisions from the regimental stores. "If they mend not their manners," adds Dyves, "I shall make bold to hang up some of them for example to the rest." [1]

Lord Hertford had come in from the west with Welsh reinforcements, and these were to form the infantry column. The plan was for Rupert and the horse to get across the Gloucester road, to prevent the arrival of succours for Cirencester, while the Welshmen assailed that town at break of day on January 7. On the first occasion it failed, owing to Hertford's late arrival. But a second expedition, on February 2, was more successful. We have a Roundhead account of it, according to which the Welsh infantry lost heavily, but were driven forward by the mounted Cavaliers behind them, shouting "On, on!" The Parliamentarians tried to hold Barton Farm, outside the town, but the Welshmen drove them out of it, and Rupert's horse were upon them before they could get

[1] Dyves to Rupert, Warburton, vol. ii, p. 103.

in through the town gates. They were chased through the streets, crying in vain for quarter; but some of them, taking cover in the houses round the market-place, kept up a steady fire, and prolonged the resistance for above an hour after the rest of the town was taken. Perhaps this exasperated the "caterpillars" of Abingdon. At any rate, the Cavaliers are accused of wholesale plunderings and burnings, and of cruelty to their prisoners, some of whom they are said to have driven all the way back to Oxford on foot.

This sudden dash at Cirencester held out a helping hand towards Hopton, who was all the time advancing victoriously from the South-west. A similar move towards the North was now projected. But this time Rupert led no raiding party; it was intended that, if possible, he should eventually unite with Newcastle himself. On April 3 he got as far north as Birmingham. It was a notoriously Puritanical town, and once again the old controversy arose about the behaviour of the Cavaliers. The men of Birmingham, who had already distinguished themselves by attacking the King's baggage train just before Edgehill and carrying off much of his plate, now put themselves in a posture of defence, though their town was without walls and quite unable to stand a siege.

The Cavaliers carried the place with a rush; and, according to the Roundhead pamphleteers, who immediately broke into a chorus of denunciation, they burned down half the houses and slaughtered the inhabitants wherever they met them. They

> rode desperately round the town, leaping hedges and ditches to catch the townsmen. . . . That night few of these ruffians went to bed, but spent it in revelling, robbing, and tyrannizing over poor affrighted women and prisoners, drinking healths upon their knees, yea, drinking healths to Prince Rupert's dog.

They did twenty thousand pounds' worth of damage.

But all this was intended for public consumption, as part of the Parliamentary propaganda. The only Royalist version of the affair is, on the contrary, contained in a private letter which was never intended for publication, and is therefore rather better evidence. According to this Royalist writer, the story of the "massacre" of Birmingham is a Roundhead myth. Only one or two houses were fired by Rupert's orders, and this was done for good military reasons, to assist his entry into the town. When, late that night, he found other streets in flames Rupert sent warnings to the municipal authorities, and did his best to help them to stay the progress of the fire. There was no indiscriminate shooting; in spite of maddening provocation, this writer would have us believe, the Royalist soldiers behaved like lambs!

At Lichfield, in the following month, it was the same story. This city was a hard nut to crack; for the Roundhead garrison had fortified the cathedral and the close and were holding out there resolutely. Rupert brought up his scanty artillery, but the few light guns which he possessed made little impression on those stout old walls. The Cavaliers dismounted and dug themselves in as close as they dared, encircling the hostile position. But the weather was against them, the trenches became rivers of mud. Digby, who was serving under Rupert (it was the last time he consented to do so), was seriously wounded while exposing himself gallantly in the front line. So was Rupert's friend Legge, who had only recently been exchanged from a Roundhead prison. The siege dragged on into a second week.

Rupert fumed at the delay. Letters from Oxford informed him that Essex, behind his back, had laid siege to Reading. He knew that he would soon be needed there. How then was he to find time for his march north? Rumours reached the Roundhead garrison of Lichfield that he had sworn, "God damn him, he would not give one man quarter"—unless they surrendered forthwith. But his uncle, the King, wrote him a model letter. Charles admitted the extreme urgency of the case, but he said, "Have a care of spilling innocent blood," and he suggested that the garrison should be allowed to march out with all the honours of war, unless they had committed "outrages" or "used violence" in the town. Rupert must have laughed at that. He could guess how the local Royalists had been treated and what the interior of the cathedral would look like by now!

Meantime he recollected that he was in a mining country, and he sent out officers who soon collected a whole platoon of expert miners. Rupert set them to work to tunnel under the walls of the close. Messages from Oxford becoming more urgent, he attempted a premature assault, which was beaten off. The Parliamentarians took one Cavalier prisoner, and him (by their own account) they murdered in cold blood, hanging his body out on a gibbet three yards from the wall, and shouting derisively to Rupert to shoot it down if he could. This was enough to exasperate a less patient man. But Rupert kept perfectly cool; and on the next day, hearing that his tunnel was completed and a mine laid under the walls, he even sent a trumpeter to the close offering to parley. The garrison replied by defiantly ringing the cathedral bells.

When Rupert sprung his mine next day he was employing a method of warfare familiar enough on the Continent and well known to veteran officers on both sides. But it was the first mine ever sprung in England, and it might be expected to have a decisive moral effect upon the common soldiery. All honour is therefore due to the Roundheads of Lichfield, who, instead of becoming panic-stricken, rallied stoutly in the breach and drove back the first assailants, and would not hoist the white flag until Rupert brought up his guns and poured such a deadly fire through the gap in the walls that flesh and blood could not stand against it. When the articles of surrender were completed Rupert watched his enemies march out, "with colours flying, trumpets sounding." There was an admiring smile on his lips, and he went out of his way to offer his personal congratulations to the officer in command upon a very gallant resistance. Even the sight of the desecrated cathedral could not change his attitude. "Il estoit tousjours soldat."

His plans were ruined, and he knew it. Without wasting another thought upon his cherished idea of a northern march—certainly without bothering his head about the charges and countercharges of burning and outrage which immediately broke out as fiercely as at Birmingham—he put a garrison into Lichfield, turned his back upon the town, and hurried south with his cavalry to the relief of Reading. He was too late. Spurring ahead with a few followers, he found Charles and his army at Caversham, just north of Reading. The King had no longer any hope of saving that town, but he hoped to bring off the garrison by making a sudden attack on the besiegers' lines. Rupert rode forward with him. Neither of them knew that Reading was already on the point of surrender.

What had happened was this. Sir Arthur Aston, the Royalist commander, was an excellent soldier and a born grumbler. Finding himself besieged by Essex in person with the full strength of the main Parliamentary army, and his own ammunition running low (though there was plenty of food in the town), he wrote despairing letters in every direction—and no doubt talked to his subordinates in the same strain. Then a tile fell on his head and put him out of action; and his successor, Colonel Richard Fielding, promptly opened negotiations with the enemy.

When Fielding heard the sounds of musketry at Caversham Bridge and the cheers of the advancing Royalists he was urged to sally out and help them. He refused. He said that he had begun negotiations, and his honour was engaged. There was nothing for Charles to do but fall back on Oxford.

There were some pretty cavalry skirmishes during that retreat. Rupert afterwards wrote a polite note to his courteous opponent Lord Essex, asking for the name of the mounted gentleman who had so eagerly pursued the Cavaliers near Caversham. He was far ahead of his own men, but when two Royalist officers, exasperated by his persistence, turned their horses' heads and rode at him, he waited for them quite calmly, shot one through the thigh, dismounted the other, and galloped off to safety before anyone else could get at him. Essex could not discover the name: the hero was as modest as he was brave.[1]

The Royalist garrison of Reading was supposed to march out with the honours of war, as the Roundheads of Lichfield had done. But as they passed through the gates they were insulted and robbed by a disorderly crowd of Essex's soldiers, who were quite out of hand, not for the first time. They arrived at Oxford exhausted and indignant, and there is no doubt that the "baser sort" among Charles's followers remembered this incident and waited for opportunities to square the account. Fielding was tried by court martial and condemned to death. He had accepted a clause in the terms of capitulation with Essex by which he handed over all Roundhead deserters in Reading to the tender mercies of their former comrades; and this so horrified the King that He refused every prayer

[1] *The Kingdom's Weekly Intelligencer*, April 25 and May 2, 1643 (Warburton, vol. ii, p. 179). The Cavalier who was shot in the thigh was the famous Daniel O'Neill, who commanded Rupert's own regiment of horse.

for a reprieve. Moreover, Fielding's brother, the Earl of Denbigh, was one of the few peers who still adhered to the Parliamentary side.

But Rupert, as a practical soldier, sympathized with this unfortunate officer and determined to save his life. With more subtlety than he usually displayed he induced the young Prince of Wales (afterwards Charles II) to approach his father with a plea for mercy. Young Charles, who adored his big cousin, readily consented, and carried out his mission so well that Fielding was pardoned and allowed to serve for the remainder of the war as a volunteer in the Royalist ranks.

The great plan of 1642–43 ceased to interest Rupert for the moment. With Essex now firmly established at Reading, it was necessary to stand on guard between him and Oxford. Hopton and Newcastle must pursue their objectives unaided. It soon became apparent that Essex would do nothing very dashing. Parliament was keeping him short of funds; his army's pay was in arrears; and he violently resisted any suggestion that he should attempt a further advance westward—and away from London. But it was important to encourage him in this defensive attitude; and Rupert therefore began a series of raids into the enemies' territory, with the object of harrowing their nerves and planting firmly in their minds the idea that they, though superior in numbers, were the defending force. In this he was singularly successful. We have a whole series of reports from his subordinate commanders describing how they had beaten up this town or that, taken what they wanted in money and munitions, burned a few houses (always with apologies and explanations to the Prince for having done so), and left behind them a chastened town council and a new respect for the King's authority.

The most resounding of these exploits was the great

ride to Chalgrove Field and Chinnor, in June 1643, which has yet to be given its proper place in the history of cavalry warfare. The Whig historians of the nineteenth century never mentioned it, except as the dismal occasion of Hampden's death. Yet it was a remarkable achievement. In the middle of June Rupert heard from a Roundhead deserter (a certain Colonel Urry) that a sum of twenty-one thousand pounds, in gold, was about to be moved from London to Thame for the payment of Essex's soldiers. Urry assured Rupert that the Roundhead outposts were half-asleep, that it would be easy to penetrate their lines and intercept the convoy. Here would be a windfall for the King's depleted treasury!

Rupert set out from Oxford on the afternoon of June 17, with seventeen hundred picked men, nearly all mounted. There were his life guards, under Sir Richard Crane; his own regiment of cavalry, under O'Neill; the Prince of Wales's, in which Bulstrode served; and Henry Percy's regiment. There were three hundred and fifty dragoons; and a body of about five hundred volunteers on foot, in light marching order, commanded by the famous Colonel Lunsford.[1] The forlorn hope was led by Will Legge. The column advanced silently through Chiselhampton and Stadhampton to the suburbs of Tetsworth. When it was dark they dashed through the town, fired at from all sides, but making no reply. Such were Rupert's orders, and his Cavaliers knew better than to disobey.

They hastened on in the darkness, through murky country lanes. Sometimes the alarm would be given, and

---

[1] This must be Harry Lunsford, who was killed at Bristol. But Colonel Sir Thomas Lunsford, who appears in Peacock's muster-rolls (second edition, p. 84) as commanding the 14th Regiment in 1640 (with "Lt.-Col. Henry Lunsford under him" and a "Herbert Lunsford" serving as captain in the same regiment), was an even more famous character. According to the Roundhead pamphleteers, Sir Thomas was a cannibal, whose favourite food was the flesh of children.

Roundhead dragoons would fire into them from the hedge-rows. There was no reply. At daybreak they surrounded Chinnor, and Legge's forlorn hope, galloping headlong into the town, made prisoners of a hundred and twenty Roundhead soldiers who were billeted there, never expecting to meet an enemy so far behind their lines. Their standard, displaying "four or five Bibles on a black ground," was handed over to Lunsford's infantry; and the cavalry galloped on, up the road over the Chilterns, in search of Essex's treasure train. But when they reached the heights a long white ribbon of empty road stretched out before them; and they knew that the convoy had been warned, and had turned off from the high-road, and taken refuge in the woods—Heaven knew where!

So they turned back to Chinnor while the morning dew was still in the fields, and the ride home to Oxford began. Rupert did not hurry. Though he was miles behind the enemy's front line he sought deliberately to draw their attack. Scattered parties of Roundheads began to pursue him, increasing rapidly in boldness and numbers. When he reached Chalgrove Field, about four miles from Chiselhampton and the bridge across the Thame, he had quite an army after him. He halted in a cornfield and drew up his cavalry, facing their pursuers, while the infantry went on and secured the bridge. The road which led to the bridge he lined with his dragoons, under Lord Wentworth. It was a pretty little trap. Rupert had nothing more to do than trot back with his cavalry and lead the enemy into it.

But the Roundheads were pressing after him with renewed ardour. Though Rupert did not know it, they had just been joined by John Hampden, the famous Parliament man, who had started the great quarrel about Ship Money. Roused from his bed by the sound of firing

Hampden had galloped to the scene of action and joined the first Roundhead horsemen he met—those of Captains Sheffield and Cross—as a volunteer. As Rupert retired across the cornfield his enemies were so close on his heels that his temper began to rise. They lined the boundary hedge he had just left, and another to his left rear, and

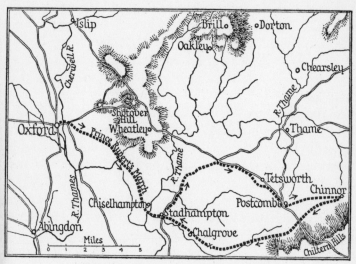

RUPERT'S MARCH TO CHALGROVE FIELD

opened a galling fire. Major Gunter, with the dragoons from Tetsworth, was in front. Their object, of course, was to delay him until reinforcements could arrive. But, as the modern historian of the Civil War remarks, "It was dangerous to play such a game with Rupert."[1] With a sudden exclamation, "This insolency is not to be endured," he turned his horse's head, spurred at the hedge, and jumped clean over it into the midst of the astonished Roundheads. Some fifteen or twenty of his life guards were quick enough to follow him. And no doubt Boy was there.

[1] Gardiner, *History of the Great Civil War*, vol. i, p. 177.

Gunter's dragoons behind the hedge fled back to where their cavalry were drawn up in the field. Rupert, following his usual tactics of giving his enemy no time to breathe, waited only for a few more horsemen to join him and ordered a charge. The Roundheads were badly caught. Their cavalry were probably equal in numbers to Rupert's, but they had no infantry support. Soon the countryside would be swarming with their reinforcements; large parties of foot were already coming up behind; but for the moment their horse were left unsupported to sustain the full weight of Rupert's charge. They did not like it. Yet they stood their ground that morning with exemplary courage—"better," says a Cavalier chronicler, "than they have ever done since our first beating them at Worcester [Powick Bridge]."[1] They even repulsed the first, untidy charge. They were probably inspired by the presence of John Hampden, who was no soldier, but a great personality.

But Rupert had held back from the first charge, while he collected his life guards about him. And with these at his heels he now came in on the enemy's left flank, and put them utterly to rout at the first encounter. Their other wing was outflanked in the same manner by Percy and O'Neill. Hampden and his party, coming up in support, were swept back with the rest. For a few moments more there was the sound of clashing steel and pistol-shots, and then the Roundheads were everywhere in flight, galloping back across the fields to the shelter of the nearest villages. It was tempting to pursue them, but Rupert, for once, called off his men. (It is interesting to note that he seems to have rallied them without difficulty.) Continuing his leisurely, cautious retreat, he moved across Chiselhampton Bridge, and established

[1] *The Beating up of the Enemy's Quarters* (Oxford, 1643; Bentley Collection, 7809).

himself on the other side of the river for the night. A party of dragoons under Colonel Washington guarded the bridge.

But the Roundheads, shaken by their defeat, made no attempt to disturb him. Their losses at Chalgrove were more serious than had at first been supposed. Forty-five were slain outright—Gunter among them. John Hampden was last seen riding from the field, evidently wounded, drooping forward over his horse's head. A few days later it became known that his injuries were fatal. He was compelled to ride for some miles before his wounds could be attended to, and by then it was too late to save him. He had friends and admirers in both camps; Charles himself was distressed to hear of his death, and would have sent surgeons to tend him.[1]

Rupert, we may guess, would not allow the death of a hostile politician to interfere with his satisfaction in a well-earned victory. Early in the morning on the day after Chalgrove Field he continued his homeward march to Oxford, quite unperturbed by the news that Essex himself was now close at hand. His horsemen, after fourteen hours in the saddle, had enjoyed a good night's rest, and the return journey was accomplished quickly. They rode into Oxford at noon on the same day, very well pleased with themselves. They had not brought back the twenty-one thousand pounds, which had been their main objective, but they had ridden a great ride, and they knew it.

In less than two days Rupert and his horsemen had made a circuit of nearly fifty miles through hostile

[1] For details of Hampden's death see Warwick's *Memoirs*, pp. 239, 241; also two excellent biographies of Hampden, *John Hampden's England*, by John Drinkwater (1933), and *John Hampden*, by H. R. Williamson (1933). Warwick makes the curious note that the reason why Hampden's wounds did not heal was that "his blood in its temper was acrimonious, as the scurfe commonly on his face showed."

country, capturing flags and other trophies, driving off scores of horses, fighting a pitched battle, killing fifty or sixty of their opponents, including one of the most prominent of the King's enemies, and returning to Oxford in triumph, with a loss on their side of precisely twelve men. It was Rupert's most spectacular feat up to date.

CHAPTER IX: THE QUEEN COMES TO OXFORD

THE Queen was coming to Oxford. Nearly four months before—in the previous March—the loyal inhabitants of the university town had heard with a thrill of her precarious landing on the Yorkshire coast. Henrietta Maria had come over in a Dutch ship, with an escort of Dutch men-of-war, which might or might not choose to fight for her if the English Parliamentary fleet attacked. They had landed her in a hurry at Bridlington Quay, with the arms and ammunition she had brought with her, and had then stood off from the shore, leaving her to look after herself. The pursuing English ships were commanded by William Batten, who was well aware of the nature of the cargo thus unceremoniously thrust ashore. He crept in close to the quay, and opened a heavy fire, directing his aim—intentionally or not—at the very house in which the Queen had taken refuge.

Henrietta Maria, who had a stout heart in her charming little body, was with difficulty induced to leave the buildings and take shelter in a ditch outside the town. Batten was firing bar shot, and his missiles whizzed over the heads of the Queen and her attendants, scattering earth and stones upon them. One of the Royal servants was killed. But the daughter of Henri IV took it very composedly. She even insisted upon returning to the house she had just left to recover a favourite lap-dog, which was asleep on her bed. It was "an old, ugly dog, called Mitte," but its mistress loved it, and it would be unkind to deny it the honour of being bracketed with Rupert's gallant boy among the dogs of the Civil War. Batten, to the general disgust, kept up his fire, until threatened by the Dutch admiral, who was still in sight. When news of the affair reached London public feeling was such that there was talk of a vote of censure against Batten in the Round-head House of Lords.[1] And more than twenty years later, when the loyal Sir William Batten was an official of the Admiralty under King Charles II, whom he had helped to the throne, this awkward incident in his earlier career was remembered against him.

Relieved of Batten's presence, the Queen had set out for York with her train of two hundred and fifty wagons, conveying arms and ammunition, several pieces of artillery, and a considerable treasure-chest. She was escorted by two thousand Cavaliers, sent from York by Lord Newcastle to attend her. It was a march of forty miles or more, but the Queen rode all the way on horse-back at the head of the troops. When they halted for meals she had food brought to her in the open, and dined there, by the side of the road, wet or fine, in full view of her Cavaliers. They called her "Mary," which was easier for their English tongues, and "God for Queen Mary!" became their rallying cry. The "She-Majesty and Generalissima," as she laughingly styled herself, enjoyed every moment of the march.

Her presence at York had an excellent effect upon the military situation in the North, and she remained there for some months, bringing many doubters over to the Royalist side, intimidating the Parliamentary leader Fairfax, negotiating with the treacherous Hothams for the surrender of Hull. But her object was always to join the King, and on May 23, 1643, she set out for Newark the first stage on her southern march. She had with her 5000 foot (of whom 2000 were to be left in Newark) and about 1500 horse, with the six guns and two mortars landed at Bridlington. But her position was dangerous. Fairfax watched her from the north and east; in the immediate neighbourhood of Newark, at Nottingham, there was

[1] Warburton, vol. ii, p. 129.

QUEEN HENRIETTA MARIA
Van Dyck
Photo Alinari

strong Parliamentary garrison under the redoubtable Colonel Hutchinson. Essex, with the main Parliamentary army, lay to the south, and it would have been easy for him to thrust a strong force across her path to Oxford. Nothing but his natural laziness had held him back. He was reported to be moving now.

It behoved the Queen to walk delicately. She showed her appreciation of the situation in writing to the King (her "Dear heart") from Newark: "Have a care that no troop of Essex's army incommodate us." Then she directed her march south-west to Ashby de la Zouch and Stratford-on-Avon, hoping to leave Essex away to her left.

But at Oxford they were aware of her coming and of the valuable help she brought with her, and were sending an army to meet her and bring her safely in. What more suitable commander than young Prince Rupert, her favourite nephew, who, as it happened, had escorted her abroad when she set out on this same journey from which she was now happily returned? So Rupert marched north again after all. He carefully interposed his forces between Essex and the Queen's line of march. So close were the outposts that skirmishes were reported every few hours. At Buckingham on July 2 Rupert was at his toilet when he heard that the enemy were approaching Whitebridge. He rushed out, half-shaved, led a successful charge, and returned a little later to deal with the other side of his face. But at this kind of warfare he could play with Essex like a cat with a mouse. After harassing the Roundheads until they were "wearied of their lives" he suddenly broke off contact, and fell back rapidly to Stratford-on-Avon, where he met the Queen. Every move had been perfectly timed. It is said that Henrietta Maria spent that night as the guest of Shakespeare's granddaughter, Mrs Nash, who was still living in Stratford.

The united armies of the Queen and the Prince moved southward at their leisure. They had no fear of Essex now. At the foot of the blood-stained slope of Edgehill King Charles was waiting for them. Broken pike-heads and helmets and bedraggled plumage—all the litter of a seventeenth-century battlefield—still lay scattered in the grass on the hillside as Rupert delivered up his charge. Charles said little to his nephew, but turned at once to embrace his brave little queen, from whom he had been separated so long. It was an affecting meeting. How much Henrietta Maria felt it we cannot tell. Perhaps she mingled a few tears with the King's. But she was "frivolous," says Gardiner, "and without any appreciation of real merit, and frequently used her influence with her husband to obtain favours for courtiers unworthy of consideration." [1] On this occasion she sparred with the lovesick King, laughingly declaring that she would not meet him alone until he had promised a peerage for her favourite Jermyn, whom she had already put in command of her troops. Charles promised eagerly. His one desire, now he had her back, was to proclaim his devotion openly by acceding to her slightest wish.

They mounted their horses again and rode on towards Oxford under a blue, summer sky, with Rupert and his Cavaliers, who had cleared all this country and made it safe for them, trotting quietly behind. At Woodstock—as though everything conspired to make the occasion happy—they were met by news of the battle of Roundway Down. This victory was the culmination of a fortnight of Royalist successes in North and South, and it deserves a few words here because Rupert, though not present himself, must have felt that it was, in a sense, his personal achievement. Lord Newcastle, in the North, had beaten the Fairfaxes from the field at Adwalton Moor,

[1] Article in the *Dictionary of National Biography*.

on June 30; and at Lansdown, near Bristol, on July 5, the united forces of Hopton, Lord Hertford, and Prince Maurice had driven Waller's army out of a strong position, and might have destroyed it utterly "had our horse been as good as the enemy's." But the cavalry of this Western army was deplorably weak. They might drive back Waller's heavily armed horsemen—among whom were the steel-clad "Lobsters" of Hazelrigg—but they could not hope to break them: they could not press home the successes of the hard-working Cornish foot. That was the position after Lansdown.

But while the beaten Waller laid siege to Devizes Prince Maurice came riding over the Western hills into Oxford, clamouring for some of Rupert's cavalry. They gave him about fifteen hundred men, under the command of Wilmot. Rupert and Wilmot were bitter enemies by now; but these were Rupert's horsemen, none the less, trained under his own eye and in his own methods as General of the Horse. They had received his historic order at Edgehill to charge without firing a shot, and they had charged and won. They had never been beaten. They rode off now, in high spirits, with Rupert's brother in their ranks—for Maurice was to serve as a volunteer under Wilmot.

On the afternoon of July 13 the besiegers of Devizes saw these fifteen hundred horsemen moving against the skyline across the height of Roundway Down, and beheld them turn gently down the slope towards the town, with every apparent intention of attempting its relief in the presence of the Roundhead army! Waller advanced his cavalry to check them. But a fierce charge, headed by Sir John Byron, hurled the cavalry back among the foot. Panicky rumours began to spread through the Roundhead ranks; these were surely not the tired horsemen of Maurice and Hertford; their methods were more suggestive of Chalgrove Field. It dawned on Waller's men that they were making the acquaintance of the famous Oxford horse. Striving to restore the situation, the "Lobsters" attempted an uphill charge, for which they were singularly ill-suited, and were beaten in their turn, and again rode over the unfortunate foot. The latter began to waver. They could see the Royalist garrison sallying out behind them from the town. In front the galloping line of Cavaliers was now close upon them. They did not wait for those terrible swords, but broke and fled in every direction, not one regiment holding its ground. Wilmot pursued them for miles, and when he had finished with them Waller's Western army, as a fighting force, had ceased to exist.

This was glorious news for the Royal party at Woodstock. Next day they hastened on to Oxford, and made a triumphant entry into the city, a gay cavalcade of lords and ladies and mounted Cavaliers, with a long train of wagons containing everything necessary for the further prosecution of the war. Victory was in the air. The bells of the cathedral and twenty or thirty churches and college chapels rang out merrily, and a continuous roar of cheering followed the procession through the streets, from the North Gate, down the Cornmarket, to Christ Church, where the King lived. In an England cruelly divided Oxford alone was unanimous—or very nearly so.

It presented an extraordinary spectacle. Such a jostle of things military and academic was never seen in a university town—and was never repeated until the khaki cadets, with their white hatbands, and the red-tabbed staff officers on 'special courses' began to crowd the streets of Oxford and Cambridge in our most recent war. Soldiers were quartered in the college gateways and in the kitchens, and lolled at their ease about the quads. There was a regiment of undergraduates, with breast-

148

plates and helmets, which paraded in Christ Church meadows, and had doubled its strength within the last few months. There was a powder-magazine in the tower at New College. There was a scheme of fortifications, devised by a B.A. of Queen's, which would soon make the city impregnable against Roundhead attacks. And since the townsmen did not seem inclined to break their backs with pick and shovel the university had been brought in: every student did one day's digging a week, and the colleges agreed to raise the sum of forty pounds weekly for twenty weeks, until the works were completed. At the same time the scholastic life of Oxford continued without interruption. The printers were busy, not only with their regular work, but with a heavy output of pamphlets (most of them now lost), in which they attempted to combat the avalanche of propaganda from London. Services were held daily in the college chapels and prayers offered up for the success of the Royal arms. Oxford, like the London apprentices, was learning to "pray heartily and fight heartily."

The Queen was at Merton. They were building a bastion in the gardens near by; but if she wished to escape from martial sounds and the din of pick and hammer there was always that private way, which can still be traced, leading through Merton Hall to the grounds of Corpus and finally to the King's own apartments in Christ Church. She had her ladies with her. The city, indeed, was full of courtiers, male and female, quartered, for lack of room, in most unlikely places— small and dingy lodgings, such as they vowed they had never seen before and hoped never to see again. But at Merton and Christ Church there was still something of the dignity of Court life. The King and Queen dined in public, and walked daily, with their ladies and gentlemen, in Merton gardens and Christ Church meadows.

Among the Queen's attendants there was one whose beauty, by general consent, easily outshone the rest. She was Mary Villiers, Duchess of Richmond, daughter of the handsome Duke of Buckingham who was Charles's favourite in the early years of his reign. Her age was twenty. Her wit and vivacity equalled the Queen's. She had inherited more than her fair share of the family good looks. Her first husband, Lord Herbert, whom she cordially disliked, had died when she was only eleven years old, and Charles I had adopted the child and brought her up with his own children. There is a pretty story to the effect that when she was still new to Court life she one day climbed a tree in the privy gardens, with her widow's weeds trailing about her ankles, and was seen from the palace windows and mistaken for some strange, exotic bird. A courtier was even sent out with a gun to secure this handsome specimen. He had approached the tree and was raising his weapon to his shoulder before he discovered his mistake. At Mary's suggestion he packed her up in a hamper and sent her to the King, with a message that he had captured a beautiful butterfly alive. And as "Butterfly" she was henceforth known in Court circles. Then, when she grew a little older, they married her to the staid and stately Duke of Richmond, who happened to be one of Rupert's staunchest friends. Most of Rupert's intimates were professional soldiers—Will Legge, Marmaduke Langdale, Gerard, and the rest—but there was some close affinity between him and this quiet, melancholy duke.

Rupert's relations with the charming Duchess were sufficiently notorious to attract the attention of the Roundhead pamphleteers, and sufficiently decorous to suggest a tragedy of unrequited love to modern biographers like Miss Eva Scott and Mrs Steuart Erskine. It is certain that they never disturbed his friendship with

the Duke. Years ago in Holland it had been proposed to
match Mary Villiers with his eldest brother, Henry, who
was drowned. Now when Rupert and Mary met again,
after many months, in the streets of Stratford, there was
something about this tall, saturnine young soldier, riding
at the head of his hard-bitten cavalry, whom he himself
had trained and led to victory, that was in itself a
challenge to her sex. Unless you count Mlle de Rohan
(who was still patiently waiting for him) or the daughter
of the Governor of Linz, he had never made love to anyone in his life. It was an easy conquest for Mary Villiers.
Prince Maurice had fallen captive to the pretty Mrs
Kirke; but Maurice was a mere platoon commander.
Mary, as she walked in the college gardens at Merton,
had the victor of Chalgrove himself striding moodily
beside her, with his big white dog at his heels. How
Rupert took it we shall never know. He hotly resented
any public references to the subject, and poor Dan
O'Neill, who talked a little too freely, was even deprived
of his command. But that proves nothing.

And after all this talk of dalliance in college gardens
let us pause for a moment to inquire exactly how long
Prince Rupert allowed himself to be detained in Oxford
after he had escorted the Queen and her ladies thither.
Three days! On July 18 his trumpets sounded through
the streets, and he was away again through the West Gate,
on the road to Bristol. That seems to give his measure
as courtier and lover. He was now to win a port for the
King. There had been a previous attempt upon Bristol,
largely of Rupert's contrivance. On the night of March 7
in this same year groups of citizens wearing white arm-
lets had assembled quietly in Christmas Street, Bristol,
and in Wine Street, intending to seize the gates and let in
Rupert's cavalry, who were waiting at the foot of Durdham Down. The plot was discovered, and the plotters

instantly executed by Nathaniel Fiennes, the Parliamentary Governor. This time, however, there was no question of plotting: Rupert intended to assault the town.

The taking of Bristol was a brief, impetuous affair, highly characteristic of Rupert and his methods, but only made possible by the weakness of English military architecture at this time. It was on the afternoon of July 23, 1643, that Rupert, with a strong force of horse and foot from Oxford, reached Durdham Down. Leaving his men in billets for the night, he rode ahead with his own life guards (under Sir Richard Crane), Washington's dragoons, and a small party of officers, to take a look at the defences. After riding for some time they came to Clifton Church, which stood on a hill-top within musket-shot of the nearest Roundhead fort. With his usual indifference to danger Rupert sprang from his horse and led the way to the church tower. From this point of vantage he could see the defences of Bristol spread out before him on either hand.

To his right—that is, to the south—flowed the broad stream of the river Avon, encompassing half the city on that side and offering a formidable obstacle to the assailants. Beyond the river lay the victorious Cavalier army of the West, waiting for Rupert's signal to attack. Maurice was with them, and Lord Hertford, and Hopton, and many others, fresh from their triumph at Roundway Down. Even as Rupert gazed in that direction his brother Maurice crossed the stream and rode up the hillside to the little church to consult with him.

Turning to his left, Rupert saw the land fortifications stretching away in a north-easterly direction, and in an almost straight line, as far as the dominating Priors Hill Fort—after which they sloped south-east, and beyond his range of vision, until they joined the river defences south of the city. They were on an elaborate scale, and had been considerably strengthened by the exertions of the present Roundhead garrison. There were bastions at frequent intervals. Between Rupert and the river was the Water Fort; immediately opposite to him, at about two hundred yards' range, was Brandon Hill Fort, crowning the highest point in the defence system; a little farther north was Windmill Fort; and between that and Priors Hill was a redoubt known as Coulston's Fort. There was one serious weakness—the shallowness of the ditch protecting the curtain wall. The ground was so full of rocks and stones that the defenders, having made their ditch a good two yards broad, had nowhere been able to dig it down much below four feet. In fact, it could be crossed without difficulty.

Rupert stood in the churchyard at Clifton, talking to Maurice, Sir Arthur Aston, and others. It was a Sunday and there was a Sabbath peace in the air. They were discussing the best positions for the besieging batteries in view of what they had just seen. Suddenly the Roundhead gunners at Brandon Hill Fort woke up to the presence of this group of strange officers on the opposite hill, hardly more than a stone's throw away. They opened fire, and sent two or three balls into the churchyard, but without hurting anyone. This was the beginning of a vigorous artillery duel which lasted until the morning of the 24th. On that morning Rupert paraded his Oxford army on Durdham Down, advancing his men, both horse and foot, to the edge of the down, so that the Roundheads in the forts might see them. Lord Hertford did the same on his side with the Western army. Mining and sapping were not to be thought of in this stony ground; but Rupert seized every empty house or other point of vantage and sent his musketeers to line the hedgerows close to the walls, so that by Monday night (the 24th) the opposing sides were exchanging volleys of musketry at point-blank range. The batteries added their deeper roar to the clatter of the small arms. " It was a beautiful piece of danger," says an eyewitness, " to see so many fires incessantly in the dark, from the pieces on both sides, for a whole hour together." "In these military masquerades," he adds zestfully, "was this Monday night passed." [1]

But Rupert had no use for masquerades. On Tuesday morning, leaving the gunners to their work, he crossed the river and had a consultation with Hertford and Maurice, at the end of which it was decided to make a general assault upon the city just before dawn on the following day. It would appear [2] that many of the Cornish officers were opposed to an immediate assault. On their side of the river the ground was not hard and stony, but soft. It would be easy to sap towards the walls. On the other hand, an assault would mean for them either crossing the river or charging over open, marshy ground with no cover from the garrison's fire. Rupert brushed these objections aside. There was no time to spare for digging, he said; the Governor, Nat Fiennes, was well known to be a coward; many of the leading citizens were on their side and longing to avenge the brutal executions of the previous March; let them but effect a lodgment anywhere inside the walls and the city was theirs. The Cornishmen said no more; but it would seem that they privately made up their minds that the glory of that lodgment should not be Rupert's.

Two cannon shots, fired from the headquarters of Lord Grandison, Colonel-General of the Foot, opposite Priors

---

[1] *Journal of the Siege of Bristol* (Warburton, vol. ii, pp. 244–245).
[2] Clarendon, vol. ii, p. 227.

Hill Fort, were to be the signal for assault. Every officer and man engaged in the attack was to wear an easily distinguishable ribbon or favour. Green was the colour pitched upon for this purpose by the Royalist leaders— no doubt because it was less commonly worn than white, red, or blue. The assailants were to be "without any band or handkerchief about the neck." The word was "Oxford"—at any rate, on the north side of the town.

But shortly before 'zero hour,' as we should call it nowadays, when the firing had died down, and that eerie, ominous silence associated with such occasions had fallen upon the opposing lines, there was a sudden sound of cheering and ragged volleys of musketry from across the river to the south. The Cornishmen had already attacked! Instantly grasping the situation, Rupert sent hurried orders to Grandison to fire off his signal and begin the general assault. Before that could be done the Cornishmen had lost heavily. Thanks to their own impetuosity, the wagons and the faggots which were to help them across the water to the walls had not yet arrived. Most of their officers were killed or wounded in the open, including Sir Nicholas Slanning and Colonel John Trevannion. Colonel Buck, who commanded on the right, struggled to the top of the wall, but was knocked over by a halberd, and died in the ditch below. The attack was a costly failure.

Lord Grandison, on the extreme north, as soon as he could fire his signal and get his infantry in motion, sent them against the curtain wall on both sides of Priors Hill Fort. They were repulsed. He then led them direct at the fort itself, and got as far as the ditch. But, owing to the attack having been begun too soon, the scaling ladders were not ready, and it was impossible to do any more. Colonel Harry Lunsford, finding a ladder belonging to

155

the enemy lying in the ditch, mounted it and got nearly to the top of the palisades; but the ladder was too short, and he had to descend, miraculously unhurt. The Royalist infantry, who were losing heavily all this time, began to bolt back to their own lines. Grandison, galloping about on horseback in an attempt to rally them, was shot through the leg and mortally wounded. It was obvious that the attack could never succeed.

Colonel Bellasys, on Grandison's right, opposite Coulston's Fort, had done no better. But just as the position seemed desperate Will Legge arrived, with news from Lord Wentworth, who commanded on the extreme right, that some of his men had effected an entry into the city between the Windmill and Brandon Hill Forts. Thereupon Rupert in person rallied the shattered infantry of Grandison and Bellasys, and sent them forward once again with Colonel Moyle, who was shouting at the top of his voice, "They run! They run!" As Rupert galloped back to fetch up the cavalry his horse was shot under him; but he rose to his feet and walked quietly on, "without even so much as mending his pace," until another horse was brought to him.

What had happened on the right was this. Wentworth had attacked, as we have seen, between the Windmill and Brandon Hill, and at first had made little progress under the enfilading fire of the two forts. But a party of his men, under the gallant Colonel Washington,[1] of the dragoons, found themselves unexpectedly in a piece of 'dead' ground, where they were invisible from both forts, and, seizing their opportunity, crept up close to the curtain wall and lobbed over hand grenades, until the defenders were frightened away. Then they rushed at the low wall, scrambled over it, and began knocking it

---

[1] He was of the same family as the American George Washington.

down behind them to make way for their comrades. A troop of Roundhead horse under Langrish had been stationed here by Fiennes to deal with just such an emergency as this. But they made their charge too late, were met by a volley of musketry, and fled back into the city. Fiennes afterwards blamed Langrish for the loss of Bristol.

Lost it presently was, though there was much hard fighting to be done before the streets could be cleared. Washington's Breach, as the place of entry was afterwards called, was commanded, *inside the lines*, by Essex Fort, but the garrison there never waited to be attacked, and the cheering Royalists, led now by Wentworth in person and joined by Bellasys and his men, with the cavalry under Aston not far behind, pressed on through the suburbs to the Frome Gate, and, right-handed, to College Green and the cathedral. They were fired at from some of the houses, and, by Colonel Moyle's order, took possession of other buildings from which they could retaliate—"so that hereabouts the fight was like scolding at one another out of windows," says a contemporary.[1]

Maurice sent over some Cornishmen to help, and the attack surged on into the heart of Bristol city. But the firing from the houses never ceased, the Roundhead *francs-tireurs* picking out the officers with deadly aim. Bellasys was wounded. The gallant Lunsford got a bullet through the heart on some steps near the Frome Gate (afterwards called Lunsford's Stairs). Moyle was shot through the groin and died in agony. Rupert was in the rear, directing his columns, keeping the Brandon Hill and Windmill Forts in check—but always so active and so ubiquitous that "it is confessed by the commanders that had not the Prince been there the assault, through

[1] *Journal of the Siege* (Warburton, vol. ii, p. 254).

mere despair, had been in danger to be given over in many places." [1]

It was now nearly five o'clock in the afternoon, and the street fighting as bitter as ever, with continued losses on the Royalist side, when a message was unexpectedly received from Governor Fiennes offering to discuss terms of surrender. This was precisely what Rupert had prophesied. Fiennes, with no prospect before him but to retire into the castle with such of his men as still stood to their arms and there endure a bitter siege behind old and crumbling walls, lacked the heart to continue. Rupert, greatly relieved, received his messengers courteously. Articles were quickly drawn up and signed, by which the Roundhead garrison was to march out the following morning with all the honours of war, leaving only their guns and ammunition behind. Bristol had fallen.

The end of the affair was less glorious than its beginning. As the victorious Cavaliers paraded the streets that night, celebrating their triumph, they were joined by some deserters from Fiennes's garrison and by many Royalist citizens of Bristol, who eagerly pointed out to them the houses of the leading Roundheads. The recent hangings had not been forgotten; nor had the outrage at Reading; nor the shooting down of so many popular officers by civilian snipers that very afternoon. Pillaging began, and went on at intervals all night, especially among the houses on the bridge, where the inhabitants were notoriously disloyal.

There was worse to follow in the morning. It had been arranged that Fiennes and his men should march out at nine o'clock, and Rupert, remembering Reading, had appointed a strong escort to protect them. But for some reason they began their march at seven, before the escort

[1] *Journal of the Siege* (Warburton, vol. ii, p. 255).

was ready, and were robbed and ill-treated by an unruly mob of Cavaliers as they passed out through the gate.[1]

Worst of all, Rupert had drawn up his treaty with Fiennes without taking the trouble to consult the Marquess of Hertford.

[1] Rupert and Maurice were accused by the pamphleteers of complicity in this outrage; but Fiennes, when excusing his surrender of Bristol before the House of Commons, went out of his way to defend the Princes against this charge. "So far from triumphing and rejoicing at these disorders," he said, the two young Palatines "did ride among the plunderers with their swords, hacking and slashing them"; and Rupert "did excuse it to me in a very fair way, as if he were much troubled at it."

CHAPTER X: THE TURN OF THE TIDE

THERE is a tide in the affairs of kings, no less than in those of common men, which, taken at the flood, leads on to fortune; omitted, all the voyage of their life is bound in shallows and in miseries. These words of wisdom, written by the greatest of the Elizabethans, might have been specially designed, by some prophetic instinct, to fit the case of King Charles I in the early days of August 1643.

Never had the situation appeared more hopeful. Rupert's victory at Bristol, says Clarendon, was "a full tide of prosperity to the King." It gave him his port in the West. It also gave him his second great opportunity to win the war. The 'pincers' plan of 1642–43 had been disappointing, but it was not a fiasco—it had not entirely failed to 'pinch.' Newcastle's Cavaliers from the North and Hopton's from the South-west never met, as designed, on the banks of the Thames to strangle the life out of London. But the former got into Lincolnshire and the latter into Sussex, and the rebel lump of the East and South-east was undoubtedly beginning to feel the squeeze. You might hear its squeals. The Roundhead leaders were loudly reproached—especially Essex, the lethargic Commander-in-Chief. Rough cartoons, depicting the Lord-General sprawling at his ease, with his pipe in one hand and his glass in the other, while the cause of the ungodly triumphed, were chalked on the London walls. The peace party raised its voice again (it had a majority in the House of Lords), and women demonstrated noisily in Palace Yard until Waller's cavalry roughly dispersed them.

It may be argued that the war party never faltered, that every fresh report of Royalist victories only hardened its determination, and that the ultimate effect of the Royalist pincers was to squeeze out of frightened London another cascade of gold into the Parliamentary war chest. But the first result of the news from Bristol was a very general discouragement. The morale of the Parliamentary side, as a whole, was shaken. The leaders were quarrelling; Essex and Waller were not on speaking terms; others were secretly corresponding with the King. Recruiting for the army fell off so alarmingly that Parliament was compelled to legalize the use of the press gangs —a confession of moral failure in itself. Even though the pincers should never meet, it looked as though a strong thrust at the heart of London might succeed this time. So thought many of the King's advisers at Oxford—and notably the Queen.

Unfortunately the Royalists were, in many respects, no happier than their opponents. They had found in their victory at Bristol as fruitful a source of internecine squabbles as the Roundheads had found in defeat. We have noted that Rupert signed articles of surrender with Fiennes without taking the trouble to acquaint his colleague, the Marquess of Hertford, with their terms. This was a failure, not only of common courtesy, but of statesmanship; for whatever Rupert may have thought of Hertford as a general (and no one could think very much) he must have known that he was a valuable and influential adherent to the King's side. His next step was to write from Bristol to the King, asking for the governorship of the captured city—an entirely reasonable request, since it was his army which had stormed the walls. So it seemed to Charles, who answered with congratulations and consent. But meantime Hertford, bitterly offended at his treatment, had anticipated Rupert's request to the King by publicly announcing that he (Hertford), as general of the Western Army, had appointed Sir Ralph

Hopton to be Governor. It was a clever move. Rupert cared not a fig for the ordinances of any imperious nobleman on either side. Though himself of the Blood Royal, he showed singularly little respect for blue blood in others. But Ralph Hopton was a soldier like himself, a gallant and efficient commander, universally esteemed. He would do nothing against him. But neither would he recognize the appointment.

When news of this impasse reached Oxford the dispute was immediately taken up among the courtiers and hotly argued, every man of them, apparently, adopting one side or the other with unnecessary vehemence.[1] The practical soldiers would be mostly on Rupert's side, the statesmen and politicians on Hertford's; and, no doubt, there was a general tendency, when disagreements arose (as they too often did), for the King's disputatious advisers to fall into these two camps. But Charles was still a king—all the sixty-three inches of him—and as soon as he realized what had happened he put an end to this dispute by one of those swift, personal interventions which might have been more frequent during the war. He went down to Bristol himself, entered the city amid the plaudits of the people, and soon brought his quarrelsome generals to reason. He made Rupert Governor, for he had passed his word on that; and Rupert immediately appointed Hopton his Lieutenant-Governor, with an intimation that this would mean the governorship in practice, since he (Rupert) would usually be away, and "would not meddle." Hopton, whose only desire was for peace accepted joyfully. And since it seemed that one cause of the quarrel was Rupert's resentment that his brother Prince Maurice, should be serving as Hertford's subordinate, the latter was persuaded to return to Oxford with the King and act as one of his civilian advisers, while

[1] Clarendon, vol. ii, p. 237.

Maurice went south with the Western army, part of which was placed under his command and part under Lord Carnarvon's.

The whole incident is a good illustration of one of the principal difficulties with which Charles had to contend —the everlasting quarrels in his council, a sort of civil war behind the Civil War. Nor can it be pretended that Rupert was at his best in the council-chamber. He approached every meeting as though it were a skirmish with the enemy. He disliked Digby so much that he opposed every suggestion that came from him as soon as it was uttered, and without consideration of its merits. His manner on these occasions was brusque and unaccommodating. His friend Sir Philip Warwick has summed it up:

> A little sharpness of temper of body and uncommunicableness in society or council (by seeming with a pish to neglect all another said and he approved not) made him less grateful than his friends wished. And this humour soured him towards the counsellors of civil affairs, who were necessarily to intermix with him in martial councils. And these great men often distrusted such downright soldiers as the Prince was, though a Prince of the Blood, lest he should be too apt to prolong the war, and to obtain that by a pure victory which they wished to be got by a dutiful submission upon modest, speedy, and peaceable terms.[1]

Thus in this moment of victory for the Royalist cause, when fortune smiled upon the Cavaliers as never before, it seemed that they could not take a step without arguing about it. The issue at the moment lay between two clearly defined policies: a dash at London, such as the Queen favoured, or a slow advance, 'mopping up' hostile towns and garrisons on the way. Rupert after Edgehill had taken the lead in supporting the former policy. Now, after Bristol, the Queen and her friends might reasonably

---

[1] *Memoirs*, pp. 227–228.

expect to find an ally in him. To their annoyance, they saw him adopt a non-committal attitude.

In fact, the case was not so simple as in the previous year. In the first place, the Royalist leaders had been made to realize the strength of local feeling in England and the limitations which it imposed upon their plans. Their soldiers had been recruited in a dozen different counties, but they were all local men, and every regiment and every troop of horse clung passionately to its own local loyalties and disliked being led far afield. Their point of view was utterly unlike that of the professional soldiers and foreign mercenaries whom Rupert had known in Germany—men who would go anywhere if the pay was good. To these peasants and yeoman farmers the war was a mere interruption of their normal lives. It seemed to them preposterous that they should be asked to march all the way to the assault of London while their own county town or native village was left behind in Roundhead hands, and their own families perhaps at the mercy of some local bully who had put up an orange-tawny scarf. Newcastle's whitecoats objected to leaving Yorkshire until Hull was taken; the men of Cornwall and Devon would not move another step into Sussex until Plymouth had been secured. And these objections were strong enough to carry the day, so that Newcastle now turned aside from his southern march, and Maurice and Carnarvon occupied themselves about Plymouth and Exeter. It was the ruin of the pincers plan. Its immediate effect was that if Charles now advanced against London there would be no relieving pressure either from north or south.

But the real crux of the matter was Gloucester. This Parliamentary stronghold contained a powerful garrison under Colonel Massey, and here again, as in the cases of Hull and Plymouth, the King's Welsh allies disliked the idea of marching eastward towards London and leaving Massey and his men unmolested in their rear, so close to the Welsh border. Rupert would worry little enough about that. But Rupert was a soldier, and it went all against the traditions of soldiering in his time to march from Bristol against London, in what was intended to be the decisive campaign of the war, without pausing to remove this danger-spot on the way. Rupert understood better than he did a year ago the difficulties and dangers of a thrust towards London. They might fail again; there might be another retreat from Brentford. Was it safe to begin the advance with an able soldier like Massey free to operate in their rear?

Massey, as it happened, whether from nerves or avarice, was beginning to wobble in his allegiance, and to throw out hints that he might be willing to sell the town. He was talking to Royalist agents, of whom Gloucester seems to have been full, leading them aside and giving them ambiguous messages for the King and for his friend Will Legge: which messages, no doubt, came eventually to Charles's ears in far more definite and hopeful terms than Massey had ever employed. But there was a general feeling in the King's council that the siege of Gloucester would probably not take very long. It would be but a brief pause, a marking time, on the march to London. And that false hope, which had no real foundation in fact, was the argument which turned the scale. Before the King left Bristol the fatal decision was taken to march against Gloucester and invest the town. Henrietta Maria smiled no more upon Rupert.

What Rupert thought of the change of plan can only be guessed at. No formal statement of his opinion exists; for all that can be discovered from the records he might never have been consulted. He was certainly not its instigator, as the Queen supposed. But he acquiesced.

It must have gone cruelly against the grain. Every fibre
of his being responded to the appeal of a direct attack.
He loved swift decisions. He longed to lead his cavalry
once again up the London road and watch the fat merchants scuttling for cover. But behind all his dash and
impetuosity there was always a core of hard common
sense, which the Queen and her friends seemed to lack.
He would fight anything but facts. On this occasion the
facts were apparently against him.

So he turned up rather sulkily at Gloucester, and stood
with the King in that gaily dressed group which waited
to receive the two Roundhead citizens who had come out
from Gloucester, in answer to Charles's summons, to
explain that though this was the most loyal town in
England it was unalterably resolved not to admit its
King. It was an extraordinary scene. Edward Hyde, who
had little of the flippant young courtier about him,
describes the two Puritan envoys as veritable caricatures
of their own party. They were melancholy-looking
personages, "with lean, sharp, and bald visages." Their
"garb and gesture" were such as "made the most severe
countenances merry." Whether intentionally or not,
they seemed to be quite ignorant of the forms of Court
etiquette. The only concession they made was to adopt
what an eyewitness describes as a "slightly kneeling"
attitude when they approached the King. Undismayed
by what was evidently a sniggering reception, they delivered their message "in a pert, shrill accent," and,
clapping their high-crowned hats upon their heads,
turned their backs and stalked off home.[1] Sounds of
undisguised hilarity must have followed them. It is
possible that Rupert's dry laugh was heard in the chorus
—but somehow one doubts it.

He did not like his situation. This was a hideous

[1] Clarendon, vol. ii, p. 243.

country for cavalry, all cut up with hedges and enclosures, and the country folk uniformly hostile. It was obvious that Massey meant to fight. They might be delayed here for weeks. Rupert urged the council to order an assault. They outvoted him. Thereupon he refused to command the besieging force, and went off to Oxford, leaving old Forth in charge. "I am afraid we shall proceed but very sleepily without you," wrote Sir Arthur Aston, of the dragoons, and he was right.

But at Oxford also there was a chill in the air. Henrietta Maria had got it into her head that there were hidden forces at work seeking to undermine her influence with the King. She had chosen to make her opposition to the siege of Gloucester a test case; and finding Rupert against her in this matter, she had cast him for the part of chief conspirator. She even persuaded herself that he had agreed to the siege, not for military reasons, but from motives of personal jealousy directed against herself. She treated him like a disguised enemy, and her hostility must have overshadowed even his happy relations with her lady-in-waiting, the Duchess of Richmond. An uncomfortable feeling that, on this particular point, the Queen and her irresponsible advisers might for once have been right would not improve Rupert's temper. He soon returned to Gloucester, where he visited the besiegers' lines and had his pot-helmet knocked sideways by a missile from the walls.

A few days later occurred the strange incident of the Earls of Holland and Bedford, which must have put an end to any friendly feelings existing between Rupert and the partisans of the Queen. These two noblemen, infected by the general depression in the Parliamentary camp, had slipped away from London and come to Oxford to interview the King. From the Royalist point of view their records were not good: the Earl of Holland was a notable turncoat, and the Earl of Bedford had recently been in command of the rebel horse. Charles I, unlike his easygoing son, always found it extremely hard to forgive disloyalty in any man. He now applied to his council for advice as to the reception of the penitent peers and "what kind of entertainment they should have." The council, after much debate—making of it another party question—agreed to admit the earls to Oxford, but otherwise provided no entertainment of any kind. In fact the new arrivals were treated like pariahs. When Holland called upon the Chancellor of the Exchequer one morning, two or three other noblemen who were present and knew him well immediately rose and left the room "without so much as saluting him." In this boycott the Queen and her friends took the lead.

Rupert, who was down at Gloucester with the King, thought it pure midsummer madness. For once he agreed with Hyde and the soberer "politicians." He correctly foresaw that such behaviour would discourage other similar desertions which might be of more service to the Royalist cause. When, therefore, he heard that the two Roundhead peers, despairing of Oxford, were on their way down to Gloucester to seek the King he put himself out to be kind to them. He even led them in personally to kiss the King's hand—whereat the Queen was "angry" when she heard. It was not Rupert's fault that Charles gave the deserters so little encouragement. Soon there were other things to think of.

The Parliamentary steamroller was approaching—the Earl of Essex, with his full strength, advancing to the relief of Gloucester. The Government at Westminster had decided that they could not allow this town to fall and the news of Massey's unexpectedly firm resistance nerved them to a special effort. Essex was appointed to command the relieving army. The new regulation legalizing press gangs were vigorously but diplomatically enforced. London was full of members of the well-to-do classes who were either neutral or definitely Royalist in sympathy; the press gangs hunted these men down, and they were clapped in prison, until they paid heavy fines or provided others to take their places in the ranks. When Essex set out at the end of August he had 8000 foot with him and 4000 horse. He took a wide sweep northward to avoid Oxford, and, passing through Aylesbury, turned left-handed to the west, and moved purposefully upon Gloucester at something rather better than his ordinary pace. Reinforcements had joined him from the North, and he was now at the head of at least 15,000 men.

Yet it was some weeks before the Royalists realized that he meant business. Wilmot's cavalry, who had been left to watch his movements, were roughly shouldered aside. At Stow-on-the-Wold he came in contact with Rupert's horsemen, who attempted to cut off his advance-guard from the main body; but the column closed up rapidly, and the Cavaliers were driven off. On September 5 he was within hearing of Gloucester, and fired four guns to let the garrison know that relief was at hand. On the 8th he marched unopposed into the town. They were down to their last barrel of gunpowder!

This march of Essex's from London to Gloucester, mostly through hostile country swept clean of supplies, was his best achievement in the war, and should not be belittled. But it is only fair to add that as soon as the King heard of his approach he immediately revised his plans, and broke up from Gloucester without offering any resistance to its relief. The new Royalist idea—whether Charles's or Rupert's or Forth's—was to let Essex into Gloucester unmolested, and then to take up a strong position across the London road by which he must return. To capture or destroy Essex would be better than to take Gloucester. He had a large army to feed, and was known to be short of supplies. There was no need to fight him. He had only to be 'held' for a few days and starvation would do the rest. It does not look like Rupert's plan—it gave singularly little scope for cavalry action—but whether it was his own or another's he cordially approved it.

The difficulty was to intercept Essex, who seemed to be unusually wideawake. After replenishing the magazines at Gloucester he marched out along the northern road to Tewkesbury, then turned abruptly in his tracks and made a rush southward to Cirencester. A pleasant surprise awaited him there, and it is interesting to note that at the very moment when the Royalists were losing the team spirit and quarrelling among themselves the fortune of war went over definitely to the other side. Essex's windfall at Cirencester took the form of a train of forty wagons laden with provisions, which had been assembled there for the use of the Royalist army before Gloucester and, by some inexcusable negligence, had not been removed when that siege was raised. The effect of this capture upon Essex's half-starved battalions was electrical, and will surprise no one who has observed what a good meal will do for the courage of soldiers on the march. "Under God's providence," wrote a Roundhead who was present, this lucky capture "was the preservation of the army till the day that we fought the great battle"—of Newbury.[1]

There was more gained than wagons by this southern march. Rupert, surprised by such sudden activity in a lethargic opponent, had for once failed to keep in touch. Essex, finding himself unpursued, hastened on southward from Cirencester, until he got on to that road that leads

[1] *Description of the Fight at Newbery*—Thomason Tracts, E. 70 (10).

from Hungerford through Newbury to London, passing Oxford at a safe distance to the south. It was an ideal route; and there was not a hostile horseman in sight! Essex wheeled to the left and began his return march to London.

But King Charles's strategy had been sound. When he broke up from Gloucester at Essex's approach he marched round the latter and established himself at Pershore and Evesham, whence he could watch proceedings and hold the inner line for the purposes of manœuvre. Whether Essex attempted to return to London by the Warwick road, which curved round Oxford to the north, or by the Newbury road, which gave the Royalist stronghold a wide berth to the south, the King could always cut across and intercept him. And this was still true on September 16, although Essex, by his sudden right-about face, had gained a day's start. It is said that Rupert lost touch through waiting for orders from the King; that he knew of Essex's march; that he had reported it to headquarters; that his cavalry were all drawn up in the darkness on Broadway Down, only waiting for the signal to pursue; that, after long delay, Rupert wandered off alone across the downs, looking for the Royal headquarters; and that, peering in at the lighted window of a cottage, he saw his Royal master seated placidly by the fire, playing piquet with Lord Percy, while Forth, the Commander-in-Chief, looked on!

We can imagine his indignation, and the scene when he broke in upon the card-players! Gardiner has well remarked that it seems very unlike Rupert to have wasted a moment waiting for orders, if he really knew of Essex's departure; still less to have wandered about in the darkness seeking an authorization to pursue. But Warburton found the story among the Prince's papers, and it is at any rate *ben trovato*. There seem to have been hot words round that piquet table; but Charles, after listening quietly, intervened to give Rupert the necessary orders, and a promise that the infantry should follow him as speedily as possible. Rupert was back with his cavalry in less than half an hour, and they rode all that night and all the next day to Faringdon, in Berkshire, without getting a glimpse of the enemy.

At Faringdon a reconnoitring party under Sir John Urry returned with the news that Essex was passing over Aldbourne Chase, intending to sleep that night at Newbury. This was heavily wooded country, inconvenient for cavalry charges on a wide front, but admirable for ambuscades. Rupert saw that he might head Essex off and force him back into Hungerford, until the Royalist infantry arrived. Riding hard, he came up with the Parliamentary rearguard among the trees, and delivered a fierce charge, which took them completely by surprise, for they had not supposed that there was an enemy within twenty miles of them. Pressing home the advantage, the Cavaliers threw the whole rearguard into confusion, and did considerable execution before the Roundheads rallied and drove them off. It was enough. Essex turned into Hungerford for the night, uncertain what lay ahead of him. And Charles, who had supported his nephew admirably, brought his tired infantry into Newbury on the following day. Once more the road to London was closed.

A crisis was approaching. Indeed it might be argued, not unreasonably, that the first battle of Newbury was the decisive conflict of the whole Civil War. The preliminary manœuvres on both sides had been exceptionally intelligent. Essex's breakaway to the south deserved to succeed; it had been frustrated only by Charles's superior strategy and by the inexhaustible energy of his General of the Horse. Yet Newbury itself was one of the most untidy, scrambling engagements of the war, and one of the most difficult to understand from the accounts handed down to us. The best explanation is that this battle marked the end of a long chase, that both sides arrived upon the scene flustered and out of breath, and that neither found time to make any proper survey of the field before going into action. Another cause of confusion was the broken character of the ground.

The town of Newbury, where the King slept on the night before the battle, was protected on its western side by the marshes to the north of the river Kennet. But on the south side of the town (and of the river) the appearance of the country altered. Walking due south from Newbury in the year 1643, one would encounter first a series of hedges and enclosures and narrow lanes, rather exceptional at that time, until, about a mile from the town, the landscape flattened out into Enborne Heath, on the Royalist left. Still a little farther south was the road by which Essex had now determined to force his way through (Newbury being blocked) to Reading and London. The Royalists had so far anticipated his intentions as to draw up their entire force to the south of the town, with Rupert and his cavalry on the extreme left, facing Enborne Heath and covering the road.

Rupert was against fighting, if it could be avoided. Essex was in hostile country and was again running short of supplies—for what are forty wagons among fifteen thousand hungry men? At Aldbourne Chase Rupert had been just in time to prevent him from breaking through. It was now only necessary to hold the fish in play. But Essex, impressed by the necessity of clearing his homeward path at any cost, had marched out from Hungerford early on the 20th, and had once more startled his opponents by the rapidity of his movements. When the Cavalier army drew into its allotted positions on that same morning of September 20, 1643, the most prominent object in its immediate front was a conical hill, over against the right centre, and so close as to command the whole Royalist line. In the hurry and bustle of last night's arrival it had been entirely forgotten! But now, in the early morning light, it could be seen that the menacing little hill was already bristling with the pikes and muskets of Roundhead infantry, and would soon be crowned by Roundhead guns.

It may be that the King, against Rupert's advice, had already decided to fight.[1] Anyhow, the Royalist position was untenable while the Roundheads held the hill. So Sir John Byron, who commanded the cavalry in this part of the line, was sent against it, and departed grumbling at the "negligence" of the staff.[2] He was instructed to co-operate with a brigade of infantry under his uncle, Sir Nicholas Byron. The ground in front was so broken up by enclosures that they decided to try and get at the hill—that fatal "little round hill in front of Cope's Hall" —from its right or southern side and made a *détour* for the purpose, scrambling through the ditches and hedges.

Falkland was riding with Byron that morning as a volunteer. He had hated every moment of the fratricidal war, and now only longed for death. As he dressed to go to the battlefield he called for a clean shirt, declaring that "they should not find his body in foul linen." He added that "he was weary of the times, and foresaw much misery to his own country, and did believe he should be out of it 'ere night." It happened that the Byrons' advance was held up at a gap which the Roundhead gunners were making their special target. As the leading troopers hesitated Falkland suddenly spurred

---

[1] Warburton, vol. ii, p. 292.
[2] He has left us (in the Clarendon MSS.) a brief account of his share in the battle, written three or four years after the event.

Lucius, Lord Falkland
From a print

forward, put his horse at the opening, and was instantly killed.

It was a sad loss, deplored on both sides. But John Byron soon had the gap widened and Nicholas's infantry made steady progress towards the hill. They never got there—though the struggle swayed backward and forward from seven in the morning till seven at night. But their relentless pressure from the south held up the advance of the Parliamentary left wing which Essex seems to have ordered early in the day. In this northern half of the battlefield there was a condition of stalemate.

Then came the advance of the Parliamentary centre and right. There exists no intelligible account of the desperate struggle in the centre, among the lanes and hedges. Some of the Royalist chroniclers have complained that their infantry behaved badly, crying out "Horse! horse!"—in appeal for cavalry support—whenever they found themselves in difficulties. "They played the poultroons," says Byron. It was obvious, indeed, that the horse could do nothing in such country. But presently the Roundhead advance reached the limits of the cultivated land, and a regiment of their cavalry (Stapleton's) emerged upon the open ground in the Royalist centre, known as Newbury Wash. Instantly it was charged and driven back among the fields. But the Royalist horse, pursuing with characteristic ardour, were caught in a long, narrow lane and shot down in hundreds by the hostile musketeers. The survivors galloped back to the open, where their commanders hurriedly rallied them to oppose the arrival of successive regiments of Roundhead cavalry.

On the extreme left Rupert—finding himself and the King's cause irretrievably committed to a pitched battle—rode forward with the main body of the Royalist cavalry on to Enborne Heath to meet the advancing right wing of the Parliamentarians. This was a broad stretch of open country, the only part of the battlefield perfectly suitable for a cavalry charge. The Parliamentarians were advancing slowly across it, the infantry consisting of two regiments of City trained bands, probably one dressed in red and the other in blue (for one or other of these was always their colour),[1] and led by old Colonel Skippon, whom we have met before. They were not professional soldiers, but neither were they the raw innocents whom we last saw at Brentford. On their right the Roundhead cavalry protected the exposed flank. The spirits of Rupert's horsemen rose prodigiously as the word was given to charge. The younger officers threw away their helmets and breastplates, and even their doublets, and galloped defiantly into battle in their shirts, with their lovelocks flying in the wind. We have no detailed account of that charge, but in a very few moments the Roundhead cavalry had disappeared from Enborne Heath. As Rupert reined in his horse in the middle of the heath the outline of the battlefield lay spread before him. He could see Essex's headquarters at Bigg's Hill immediately in front of him, and farther away to the right the Parliamentary baggage and reserves, comfortably tucked away among the enclosures where no hungry horsemen could get at them.

There remained these London regiments. They were retreating steadily to their left rear, seeking the cover of the hedges which had so well served their friends in the centre. Rupert charged them again and again. His cavalry must have surged round them like the French round our squares at Waterloo; we can readily believe the contemporary statement that the Cavaliers rode, time after time, right on to the pikes. According to one

---

[1] "300 redcoats and 200 blue and 200 mixed-coloured coats," says a pamphleteer, describing the appearance of some of the London recruit (Thomason Tracts, E. 74 (4)).

account the Royalist infantry of the left came up and joined in the attack, and some of the King's guns—they were few and ill-served—blew holes in the red and blue ranks. But nothing could break the spirit of those gallant apprentices. They were hungry and resentful—for their cavalry had ridden off and left them without striking a blow—but they kept their ranks, and laughed and cheered at old Skippon's jokes, and at last they found the hedges at their backs and slipped into cover and comparative safety, the real heroes of Newbury.

It is universally agreed that the many loyal gentlemen who served the King that day fought with equal bravery. It was a soldiers' battle, and from Lord Forth (who commanded under the King), Rupert, Wilmot, and Sir John Byron of the horse, Sir Nicholas Byron of the foot, and regular officers like Will Legge, Astley, Daniel O'Neill, Gerard, Lucas, Lisle, down to volunteers like Falkland and Richard Fielding (late governor of Reading) they showed themselves as gallant soldiers as ever lived. Their losses were heavy, including the young Earls of Carnarvon and Sunderland. But it would be absurd to deny that their conduct—at any rate in the higher ranks—did more credit to their hearts than to their heads. The battle had now reached a stage at which some intellectual effort at headquarters was obviously required. Essex's advance had been checked, but not stopped. It bulged forward in the centre to the edge of Newbury Wash, but at either end it was bent back—brought to a stand.

To the modern critic it seems that the southern end of the fighting line, where Essex had his only serious chance of breaking through, and where Rupert's horse had swept Enborne Heath clear of the enemy, was the position from which a flank attack might most easily be pressed home, with disastrous results to the Roundhead centre. Nothing of the kind seems to have been attempted. The Royalist

177

leaders do not appear to have realized the advantage of their position in this part of the field, nor even that this southern road needed defending as much as the northern one through Newbury. The only turning movement they attempted was from the north in the valley of the Kennet, and they were nearly round the enemy's left flank before Skippon, who was acting as second-in-command, detected them and brought up infantry to restore the line. An attempt on his part to force a passage across the Kennet was repulsed in its turn.

It was getting dark. The struggle had continued all day without ceasing. But even Essex's white hat, which his friends had vainly urged him to remove as affording too good a target, was difficult to distinguish now. And perhaps it was the failing light—or just his proverbial luck—that saved Rupert's life when the Roundhead Sir Philip Stapleton rode up alone to a group of Cavaliers, where Rupert was standing talking to Digby, and, after coolly looking them over to identify his man, fired his pistol in the Prince's face at the range of a few feet. He missed—but he cantered back safely to his own lines, with the bullets of the outraged Royalists singing round his ears.[1]

When the opposing lines could no longer see each other the exhausted infantry threw themselves down where they stood, on the trampled grass, and slept. It must have been a miserable night for the Parliamentarians, for their stomachs were still empty, and their enemies still lay between them and London. It was not till an hour before dawn, as they stood stiffly to their arms, that the good news came in from the outposts—the Royalist positions were empty! The King had drawn off into Newbury during the night.

He had run short of powder. The authorities are no

[1] Whitelocke, *Memorials*, p. 74.

unanimous on the point (Clarendon, for instance, says nothing about it), but the balance of evidence, both Roundhead [1] and Cavalier, points to this failure of ammunition as the primary cause of the Royal infantry's retreat. The cavalry were held in readiness all night. Rupert never dismounted from his horse. And as soon as he heard in the morning that Essex had passed to the south on his way to London, he went fiercely after him, and overtook his rearguard in a tangle of country lanes about Aldermarston. The names of so many of these roads have been altered that it is extraordinarily difficult to fix the scene of this last encounter of the Newbury campaign; but it was somewhere towards Padworth that the first charge was made, and many of the London apprentices and of Rupert's horse lie buried in Padworth churchyard. There was great slaughter of the foot, and panic cries of "Away, away! you are all dead men!" George Lisle brought up a thousand musketeers in time to pour a murderous volley into their retreating ranks. Many prisoners were taken. But the time arrived when the Cavaliers' horses were ridden to a standstill, and not even their young leader could inspire them to another charge. Essex, with his main body, struggled on through Reading, and so to London, tired and scarred, but safe. The second opportunity of the war had been missed.

---

[1] For instance, Thomason Tracts, E. 69 (10).

CHAPTER XI: BEFORE MARSTON MOOR

THE story of Prince Rupert's career in the autumn and winter following the first battle of Newbury is mainly a record of battles and sieges. To represent him as primarily interested in anything else is to distort the facts, as disclosed by his correspondence and by the very full record of his movements which Warburton has compiled—and might have made even fuller —from the Prince's private papers. There is no reason why the story should be dull, for every military operation undertaken by Rupert was typical of his methods and illustrative of his character. A charge of dullness may be brought against his biographer, but never against Rupert himself. Yet it is fortunate that he was so fully occupied, for he had enough anxieties of other kinds to have engrossed the full attention of any ordinary man.

In the first place Prince Maurice fell seriously ill at Exeter. Rupert, who had an elder brother's affection for this wild but loyal youth, sent doctors to nurse him back to life—to the disadvantage of the cause, for Maurice was no general, and his soldiers were always out of hand. The doctors reported that the young prince was suffering from "the ordinary raging disease of the army," which, from their description, was very like the paratyphoid which so much reduced the strength of the British army in our latest war. His surprisingly quick recovery may have been due to the fact that the doctors, "concluding the disease to be venomous, do resolve to give very little physic, only a regular diet and cordial antidotes." They sent reports to Rupert every two or three days.

And then there were the intrigues at Court. During a large part of this period Rupert was in Wales, organizing the King's affairs there, and corresponding with Lord

Ormonde in Ireland about the shipment of Irish regiments to serve in the Royalist ranks. Before his promotion to be "President of Wales" he had made a dash northward from Oxford on October 15, and had taken Bedford and put a garrison into Newport Pagnell, with a view to threatening the Parliamentary communications with the north and at the same time guarding the Royalist road between Oxford and York. And he had narrowly escaped from a Roundhead ambush at Aylesbury, being tempted to march against that place by the promises of an ex-prisoner, named Ogle, who professed to have 'squared' the governor. But Rupert became suspicious, seized the first messenger from the town, and discovered the sort of welcome prepared for him. He tried to make the appropriate retort by marching round Aylesbury and attacking the ambushed Roundheads in the rear; but the flooded river stopped him, and he retreated to Thame in terrible weather, losing many of his men on the way by drowning and exposure.

Among the mountains of Wales he became more conscious even than at Oxford itself of those obstructive influences at Court. Digby was his implacable enemy; so were Percy and Ashburnham and their new ally, O'Neill. Arthur Trevor, who was as much his friend as Ormonde's, sent long confidential reports; Richmond and Will Legge helped to keep him informed. Jermyn, though the Queen's favourite, was always on Rupert's side, and did much to compose the differences between Henrietta Maria and her nephew. The King's Secretary, Nicholas, was at any rate not hostile. Yet supplies ordered by Rupert somehow failed to arrive—or they would be sent to Worcester, when he wanted them at Shrewsbury, and no one could discover why. Rupert himself drove his friends to despair by forgetting to answer letters, by signing bills of exchange without letting anyone know, and by making wildly extravagant demands—no doubt on the familiar principle that if he asked for more than he wanted, to be delivered immediately, an adequate supply might be expected to reach him about the time when it was really required. But it was hard on Trevor and Jermyn. The former wrote to Rupert:

> His Majesty was very well pleased at your letter, and so was my Lord Jermyn, until he found your wants of arms and ammunition; at which, after a deep sigh, he told me: "This is of more trouble to me than it would be pain to me at parting of my flesh and bones."

Rupert had taken over his new command on February 6, 1644, when he established his headquarters at Shrewsbury. It must not be supposed that he was inactive there. On the contrary, he opened communications with Ormonde, arranged to get some Irish regiments over, and in general pumped new spirits into the Royalist cause in Wales. But it was not the kind of employment that suited him, and we cannot doubt that he welcomed every interruption. The first of these occurred as early as March 12—only five weeks after his arrival—when he was called away to the relief of Newark. Piteous appeals for help had been coming into Oxford from the north. The negotiations (which need not detain us here) between the Scots and the Presbyterian Parliament at Westminster had been brought to a successful conclusion, and the northern counties of England were threatened by an invading Scottish army, intervening in our Civil War— decisively, as it turned out—on the Parliamentary side. Newcastle wrote that they were already at Morpeth, and that they numbered at least fourteen thousand men. He called loudly for help.

In the meantime the Fairfaxes had been making progress in Cheshire and Lancashire and in the East Riding of Yorkshire. There was now a long stretch of hostile territory through Leicestershire and Northampton to the eastern counties and London, splitting the Royalist part of England in half. In the midst lay Newark, which was generally looked upon as a key position; and Newark was now closely besieged by the Roundhead leaders Sir John Meldrum and Lord Willoughby of Parham. Rupert, as we have seen, had always been keenly appreciative of the importance of keeping open this northern road. He knew that Newark was at its last gasp—it must be relieved quickly or not at all. Newcastle could wait. He set out immediately with a small following—there had been no time or money to collect more—and Essex, as soon as he heard this alarming news, sent a column of mounted men in pursuit. "The strength that followeth your Highness," wrote Ashburnham from Oxford, "is nine hundred dragoons and one regiment of horse, which I hope will all be damned." [1] The peril of Newark seemed to bring these squabbling Royalists together: O'Neill was serving cheerfully in Rupert's relief force, and was presently to save his commander's life.

Rupert wasted no time. Leaving Shrewsbury on March 13, he pushed forward to Chester, picking up Royalist garrisons wherever he could on the way, and on the 15th was at Bridgnorth with a respectable following. He dined here with Lady Beeston, and after the meal informed the unfortunate lady that she must immediately pull down her ancient baronial castle, lest it should prove useful to the Roundheads—and he waited to see it done. Five days later he was at Bingham, almost within sight of Newark. At two o'clock on the following morning he mounted again, and galloped madly forward with his cavalry, leaving his scanty infantry and artillery

[1] Warburton, vol. ii, p. 392. Whether damned or not they accomplished nothing.

to struggle along behind as best they could. After ten miles of hard riding they were close to the beleaguered town, and could reduce their pace.

There was a full moon, bright and clear, as Rupert's cavalry, turning aside, rode gently along the country roads, making a circuit of Newark in order to reach Beacon Hill, from which they could look down upon the enemy's positions. About the same time that Rupert started on this last ride a galloper had come in to Meldrum's headquarters, sent by Colonel Hutchinson, the Roundhead Governor of Nottingham, to warn him that he was about to be attacked. Many such warnings had reached him before, but he had refused to believe them. He had an excellent intelligence service, and was well aware of Rupert's advance from the south. But he had 5000 foot under him and 2500 horse, and he knew that Rupert had started for Newark with only 1000 Irish volunteers on foot and 120 musketeers, and about 400 picked horsemen, composed of his own life guards and some of the Prince of Wales's regiment. He could not believe that Newark was his aim. It was true that Lord Loughborough had joined him at Ashby de la Zouch, and General Porter a little later, with numbers vaguely estimated at 1500 to 2000 men; but even then his cavalry were less numerous than Meldrum's, and his infantry and guns must still be miles away down the road.

Still, Hutchinson was a serious man—perhaps the most serious ever immortalized by a disconsolate widow—and his castle of Nottingham was only a few miles north of the southern road by which Rupert was said to be advancing. Meldrum accepted his warning. He had been approaching the walls of Newark in a leisurely way by means of trenches and saps, expecting the half-starved garrison to surrender at any moment. He now withdrew his men from their earthworks and began to assemble them in

the moonlight round the fortified position, known as
"the Spittle," which lay behind his lines towards the
foot of Beacon Hill. What he did not know was that
Rupert had succeeded in communicating with Sir John
Henderson, the commander of the Newark garrison.
Employing a home-made cipher, he had written, "Let
the old drum on the north side be beaten early on the
morrow morning." "Old drum" meant Meldrum, and
Henderson at once understood that he was to sally out
next morning and beat up the besiegers' quarters. He
prepared to do so.

It was between nine and ten in the morning when
Rupert's cavalry appeared upon the heights and looked
down on the panorama of the siege of Newark. What
proportion of the Prince's mounted men were with him
it is impossible to say, but they must have been inferior
in numbers to Meldrum's horse, behind whom stood his
5000 infantry and the guns. "Rupert's sole notion of
tactics was to charge," says Gardiner,[1] but he has the
grace to add that on this occasion he "could have found
no better." Rupert well understood the moral effect
that must have been produced by the sudden announce-
ment of his presence, and by the hasty retreat from the
trenches in the small hours. He instantly gave the order
to charge, and came down like an avalanche upon the
nearest Roundhead horsemen. There was a desperate
hand-to-hand encounter. According to Mrs Hutchinson
—a very prejudiced witness—Colonel Thornhagh, with
the Nottingham horse, made a gallant counter-charge,
and even broke through the Cavaliers opposite to him,
but the Lincolnshire horse "run away."

Rupert was never in more danger of his life. The
story goes that "three sturdy Roundheads" assailed him
at the same time. The first he slew with his own sword;

[1] Vol. i, p. 373.

the second was shot by one of his attendants; the third
had hold of his collar, and was attempting to drag him
from his horse, when O'Neill, coming up behind, slashed
off the man's hand at the wrist.[1] Then Crane and the
Prince's life guards came with a rush, sweeping the enemy
before them. The Parliamentarians, horse and foot, fell
back on the Spittle. But their position was now hopeless.
The Newarkers had sallied out and entrenched themselves
on Meldrum's flank; Rupert had seized the bridge across
the river which gave access to the only road by which he
could retreat; the Royalist infantry and guns were
beginning to arrive. With no prospect before him but to
starve slowly in this fortified post, Meldrum turned to
Charles Gerard, who had been wounded and taken
prisoner; and Gerard was presently seen limping across
the open ground towards the Royalist ranks with proposals of peace. Rupert graciously gave the enemy leave
to depart, but without any of their arms or baggage, all
of which fell into his hands. Thus he won what Clarendon
well calls "as unexpected a victory as any happened
throughout the war." [2]

The reactions at Oxford were not without humour.
This stimulant was just what the politicians needed, and
it rather went to their heads. Letters of congratulation
poured in upon Rupert. Even the King could not refrain
from describing the relief of Newark as "no less than the
saving of all the north"—which, of course, it was not.
The good Arthur Trevor wrote almost incoherently
begging to join with "the courtier, the scholar, people
of all ages, all sexes, all faculties, bells and bonfires" in
congratulating Rupert, "all on this side of idolatry.
Digby, at even greater length, expressed his sense of
Rupert's "courage and excellent conduct," which "hat

<hr>

[1] Webb, vol. i, p. 385.
[2] Vol. ii, p. 357.

made fortune your servant to a degree beyond imagination," and added that the King was to be congratulated upon having secured the services of such a general. In sober fact Rupert's spectacular success achieved little, because he could not follow it up. He had no army. The demoralized enemy abandoned Lincoln, Gainsborough, and Sleaford, and prepared to defend the remainder of the Eastern counties against his expected attack. But all Rupert could do was to restore to the Royalist garrisons in the West the innumerable small detachments out of which he had constructed his victorious little 'army,' and then retire into Wales to resume recruiting. When he had a real army of his own he would resume his Northern campaign.

Oxford, in spite of its raptures, was not very helpful. On April 3, less than a fortnight after the relief of Newark, Rupert was incensed by an order to leave his work in Wales and go to Oxford in order to escort the Queen to the South (she was expecting a baby). Next day the order was countermanded. But he was indignant; and was further annoyed by a proposal that the young Prince of Wales should be sent to Bristol and given the title of Commander of the Army in the West. Rupert objected to both propositions, which, of course, were supported by Digby and the civilians. He could not see why the Queen need move; and the little Prince, to whom Rupert was a hero, formally refused to take any step "wherein he has not your Highness's approbation." For the moment Rupert got his way. But he does not seem to have behaved very graciously, and Jermyn, who was trying to patch up a peace between him and Digby, gave up the task in despair. As Clarendon says in this connexion,

he who too affectedly despises or neglects what is said of him, or what is generally thought of persons or things, and too stoically contemns the affections of men, even of vulgar (be his other abilities and virtues as great as can be imagined), will in some conjuncture of time find himself very unfortunate.

At the same time he admits that Rupert's "unpolished roughness" in these controversies was mainly due to the fact that "his heart was so wholly set upon actions of war." That was true. His heart was now set upon going to the rescue of the Northern Royalists, and he may well have brushed aside these other matters—to use Warwick's words—"with a pish."

On April 25 he came to Oxford of his own free will, to consult with the King and his advisers about the impending campaign. He urged that the army which he had just raised with so much difficulty should be left intact for the Northern adventure, while the King maintained his position in the centre of England, behind the semicircle of garrisoned towns which protected Oxford against any Parliamentary advance from London. The King's advisers agreed. Rupert had hardly left Oxford for the West when they decided, against his advice, to dismantle Reading. But in principle they agreed. Every fresh piece of news inspired Rupert to hurry. Newcastle had sent his cavalry away from York, and was settled down there with his infantry, preparing to stand a siege by the advancing army of the Scots. The Earl of Manchester, in East Anglia, had plucked up courage to recover Lincoln and Gainsborough, and was already marching northward to join the Fairfaxes and the Scots at the siege of York.

Rupert had left Oxford on May 5. On the 16th he led his army out of Shrewsbury on the way to York. It consisted of 2000 horse and 6000 foot, the latter including his own infantry regiment, two other English regiment in green coats, Lord Byron's regiment from Chester various detachments of Welshmen, and four or five Irish regiments, none of them up to strength. It will be seen

188

that the proportion of foot was unusually high, but he intended to collect more cavalry on the way. On the 25th Rupert took Stockport, and on the 28th attacked the Roundhead stronghold of Bolton. Close to Bolton was Lathom House, where that brave lady the Countess of Derby, with a tiny garrison, had for nearly three months been holding out against a large besieging force under a local Roundhead lawyer named Rigby.

Lathom House was well situated for defence. Beyond the surrounding moat the ground was high, so that the besiegers could not shoot at the house direct without bringing their cannon to the top of the rise, where they became easy targets for the defending gunners. But they threw many shells into the house from their mortars, reducing parts of it to ruin. Yet they could not break the nerve of the gallant defenders, who continued to make vigorous sallies almost up to the date of Rupert's arrival. At Rupert's approach Rigby drew off into Bolton with his whole force—a fact of which Rupert was unaware until his advance-guard (consisting of Colonel Tillier's green-coats) encountered strong resistance in the suburbs of the town. The first Royalist assault was repulsed with loss, and the elated Parliamentarians made the mistake of hanging one of their Irish prisoners from the walls. Nothing angered Rupert more than this pretence that the King's Irish allies were mere rebels, not entitled to the ordinary decencies of civilized warfare. Springing from his horse, he led on the next wave of assailants himself, and such was the spirit he could always inspire that his infantry quickly opened a way for the cavalry to charge into the town.

Among the foremost horsemen was Lord Derby him-self, burning to avenge his Countess's long ordeal; and almost the first person he met was one of his own former servants, a man named Booth, now a captain in the

Roundhead army, who had deserted from Lathom House and won promotion by the skill with which he directed the besiegers' artillery. Derby killed him joyfully. There was less excuse for the other killings, which continued for hours as the panic-stricken defenders bolted from street to street—still less for the plundering of private citizens' houses, which Rupert did not check. But the spirit of the war had changed. Bolton was Roundhead to a man, and "the goods of the town were the soldiers' reward" sums up the Royalist attitude.[1] A pleasanter feature of the affair was Rupert's visit to Lathom House, where he formally thanked the Countess for her service to the King and handed over to her the flags of Rigby's beaten army.

All Lancashire was not Roundhead. At Wigan, Rupert's next stop, the streets were strewn with flowers, and he passed through like a Roman conqueror. But at Liverpool he had to shoot holes in their mud walls before he could get into the town—only to find that most of the garrison had escaped by sea. There was more plundering at Liverpool. Having secured that port—which was convenient for the arrival of Irish reinforcements—he turned inland towards York on the last stage of his journey.

At York the Roundhead generals Manchester and Fairfax and Leven, the Scot, and Leslie and Oliver Cromwell were in earnest consultation. Their politicians had been worrying them. Vane had come all the way from London with an urgent request that Manchester and Fairfax should march into Lancashire and put a stop to Rupert's depredations. He had also in his pocket proposal that King Charles's abdication should be formally demanded; but this the generals rejected with horror. They also refused point-blank to stir from the

[1] Carte MSS., X, f. 664. Or, as Defoe puts it, in his ingenious historical reconstruction entitled *The Memoirs of a Cavalier*, "our men got some plunder here, which the Parliament made a great noise about but it was their due, and they bought it dear enough."

leaguer of York. They understood the position—and
their own strength—better than Vane did. They knew
that while that great Commoner was on his way north
Rupert had been joined by Lord Goring with 5000 horse
and 800 foot—the former including Newcastle's cavalry,
under Sir Charles Lucas, which had been sent out of
York when the siege began. But they also knew that,
even with this addition, Rupert's total strength, when he
started from Liverpool for York, was only 6000 foot and
7000 horse. Under their own command in the besieging
lines they had 27,000 men, of whom about 7000 were
cavalry. Their cavalry were equal to Rupert's; their
infantry easily outnumbered his whole army! And they
had sent for Meldrum and other Roundhead commanders
in the North, who might yet arrive before battle could be
joined. It is true that the air was full of alarmist rumours
about Rupert's "vast army," [1] so numerous that it was
"not to be numbered." [2] After the battle Cromwell
himself talked in the same strain. But he and his colleagues knew better. And they came to the obvious and
not particularly heroic conclusion to stand where they
stood. If and when Rupert appeared, they said, they
would leave their works and fight him and, "if it please
God," drive him off.[3]

Rupert and his 13,000 came on. When he reached
Knaresborough, about seventeen miles from York as the
crow flies, the Parliamentarians abandoned their siege
works and fell back upon Marston Moor, which was
directly in his line of march. But Rupert swerved to the
north, and arrived at the gates of York without accident
on July 1. He had outmanœuvred his opponents. There

---

[1] Carte MSS., XI, f. 444. "Prince Rupert with a vaust armey went
raise the seidge of York" (Captain Clarke to Captain Bartlett).
[2] Thomason Tracts, 164.
[3] Napoleon once remarked that God was usually on the side of the big
battalions.

was nothing to prevent him from taking off the garrison, refusing battle, and marching south, south-west, or east, as he pleased. It was the obvious policy to pursue, in view of his inferiority in numbers. With his veteran light cavalry he could march faster and fight a better rearguard action than any Parliamentary army in the field.

He did nothing of the kind. On the contrary, he insisted upon forcing a general action, in opposition to the advice of Newcastle and every senior officer he consulted. The King had written to him as follows:

NEPHEW,

First, I must congratulate with you for your good successes, assuring you that the things themselves are no more welcome to me than that you are the means . . .

But now I must give you the true state of my affairs, which, if their condition be such as enforces me. to give you more *peremptory commands* than I would willingly do, you must not take it ill. If York be lost I shall esteem *my crown little less*, unless supported by your sudden march to me, and a miraculous conquest in the South before the effects of their Northern power can be found here. *But if* York be relieved, and *you beat the rebels' army* of both kingdoms, which are before it, then (but otherwise not) I may possibly make a shift (upon the defensive) to spin out time until you come to assist me. Wherefore *I command and conjure you*, by the duty and affection which I know you bear me, that, all new enterprises laid aside, you immediately march, according to your first intention, with all your force to the relief of York. But if that be either lost, or have freed themselves from the besiegers, or that, for want of powder, you cannot undertake that work, that you immediately march with your whole strength, directly to Worcester to assist me and my army; without which, at your having relieved York by beating the Scots, all the successes you can afterwards have must infallibly be useless unto me. You may believe that nothing but an extreme necessity could make me write thus unto you; wherefore, in this case, I can in no way doubt of your punctual compliance with

Your loving and most faithful friend,

CHARLES R.

Whatever one may think of the phraseology of this famous letter, there can be no doubt—and the King's advisers themselves, if they had paused to consider, could have had no doubt—of the impression it would make upon the mind of Prince Rupert. He took it, of course, as an order to fight. At Oxford Sir John Culpepper, the King's friend, who had not been consulted about the letter but had heard of its contents, hurried to the royal apartments and asked whether it had been dispatched. Charles replied, "Yes." "Why, then," exclaimed Culpepper, "before God you are undone, for upon this peremptory order he will fight, whatever comes on't." It is extraordinary that none of the others seems to have understood Rupert well enough to realize that.

At York that courteous and intelligent nobleman the Marquess of Newcastle advanced such arguments as occurred to him against the unequal combat. Rupert waved him aside; he had the King's orders, he said— and he moved out towards the Roundhead position on Marston Moor without even waiting for Newcastle's men to march with him. Yet he somehow found time to draw up a plan of the battle as he intended that it should be fought. Newcastle's military adviser, Lord Eythin, was an old acquaintance of his; as General King he had given the young Rupert too much advice and too little practical assistance in the campaign in the Palatinate six years before. Rupert now showed him his plan. "By God, sir," was the answer, "it is very fine in the paper, but there is no such thing in the field!"

Now, when Rupert's column appeared upon Marston Moor, the Parliamentary generals were in full retreat towards the south. They were not running away. On the contrary, they never imagined that Rupert would venture to offer battle. But he had outmanœuvred them and relieved York, and in these circumstances they had decided to fall back upon the Ouse and secure the bridges while they waited to see what his next move would be. But when they heard the glad news of his advance they promptly and "merrily" turned back and went to meet him. By this time he was near the end of the moor, above the road that leads from Tockwith to Marston. Newcastle was coming up behind with the garrison of York, and when the two armies were united Rupert moved down the gentle slope, and halted a little above a narrow ditch which ran all along his front, separating him from the oncoming Roundheads. The ditch was an insignificant obstacle: in some places there were bushes on its banks, where musketeers could take cover, but it was everywhere easily fordable by cavalry, and in the centre of the field it could hardly be said to exist. Rupert deployed his troops in order of battle.

They were 17,000 men against 27,000.[1] Rupert, as Commander-in-Chief, held the place of honour on the right wing; Newcastle commanded the centre, with Eythin and Tillier under him; Goring led the Royalist horse on the left. It was the conventional formation of a seventeenth-century army, and conformed precisely with the dispositions of their opponents on the other side of the ditch. But there exists in the British Museum [2] an elaborate order of battle drawn up by a Dutch soldier named de Gomme, who served under Rupert at Marston Moor; and Professor Firth has, not unreasonably, suggested that de Gomme's plan must have been based, to some extent, upon the rough sketch which Rupert showed to Eythin. It is an important document, and contains points of special interest for Rupert's biographer. Th

---

[1] A Roundhead observer (*Fairfax Correspondence*, vol. i, p. 11) estimated the Royalists at only 15,000. I follow Professor Firth in h paper read before the Royal Historical Society on November 18, 189 (*Transactions*, New Series, vol. xii, p. 18 *et seq.*).

[2] Additional MSS., 16370, f. 64.

cavalry of the right wing were drawn up in only two lines, the first (1100 men) consisting of the regiments of Lord Byron,[1] Colonel Urry, Sir William Vaughan, and Colonel Trevor, and the second (800 men) of the regiments of Lord Molyneux, Sir Thomas Tildesley, and Colonel Leveson. Colonel Tuke's regiment guarded the right flank and Rupert's own regiment (a mere 400 or 500 men) the left. But the point that springs to the eye is that the cavalry lines are *broken*, in violent contrast with Rupert's method in every previous fight. There are wide spaces between the squadrons. And groups of musketeers are posted *on foot* to fire through those spaces at the opposing cavalry! We are back at the method of Gustavus Adolphus, discussed in Chapter IV. Rupert's shock tactics, which have never failed him yet, are suddenly abandoned at the most critical moment of the war.

It seems incredible, and it may be untrue—though it is beyond doubt that Goring adopted these Swedish tactics on the left wing. The authorities are vague and contradictory. But it must be remembered that Rupert was not merely the commander of the right wing, but the Commander-in-Chief of the army. His own position was behind the centre; and it may very well be that the actual ordering of the ranks on the right wing was left in the hands of some of the experienced soldiers serving under him. Urry has been blamed for it, since he "had the marshalling of the horse in the Prince's right wing."

Some suspected Colonel Urry (lately converted to the King's party) for foul play herein; for he divided the King's old horse, so valiant and victorious in former fights, into small bodies, alleging this was the best way to break the Scottish lancers. But those horse, always used to charge together in whole regiments or greater bodies, were much discomposed with this new mode, so that they could not find themselves in themselves.[2]

[1] Formerly Sir John.
[2] Royal Historical Society's *Transactions*, New Series, vol. xii, p. 32.

If Rupert himself gave any such order it can only have been because he was inexplicably losing faith in his own horsemen and in his own chosen method of attack. Or was it that he was deliberately adopting defensive tactics, knowing that he could not win?

It was too late to change now, in any case. Indeed, it was almost too late to fight. The evening was already drawing in and the sky dark with storm clouds when Rupert, standing up in his stirrups and staring forward over the heads of the Royalist ranks, asked abruptly, "Is Cromwell there?" They told him that the East Anglian General commanded the cavalry of the Roundhead left, with David Leslie, the Scot, serving under him. Rupert seemed satisfied. Another glance at the dark masses of the enemy, and at his own tenuous line, with the white coats of Newcastle's infantry showing up in the centre, and he turned cheerfully to the Marquess, who was beside him. "We will charge them to-morrow morning," he said. Then he dismounted from his horse and went and sat on the grass, and began to eat some meat which his servants brought him. Most of the Royalist cavalry followed his example, seated by their horses' heads. Lord Newcastle lit a pipe.

There was a sudden burst of small-arms fire from the right. Messengers came running. Cromwell's dragoons were driving the Royalist musketeers from the bushes round the ditch. His cavalry of the New Model were advancing in line behind them. Rupert sprang to his feet and ran towards his horse. For the first time in his life he had lost the initiative.

CHAPTER XII: CROMWELL

COLONEL OLIVER CROMWELL — that ugly, moon-faced, excitable, verbose, thoughtful man, that grimly efficient product of mixed Welsh and English ancestry (for the family name had been changed to 'Cromwell' from 'Williams')—Colonel Cromwell (as he then was) had been present at Edgehill, and had watched Rupert's horsemen in action. He had seen these newly raised cavalry crash through the Parliamentary left wing as through paper, gallop into Kineton, plunder the baggage, and ride back to Edgehill just in time to prevent victory from being turned into defeat. He saw it all happen, and a little later he unburdened himself as follows to his friend and relative John Hampden:

> Your troops are most of them old, decayed serving men and tapsters and such kind of fellows, and their troops are gentle-men's sons and persons of quality. Do you think that the spirits of such base and mean fellows will ever be able to en-counter gentlemen that have honour, and courage, and resolu-tion in them? . . . You must get men of a spirit, and take it not ill what I say—I know you will not—of a spirit that is likely to go on as far as gentlemen will go, or else you will be beaten still.

(Harsh, undemocratic common sense, highly characteris-tic of the future dictator of England!)

The first point that occurs to the modern critic is that Cromwell seems to have noticed only the *moral* superior-ty of the Royalist horse. He set himself to put that right, and succeeded to a marvel, for as an organizer and in-spirer of men he stands in the front rank. But it never, apparently, occurred to him that Rupert's shock tactics might have had more to do with the success of his charge than the genealogies of his troopers. He must surely have noticed that there were no pauses to fire volleys, and

197

that the Cavalier onset gained greatly in impetus by the omission of these preliminaries. If he did notice it he does not say so. The truth is he was not deeply interested in cavalry tactics. He was interested in the organization, clothing, equipment, discipline, and, above all, in what we nowadays call the morale of his men. When he had attended to those points he thought that he had done all. And, in the peculiar circumstances of Marston Moor, so he had. "Cromwell's success," says one of his military admirers, "was due more to the care with which he had raised, organized, and disciplined his men than to superior tactical skill." [1]

Such a leader would not be the man to depart from the seventeenth-century text-books. It is fair to repeat here that he reduced his cavalry to only two ranks. And he seems to have followed Gustavus in teaching them to fire from the saddle, so that a volley could be discharged without coming to a dead stop. But he still interspersed their ranks with musketeers, and he still called it a "fierce" charge when they fell in among their opponents at "a pretty round trot." [2] Such a 'charge' would have aroused laughter among Marlborough's cavalry leaders sixty years later. Here, again, it must be admitted that the heavily armed cuirassiers charged at the trot down to the end of the eighteenth century. But Cromwell does not seem to have realized that speedier horsemen would have had any decisive advantage. He does not seem to have grasped the idea of shock. He was no innovator, as Rupert—perhaps in spite of himself—most certainly was. And it was sheer luck for him, a miracle of luck, that in his first encounter with Rupert's magnificent light cavalry he got the initiative, so that he could push his solid cuirassiers up against them, in such a way that they

[1] T. S. Baldock, *Cromwell as a Soldier*, p. 517.
[2] See p. 70.

OLIVER CROMWELL
From a portrait by Samuel Cooper at Sidney Sussex College
Photo W. F. Mansell

could not charge at him, but were brought to a stand and gradually worn down in the protracted *mêlée* by superior weight and equipment.

The Ironsides—Rupert is said to have given them the name after the battle—splashed heavily across the intervening ditch, and had closed with the front ranks of the Royalist horse almost as soon as the men could get into their saddles. There was a great heave towards the rear; then a counter-effort, which restored the position; then another heave, and they stuck, and "stood at the sword's point a pretty while, hacking one another." [1] It was one of the vital moments of the Civil War. The struggling horsemen were vaguely conscious of a roar from the right, which showed that battle had been joined all along the line; but they had no time to look. "In a battle," wrote one of the Royalists, with engaging frankness, "the next man can hardly make a true relation of the actions of him that is next him, for in such a hurry and smoke as in a set field a man takes notice of nothing but what relates to his own safety." [2] But it was clear that good feeding, and regular pay, and stout helmets and equipment were beginning to tell. The Ironsides "leant" upon their lighter opponents,[3] and when they could do that there was no stopping them. The Cavaliers were being slowly shouldered off the field. The regiment of Colonel Urry, who was the author of the new defensive formation which had landed them in this pickle, was one of the first to go. Lord Byron's broke about the same time—and, in Rupert's absence, Byron was probably in command of this whole right wing.

These two regiments were on the right of the first line.

[1] *Transactions* of the Royal Historical Society, New Series, vol. xii, p. 45.
[2] Bulstrode, *Memoirs*, p. 84.
[3] Mr Belloc's phrase.

The left held a little longer—but only a little. As Rupert came galloping round from behind the centre he met his own regiment, his invincible horsemen, who had been on Urry's left, in full retreat, their backs to the enemy. He roared at them " 'Swounds, do you run? " And then—

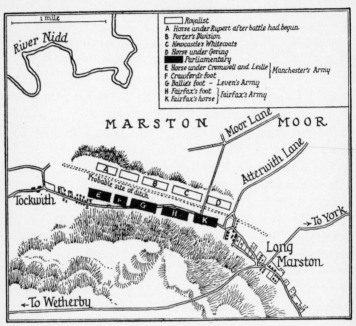

THE BATTLE OF MARSTON MOOR

his voice rising hysterically—"Follow me!" They swung their horses round obediently, tried in vain to gather speed for a charge, and before they knew it were once more crushed against the iron wall of Cromwell's cavalry —for it was to him personally that they had been opposed. Again they took the strain, thrusting and hacking. It was too late. For a moment it seemed that they might hold. But David Leslie had thrust his rough Celtic cavalry, mounted on "little light Scottish nags," in between the horse of the Royalist right and the infantry

200

of the centre. He took Rupert's men in the flank—and that finished it. The Royalist right wing was thrust from the field, broken into flying fragments. They had tasted their first bitter draught of defeat.

And then Cromwell's discipline and training brought its reward. He halted his victorious army. He detached part of it to pursue the beaten Cavaliers, and with the larger part swung round to his right to see how the rest of the battle had gone. A mounted officer with a small following came towards him. It was Sir Thomas Fairfax, who had ridden right across the battlefield, past the Royalist reserves, without being recognized. He had a sword cut across the face, and the front of his uniform was soaked with blood. He told what he knew.

The Roundhead army had advanced all along the line. The infantry in the centre or "main battle" had crossed the ditch, driving out the musketeers and capturing a few guns, and had gone forward at a pace described as "a running march" against the Royalist foot, whom they outnumbered by two to one. At first they had some success, but when they came against Newcastle's white-coats in the second line there was a different story to tell. This famous brigade had been going through a bad time. It had just suffered the discomfort and nerve strain of a siege, and its pay was so scandalously in arrears that on this very morning of Marston Moor it had mutinied in the streets of York. This outbreak, quickly suppressed, had delayed Newcastle's march, so that he only overtook Rupert on the edge of the moor; it must have influenced the Prince in his decision not to attack that night; and it may also have had something to do with the defensive formation adopted by his cavalry. Such is the influence of the money-bags in every crisis of history! But the gallant whitecoats did their best to make up for it now. Outnumbered as they were, they threw back the Roundhead infantry, driving some of them across the ditch in disorder. They advanced in their turn, and gained ground rapidly.

On the Roundhead right the advancing cavalry, under Sir Thomas Fairfax, found themselves in very difficult country, covered with furze-bushes and intersected by ditches and narrow lanes. (Fairfax's mounted Scottish auxiliaries on this wing were armed with lances, which they found worse than useless.) Goring commanded the Royalist left, and, as on the other wing, his horse were supported by parties of musketeers, who made good use of the cover. Fairfax himself, with 400 horse, struggled through to the open moor, and drove off the Royalists immediately opposite to him. But when he turned back he found all the rest of his wing in retreat, with Goring at their heels. Some of the fugitives, turning towards the centre, rode over a regiment of their own infantry and over the Scottish reserves, throwing them into confusion. Goring, keeping up the chase, found the Parliamentary baggage and plundered it in the time-honoured manner. (He must have wondered where Rupert was!) But many of his regiments got back to the field in time to join in the infantry attack on the Roundhead centre.

Of that great, unwieldy mass of Parliamentary infantry, more numerous than all their opponents put together, the most part were scattered about the moor in every stage of retreat, some still formed as regiments, some in small parties, holding loosely together. But five or six Scottish battalions on the right of the centre stood firm and unshaken, at the point which they had reached in the first advance. They repulsed three charges by Sir Charles Lucas's cavalry—in the last of them Lucas himself was unhorsed and made prisoner—they firmly withstood the advance of Newcastle's hungry but victorious whitecoats. As Cromwell looked across the field from the left wing selecting his line of attack, he must have seen these five or six regiments standing like a rock amid the successive waves of their assailants.

He began to move steadily across the field from west to east, rather in the manner of a steamroller, crushing all opposition before him. Crawford's and Manchester's foot, forming the Parliamentary left centre, had advanced with him, and shared in his success; and they now turned when he did, and moved across the field on his right. The scanty Royalist infantry recoiled before this flank attack. One by one their regiments were overwhelmed or saved themselves by flight. Newcastle's whitecoats took up a defensive position, and prepared to sell their lives dearly. The irresistible Roundhead advance surged round them—then over them. Before this happened Cromwell and his Ironsides reached the farther end of the field and found themselves facing southward, in almost exactly the same position which Goring had occupied earlier in the day as he waited for Fairfax's attack. Cromwell was now waiting for Goring.

When the latter returned from his pursuit he did all that a brave soldier could, in such circumstances, to save the day. Uniting his cavalry with Lucas's, he prepared to meet the Roundhead attack, which presently came rolling down the hill towards him. We have no detailed description of this last encounter. The Parliamentarians were the assailants, and we are told that they advanced with such steadiness, after a tiring day, that Leslie, the Scottish veteran, who was present (according to the Scots he was the leader, rather than Cromwell), exclaimed that these were the best troops in Europe. It was all over by nine o'clock. Goring's cavalry had disappeared, and the triumphant Roundheads were pursuing the flying remnants of the Royal army across the darkened moor towards York.

The losses, as far as the cavalry were concerned, had been surprisingly small. Rupert, as he drew off across Marston Moor, shouting angry orders into the darkness, slowly collecting the dim, broken masses of his horse, was in a mood of exasperation. He had been cheated. He blamed Lord Byron, who was said to have made a premature charge (it is not clear when). But the truth is that Rupert had been caught unprepared—and he must have known it—caught and smothered by superior numbers. The Roundheads boasted that the bodies of the dead Cavaliers lay scattered all along the road for three miles that side of York. On the field of battle the whitecoats lay silent where they had stood. Rupert knew that somewhere among the corpses was the small, limp body of his faithful friend Boy. He had meant to leave him behind for once, but the dog had broken away from his keepers and followed his master on to the battle-field. There he met a soldier's death, probably trampled under the horses' hoofs in the cavalry *mêlée*. The London pamphleteers raised a loud hymn of praise at the death of "the accursed dogge."

Riding to York, the Prince found Eythin and Newcastle there. They were in a mood of despair. The following dialogue took place:

> Says General King [Eythin], "What will you do?"
> Says the Prince, "I will rally my men."
> Says General King, "Know you what Lord Newcastle will do?"
> Says Lord Newcastle, "I will go into Holland." [1]

Newcastle added that all was lost and that he "would not endure the laughter of the Court." So Newcastle and Eythin mounted and rode for the coast. Sir Thomas Glenham, with the remnants of the infantry, was left to hold out as long as he could in York. Rupert moved off

[1] Warburton (quoting from Rupert's diary), vol. ii, p. 468.

on the Thursday morning at the head of 6000 cavalry. He rode boldly past Marston Moor and, turning south, made for Shropshire and Wales. Cromwell had been wounded in the throat during the cavalry combat, but he had tied a bandage round his neck; and now, when he heard that Rupert had passed, he came out upon the high-road with his Ironsides and attempted to overtake him. He was easily outpaced, and presently returned to the siege of York. Rupert rode on southward. He did not understand—nobody yet understood—that the war was lost. But he carried with him, and never afterwards parted with, the King's letter, which he had accepted as an order to fight at Marston Moor.

Rupert made a short halt at Richmond, where he was joined by scattered bodies of mounted Cavaliers from Marston Moor who had been drifting about the country-side. As he moved farther south he came into a different atmosphere. There was a spirit of optimism in the air. The King himself had defeated Waller at Cropredy Bridge, and was now preparing to move into the South-west and compel the surrender of Essex's army at Lost-withiel. The Oxford Royalists, delighted at the ease with which their King had outmanœuvred and outfought his two immediate opponents, were inclined to look upon Marston Moor as a mere regrettable incident some-where up north—too far from the heart of things to affect the issue of the war. They could not see that the loss of the North meant the loss of all, if only because money could no longer be drawn from thence. They were more interested for the moment in the disgrace of Wilmot, who had tried the King's patience beyond breaking-point, and in the elevation of Goring, who was, not undeservedly, the hero of the hour.

Rupert seems to have had little share in these intrigues, though Wilmot blamed him for everything. The disgrace of Wilmot was accomplished with rather unnecessary theatricality. He was arrested while actually on parade with his men, with whom he was not unpopular. There were murmurs in the ranks, and might even have been a mutiny, if the King himself had not ridden to the head of each regiment and assured them that the arrest was only temporary and had the approval of Prince Rupert. The introduction of Rupert's name quelled the mutiny, but won him the hatred of all Wilmot's friends. "He plays the courtier," wrote O'Neill, and "is known to be the *primum mobile* of that mischief." [1] In fact, he went on into Wales, and continued his recruiting there, in a mood of black depression.

The news of the second battle of Newbury, when Charles slipped out from between the two armies of Manchester and Cromwell, which ought to have crushed him like an eggshell, brought Rupert from his retirement. He arrived too late for the battle, but had an interview with the King, and was shortly afterwards appointed generalissimo of the Royalist forces in place of old Forth (now Earl of Brentford). Charles obviously felt that something was going wrong with the morale of his army. At the moment when he had just scored his two outstanding personal successes of the war it was an irritating reflection. He had got rid of Wilmot, and was now in a mood to make a clean sweep. How he had tolerated Forth so long is a mystery to the historian. Clarendon has summed up that veteran's abilities at this time:

> He was still a man of unquestionable courage and integrity yet he was now much decayed in his parts, and, with the long continued custom of immoderate drinking, dozed in his under standing, which had been never quick and vigorous, he havin

[1] When Rupert's friends were in the ascendant at Court he wa accused of "playing the courtier"; when they were not he was blame (by Hyde, for instance) for being a rough soldier and paying insufficie attention to the arts of peace.

been always illiterate to the greatest degree that can be imagined. He was now become very deaf, yet often pretended not to have heard what he did not then contradict, and thought fit afterwards to disclaim. He was a man of few words and of great compliance, and usually delivered that as his opinion which he foresaw would be grateful to the King.

Such a Commander-in-Chief was better out of the way. The King was once more engaged in negotiations with the Parliament, this time over the proposed Treaty of Uxbridge. But the Parliament's terms were impossible— as harsh as any that were offered him after Naseby. In the long list of persons to be exempted from the general pardon occurred the names of Prince Rupert and his brother Maurice, and Whitelocke (who was one of the Parliamentary commissioners) records that the two young Palatines laughed loudly when the list was read out. Yet we know that Rupert did his best to promote the treaty behind the scenes. He was already coming round to the view that the King could no longer hope to win the war by force of arms.

But promotion in rank could not cure his depression. His correspondents speak of his "profound melancholy." His post-bag was enormous. As generalissimo he was receiving not only all the correspondence proper to general headquarters, but innumerable personal appeals from Wales, where he had so long been in charge of the King's affairs. The difficulty was always to get money and supplies. The King was so short of cash that when he sent the Prince of Wales to Bristol the boy had to live at Hopton's personal expense. And on top of all this came the galling intelligence that Rupert's curly-headed elder brother, Charles Louis, had arrived in London and was making himself agreeable to Parliament, talking of "Popish schemes" (presumably his brother's or his uncle's) and assuring the rebels of his undying attachment to the Protestant cause—he who had suffered nothing for it compared with Rupert's captivity at Linz! Worst of all was the feeling that his side was losing the war. It was curious how the skirmishes began to go against them—those weekly, and almost daily, little affairs between rival parties of Roundheads and Cavaliers. The Royalists had once held a definite advantage here— chiefly because there were no mounted men in the field who would stand against Rupert's horsemen. But things had changed, almost imperceptibly. The horsemen were still there, but the generalissimo could not lead them on every foray. Gage was heavily repulsed, and himself slain, in an attempt upon Abingdon. Goring, with something of the old Cavalier spirit, made a dash at Farnham and seized the place; but he could not collect enough money to pay his troops with, and to avoid another mutiny fell back into the West. At the same time the Roundheads began to take the offensive. A cold, keen wind from East Anglia was stirring them into life, and the name of Cromwell appeared with increasing frequency in the military reports sent in to headquarters. Thus ominously passed the winter of 1644–45.

On April 2 old Essex—in actual fact he was only fifty-four—resigned under the terms of the Self-denying Ordinance, and his place in the Midlands was taken by Oliver Cromwell, with the men of his New Model army behind him. He at once began 'mopping up' outlying Royalist garrisons, following Rupert's methods to a large extent, but with a kind of pious ruthlessness and thoroughness all his own. Sometimes he was repulsed; more often he succeeded, either by bluff or force of arms. An outstanding example of the former was the surrender of Bletchington House, only six miles north of Oxford Fairfax and Cromwell had undertaken two daring raid with their New Model: the former plunged southward passing through Winchester to Blandford, and back *via* Salisbury; Cromwell, starting from Windsor, was making a circle round Oxford, moving first from east to north. At Islip he defeated a party of Royalists, some of whom took refuge in Bletchington House, which Colonel Windebank held for the King.

Cromwell had only cavalry with him, between two and three thousand at the most, and nearly all of them lightly armed, since their principal business on this occasion was raiding and rounding up cattle. But he put his few dragoons in front, and rode boldly up to Bletchington House, demanding its surrender. To his surprise and delight, Windebank at once agreed to evacuate the place, leaving sixty or seventy horses, with some arms and ammunition behind him. "I did much doubt the storming of the house," says Cromwell, "it being strong and well manned, and I having few dragoons." But he got it by bluff—"by dragoons and fierce countenances." [1] The pusillanimity of Windebank was never explained. It was said that his young wife and some of her friends from Oxford were frightened, and that he did not want to subject the ladies to the terrors of a siege. But with assistance so close at hand and such an inadequate besieging force before him, without infantry or guns, the leaguer could hardly have lasted twenty-four hours. When he reached the Royal headquarters the unfortunate man was tried by court martial, found guilty, and promptly shot, with his back to the wall of Merton College. His fate seems to illustrate, in the first place, the decline in the Royalist morale and, in the second, the devastating psychological effect of a certain "fierce counance" turned up menacingly from the other side of the moat at Bletchington.

On May 7 the campaign proper of the year 1645—and

[1] Carlyle, vol. i, p. 180; Warburton, vol. iii, p. 76.

the last campaign of the Civil War—began with a flourish of trumpets. The King rode out of Oxford with Rupert and Goring. He was bound for the North. Yet, with that fatal passion for dividing their slender forces which had dogged the commanders on both sides ever since the outbreak of the war, he was taking only part of his total strength with him. The Parliamentary leaders had been equally at fault—indeed, they were much more to blame, for, with their numerical superiority, they might have crushed the King at any time during the previous eighteen months if they had possessed the intelligence and foresight to direct their whole weight against him. But they were divided again now.

Charles himself was a good strategist, and no one will ever know what might have happened had he also been born with the gift of swaying men at the council-table. But once again his generals had disagreed. Some of them urged him to march south and attack Fairfax, who was relieving Taunton. Rupert and Langdale were for a northern march : they realized the importance of the North, and Rupert had in his pocket a firmly worded petition from the splendid cavalry he had brought away from Marston Moor, begging to be allowed to return to the relief of their own home lands in Yorkshire. It was a display of that old local spirit which had more than once inconvenienced the Royalist leaders, and which Cromwel had just eliminated from the Parliament's New Model Charles compromised. Goring turned off to the wes and south; Rupert and the King continued northwar towards Evesham, Droitwich, and Market Drayton.

The Royal army had been barely a fortnight gone whe Fairfax appeared before the walls of Oxford and cool laid siege to the place. That was part of the Parliamer tary plan. But it was also part of the plan that the Rounc heads in Oxford should rise in revolt or covertly betra the place to its besiegers. Nothing of the kind happened, and it seemed that Fairfax had a difficult task before him. Another part of the Parliamentary plan was that Leven, with the Scottish army from Marston Moor, should oppose the King's northern march; but upon the receipt of bad news from Scotland, where Montrose was winning a series of victories, Leven moved off rapidly towards the Border, leaving Charles to do as he pleased.

It seemed at first an inviting prospect, full of brilliant possibilities for the future. But soon after passing Market Drayton Charles was overtaken by messages from Oxford calling for help. The siege was less than one day old, but Secretary Nicholas declared that supplies would only last a few weeks. It was the old, maddening difficulty of money and supplies. Now it had prevented his northern march, just when the road was unexpectedly cleared. Charles turned reluctantly southward, sending urgent messages to Goring to join him. It was about this time that somebody—possibly Rupert—suggested that a useful addition to the stores of the Royal army might be acquired by attacking the wealthy town of Leicester. Rupert had been there before; he might be said to know the way in. The wealth of the town was more imposing than its military defences; and the garrison placed there by the Parliament was, from all accounts, absurdly small.

Rupert's advance parties appeared outside the town on May 28. On the 30th he brought up his guns, and had blown a breach in the walls before midnight. Instantly he ordered an assault, and his forlorn hope was in the streets of Leicester before it was light. There were scenes of wild excitement—it was Rupert's last exploit of the kind. About a hundred Roundheads were killed, and, though some women and children were found among the dead, even the Parliamentarians admitted that they were probably slain by accident. But the pillaging of the shops and houses was deliberate enough, and a long train of wagons loaded with plunder followed the hungry Cavaliers out of Leicester.

They continued southward as far as Daventry, and there Charles got the news that the first object of his right-about face had been accomplished. Fairfax had abandoned the siege of Oxford. What he did not know was that Fairfax was now moving northward in search of him, with a full licence from Parliament to seek out and fight the King's army wherever he should find it. He did not know that Cromwell, with a small following of horse, was hastening across England from East Anglia to join Fairfax. He did not even know that his enemies now outnumbered him by nearly two to one. His military advisers—including Rupert—completely underestimated the importance of the New Model, both as regards numbers and quality. His Privy Council at Oxford, after renewing their old quarrel about whether he should march north or south, had now come to the unanimous decision (and communicated it to him) that the best plan would be to invade East Anglia!

Every leading man on the Royalist side seemed suddenly to have lost all sense of realities. They did not know that Cromwell had suddenly been appointed Lieutenant-General under Fairfax; or if they knew they did not understand or care. They believed (according to one of the King's letters) that the Parliamentary generals were quarrelling fiercely among themselves, when in fact they had never been so closely united. On June 12 the King was enjoying a day's hunting in Fawsley Park. That same evening his patrols came unexpectedly in touch with Fairfax's advance-guard. A few hours later Cromwell and his six hundred horsemen from East Anglia rode into Fairfax's camp, and were greeted by the soldiers with "a great shout."

CHAPTER XIII: NASEBY AND THE END

THE two armies were manœuvring for position among the hills near Naseby. To speak more strictly, the Parliamentarians were manœuvring, while the Royalists were merely advancing. Fairfax, as soon as he found that he was about to be attacked, was at pains to choose his ground. He was drawn up at first on a hill near Dust Hill, well to the north of Naseby, with wet, boggy ground in front; but, seeing the difficulty of using his superior weight in cavalry on such a surface, he fell back from the ridge of the hill to a position farther west and south, at the highest point of the plateau, and quite close to Naseby. On Cromwell's advice he then withdrew some hundreds of yards behind the summit, in order that the Royalists, advancing from the other side, should not perceive his vast superiority in numbers. For if they did perceive it he could not imagine that they would be mad enough to attack. Fairfax was a practical soldier.

The Cavaliers came on with their usual gay courage, marching to their last battlefield. It seems certain that they were unaware of the great strength opposed to them. In any case, it would probably not have deterred them. The Cavaliers had always been outnumbered. Rupert had disliked this southern march from the beginning: he had wanted to go on north, and smash the Scots, and recover those rich recruiting districts from which Langdale's and many of his own troopers had been drawn. But he had seen the necessity of easing the pressure on Oxford, and had found the taking of Leicester a pleasant interlude. Whether or not he was in favour of giving battle at Naseby it is difficult to tell, since the authorities are at variance.[1] Most probably not. But, having arrived on the field of battle, he pressed forward with his accustomed *élan*. He had sent his patrols out early that morning under his official scoutmaster, and, getting no satisfactory report from that officer—who seems to have ridden only a mile or two—he had himself mounted and cantered southward, until he could plainly see the Roundhead formations about the ridge of Dust Hill. They were not there now, though a few of their skirmishers were pushed forward down the slope of the next hill, farther south, and greeted the Royalists with a scattered fire of musketry. Rupert scented battle in the air. He pressed on eagerly. It is perhaps unfortunate that he had been compelled to do his own scouting. Every time he had seen the enemy they were a little farther back, and he now decided that they must be in retreat. The official scoutmaster, from what we know of him, would not have jumped so easily to an optimistic conclusion.

The Roundheads, as we have seen, were stationed a little behind the highest point of the plateau. Most of them were standing in a fallow field; but far away on the left there was a hedge running at right angles to their position, and Ireton, who commanded the cavalry on that wing, had lined it with dragoons to protect his flank. The position of honour on the right was held by Cromwell, the Lieutenant-General, and beyond him again there were warrens, where cavalry action would be difficult. The foot in the centre were commanded by Skippon, under Fairfax. But it should be noted that the Parliamentary army was formed in only two lines, and therefore extended over so wide a front that the danger of outflanking by an inferior force was negligible.

---

[1] Walker, *Historical Discourses*, p. 129 (1705), seems to give the best view. Parliamentary pamphleteers who represented Rupert as spoiling for a fight really knew nothing about it.

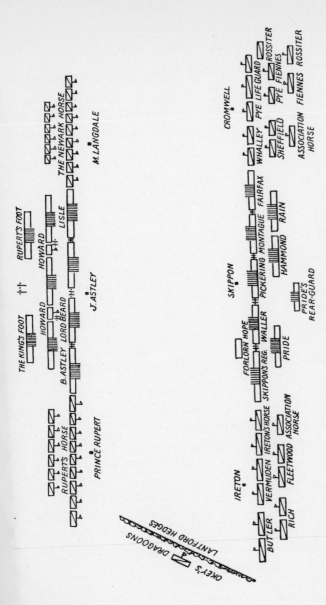

ORDER OF THE ARMIES AT NASEBY

*Based on Sprigge's contemporary map as reproduced in "Cromwell as a Soldier," by T. S. Baldock, by permission of
Messrs Kegan Paul, Trench, Trübner and Co., Ltd.*

The Cavaliers came on rapidly. With Rupert on the right wing rode his brother Maurice, and many an old comrade—though honest Will Legge was left behind at Oxford, as governor of that city. Rupert's good friend Sir Marmaduke Langdale, with the Northern horse, commanded the left wing. The infantry in the centre were led by old Sir Jacob Astley. As they breasted the gentle rise the whole Parliamentary army advanced and appeared in its full strength only a few hundred yards above them. Rupert found himself leading less than 2000 light horsemen uphill against 3400 heavily armed cuirassiers of the New Model under Ireton. On the left wing Langdale was making a similar attempt with 1500 sabres against Cromwell's 3600. In the centre the Royalist infantry, numbering about 3500, mostly Welshmen, would soon be at thrust of pike with 7000 Parliamentarians—a solid mass of scarlet, the new redcoats, trained in Windsor Park, under the walls of the King's own palace, and wearing the colour that thenceforward became traditional in the British Army.[1] It was a mad attempt—madder than at Marston Moor—but it was too late to turn back now.

Rupert was the first to give the signal for the charge, and his Cavaliers were soon pricking up the hill towards Ireton's horsemen, who, for the most part, sat stupidly waiting for them. Well ahead rode the young Prince, conspicuous in his bright red cloak—which he had not discarded on this occasion—his dark hair flying in the wind behind him. It is evident that this was a typical charge on the Edgehill model. We hear nothing of musketeers interspersed among the horse as at Marston Moor—neither on Rupert's wing nor on Langdale's. Rupert had obviously ordered his horsemen to hold their fire and rely entirely on the speed and shock of the charge

[1] With blue, yellow, or green facings, according to each colonel's taste.

with cold steel, until the enemies' backs were turned. They never checked for a moment: not even when they began to pass the hedgerow on their right and the dragoons behind it opened a brisk fire, emptying many saddles. They went straight on at Ireton's cuirassiers—2000 riders against 3400—crashed in among them, broke their ranks, and drove them from the field. It was Rupert's last great charge and probably his finest.

Following up the pursuit with their usual impetuosity, Rupert's horsemen came out upon the road to Naseby, well behind the battlefield, and presently encountered the Parliamentary baggage, with its baggage guard, strongly posted. Rupert rode forward to look at them, and was surprised to be greeted by the commander of the baggage guard, who advanced from his own lines with a friendly inquiry as to how the battle was going. It appeared later that he had mistaken Rupert for Fairfax, who had recently affected a red cloak. He was now sent back with a demand for the surrender of the baggage, but his men very properly replied with a volley of musketry, and Rupert drew off. He knew that he had no time to spare. Collecting all the Royalist cavalry in sight, he turned back towards the scene of action. And some of Ireton's regiments—Ireton himself being wounded and a prisoner—were rallied by their officers and followed him.

These uninspired, conventional seventeenth-century battles—and, as Fortescue remarks, Naseby was not even a "well-managed fight"—fall automatically into three parts. Having glanced at the right wing, we proceed to the centre of the field. Here the Royalist foot had made such good speed up the slope that they must have been near the crest of the hill when Rupert's charge went home on their right. The result was—and it was as well, perhaps, for the Welshmen's nerves—that they came suddenly upon their opponents, and only contemplated the full strength of those serried ranks for a few moments —just time enough to exchange a single volley—before they closed. Then, says Clarendon,[1] "the King's foot, according to their usual custom, falling in with their swords and the butt ends of their muskets . . . did very notable execution." In Sprigge's map parties of horse are shown among the foot on the Royalist side; it seems an unlikely arrangement, and we hear nothing of them when the battle was joined.[2] It is to the Royalist infantry, always outnumbered, often neglected and half starved, that the whole credit for this valiant attack is due. And it is interesting to note how their aggressive methods matched the tactics of their cavalry.

Now with their swinging swords and muskets they put the enemy into "great disorder and confusion." Against odds of roughly two to one they struggled gamely forward, shouting "God and Queen Mary!" which was the Naseby battle-cry. The Parliamentarians began to give way, and the regiments on the left of their front line, where Rupert's victorious charge had left the flank unguarded, broke off altogether and ran to take shelter in their second line. Skippon was wounded. Help came just in time. That vigilant officer Colonel Okey had been in command of the Roundhead dragoons behind the hedge on the extreme left, and, as we have seen, had fired ineffectually into Rupert's cavalry as they galloped past. He now saw an opportunity of more useful service Quickly remounting his dragoons, he led them forward across the open space where Ireton's horse had been and poured a volley into the flank of the advancing Royalis

---

[1] Vol. ii, p. 507.

[2] Sprigge was a chaplain in Fairfax's army, and may very well hav been wrong about the Royalist dispositions, though he is one of our be authorities for Naseby.

infantry, pulling them up short. The battle was thus restored at this point, and the issue of the infantry combat remained yet in doubt.

We repair to the other wing. Cromwell, seeing Langdale's small force trotting up the hill towards him, did not, like Ireton, wait to be attacked. He moved promptly forward, and charged downhill upon his opponent. Langdale waited to fire a volley. Cromwell, who was quite as academically minded in these matters, fired a volley in return. Then they came together—probably at the trot. But speed matters less if the ground and everything else is in your favour. The inevitable happened. The numerically inferior and more lightly armed body was pushed rapidly downhill, until the strain became insupportable, and the Northern troopers broke away in small parties and galloped for safety behind the Royal centre, where the King himself was in command of the cavalry reserve. Many others of them fled from the field, pursued by Cromwell's Ironsides.

Cromwell, as usual, had his men well in hand. He detached a sufficient force to keep Langdale's retreating horsemen on the move; with the rest he turned against the King's reserve. This consisted entirely of picked men, mostly gentlemen, and presumably well armed and mounted. True they numbered only 500, but a well-timed charge might have temporarily restored the fortunes of the day. Charles, mettlesome as ever, placed himself at their head and led them forward against the victorious Ironsides. Then occurred one of the most extraordinary incidents of the Civil War. The Scottish nobleman Lord Carnwath galloped forward from the ranks, seized the King's horse by the bridle, and with a cry of "Would you go to your death?" followed by "two or three full-mouthed Scotch oaths," led him off to the right. Carnwath seems to have been an honest but stupid person, "not one from whom the King would have received counsel in such a case." [1] But Charles, taken by surprise, was too astonished to resist.

Now, whether because of Carnwath's action or for some other inexplicable reason, the order was given and repeated along the line, "March to the right hand!" Checked in full career and attempting to execute this unexpected order, the Cavaliers fell into confusion; confusion changed to panic; and before the King fully realized what had happened his gallant reserve were in disgraceful flight, sweeping him along with them. Without a moment's hesitation Cromwell once more changed direction with his main body and assailed the Royalist foot in the rear. He rightly judged that he could afford to disregard the King and Langdale, who would be fully occupied in rallying their men. The long lines of infantry were still swaying together in hand-to-hand struggle all along the crest of the hill. The two first lines of Royalists were being forced back, though they rallied desperately again and again. But, unlike the Parliamentarians, the Royalists had a third, though much abbreviated, line of foot, consisting of only two regiments, the King's and Prince Rupert's. These seem to have come into the fighting line and stopped the Roundhead advance just before Cromwell made his first charge against their rear.

The effect of that charge was shattering. The Roundhead foot, seeing it, pressed downhill with renewed ardour. Okey's dragoons, on the Royalist right, poured in another volley. It was on that side that the Royalist line first began to lose its cohesion, as regiment after regiment broke away from the unequal contest and retreated down the hill. On the other side—that is, on the Roundhead right—the slaughter had been less, and Fairfax's own

[1] Clarendon, vol. ii, p. 508.

regiment, on the extreme right of the line, was comparatively fresh when he sent it forward again against Lisle's tired infantry, who were its "opposite number." The latter were driven back in disorder, and we hear of them no more. But just behind them was Rupert's own regiment of foot, his redcoats, and these stood like a rock. They repulsed Fairfax's men in front; they beat off charge after charge from the Ironsides at their backs. Soon they were the only Royalist regiment of foot holding its ground: all the others had dispersed. It is said that Fairfax sent for his own mounted life guards to deliver the final charge. At last it was done, and Rupert's redcoats lay dead in their ranks like the whitecoats at Marston Moor. The Royalist infantry were irretrievably shattered.

Meantime Rupert's horse had been streaming back on to the battlefield. The Prince, as he reached the fatal ridge, could see the infantry still struggling for their lives on the hillside, surrounded by hostile horse and foot. Far away the King and Sir Marmaduke Langdale had got their men into line and were preparing for another cavalry effort. Rupert rode over and joined them, so that presently there appeared to be quite a formidable line of mounted men ready to renew the fight. Their losses had been slight, though the morale of some of them had been badly shaken. Facing them (and between them and their luckless infantry) were the ordered ranks of Cromwell's Ironsides. Ireton had somehow escaped from his captors, and, with blood streaming down his face, was forming his rallied regiments on Cromwell's left. There was a pause. If Rupert's Cavaliers could have spurred their tired horses into another gallop now; if the King and Langdale could have inspired their demoralized followers to some deed worthy of the occasion—they might even then have made a draw of it. It was not to be. Cromwell

advanced first, calm and resolute, strong in the knowledge
of his superior discipline and irresistible numbers. The
discipline and the resolution indeed were his, and highly
characteristic of his genius; but, having provided them,
even an Essex could hardly have lost this field. The
attenuated ranks of his enemies wavered at his solid
approach. Before he could get at them they turned as
with one accord and began to ride off the field, most of
them making for Leicester with the King, others for
Newark (these were the Newark horse from Langdale's
command), others galloping aimlessly across the countryside. Fairfax and Lambert pursued vigorously; but the
King, with Rupert and Maurice, reached Leicester well
ahead of them, and afterwards continued his retreat
through Lichfield and Bewdley to Hereford.

Cromwell turned on the flying remnants of the Royalist
foot and began to cut them to pieces. He had killed a
thousand before he was done, and captured five times
that number of prisoners. Then he closed in on the
helpless mass of the camp followers: the pedlars, pro-
stitutes, and goodness knows what, who trailed behind
every seventeenth-century army. Some rode in carriages;
some were mere "vermin on foot." [1] The scene that

[1] Sir James Turner, a contemporary authority, in his *Military Essays*,
p. 276, states that it was the practice to divide the women followers into
three companies, with a marshal to order their ranks. The senior officers'
wives went first in coaches, those of the junior officers' next on horseback
and the women (married or unmarried) of the common soldiery on foot
Sir James argues that soldiers were better behaved, better fed and care
for, especially at a siege, if they had their wives with them. He goes on t
describe with strong disapproval a practice attributed to the Duke o
Alva in regard to *un*married female camp followers : the Duke is said t
have divided them into four "squadrons" according to their looks; th
first were ordered to have no dealings with any but senior officers, th
second only with subalterns, the third with non-commissioned officer
while members of the fourth "squadron" were severely punished if the
cast their eyes upon any above a private's rank. Each "squadron" ha
its own banner and its "she-cornets" to enforce discipline. "A practice
adds Sir James, "which with an impudent face loudly cried defiance
both Religion and Moral Honesty!"

followed was too hideous to dwell upon. The Puritan soldiery divided from the rest those women whom they thought were Irish Papists—though it would seem that there were several English officers' wives among them— and murdered them in cold blood. Those whom they chose to regard as English they merely mutilated, slashing their faces. In London they had been fed with Press propaganda about the inhuman barbarity of the Irish. Months ago, before Rupert marched north, a certain Captain Swanley, having captured a boat-load of reinforcements coming over from Ireland to help the King, made prisoners of the English, but tied the Irish back to back and threw them into the sea. A little later thirteen of Rupert's Irish auxiliaries were hanged without trial by a Parliamentary commander. Rupert promptly replied by stringing up thirteen of his Roundhead prisoners, and the trouble thereupon ceased as far as he was concerned. But the point to notice is that Essex, his mild-tempered opponent, wrote in a tone of pained surprise to know by what law he had treated the Englishmen like Irishmen. Rupert replied that it was "simple soldiers'" law, and that he would do it again.

The battle was ended. The King had brought off most of his cavalry, but all his guns and ammunition and baggage, including his private papers, had fallen into the enemy's hands. His infantry had ceased to exist. Gerard joined him at Hereford with a few thousand men, and the uncertain Goring was still at large. But for any serious purpose he could no longer put an army in the field.

Yet the strange fact is that he would not recognize the extent of his calamity. While the Roundhead armies roamed the countryside unchallenged in every part of England except the South-west Charles ambled placidly out of Hereford and went to stay with his good friend the Marquess of Worcester, the Catholic nobleman who had sacrificed everything for his cause. And here he stayed for three weeks, resting himself after his exertions and taking part in "sports and entertainments," while the Royalist garrisons all over England fell one by one into the enemy's hands. At first sight it might almost be mistaken for stupidity or dull despair. It was nothing of the kind. There was in Charles's character a core of steel, upon which not all "the slings and arrows of outrageous fortune" could make the least impression. The Whig historians of the eighteenth and nineteenth centuries agreed to call it "obstinacy." Modern critics have usually found a kinder word. Charles was, before everything, a man of principle. He had not drawn the sword at Nottingham in any light-hearted mood, though his enemies pretended to think so. He had drawn it on a point of principle, and while that remained in doubt he would never willingly sheath it. Military defeats were unfortunate, regrettable; but they could not settle the real issue. Charles always looked for a moral victory. Who shall say that he was wrong? For it can hardly be denied that he got his moral victory in the end, though it was not until after his own martyrdom.

It would be hard to imagine any attitude of mind more opposed to Rupert's practical temperament. Rupert knew that, in a military sense, the war was lost, and it was not his habit to think of wars in other than military terms. He knew the signs. He was still in the West, seeking recruits among the loyal Welsh, and every day finding it harder to get them as the bad news spread abroad. At the King's suggestion there was a meeting between uncle and nephew at Blackrock on July 22, five weeks after Naseby. Charles was still talking of reinforcements from Ireland. Rupert—though he would have agreed with Byron's opinion, that, since the Parliament had called in the Scots, there could be no moral objection the King engaged the Turks—probably listened now in discouraging silence. But the main subject of the conversation was the King's immediate plan of crossing the Severn with the remnants of his army (perhaps five thousand men) and marching south to help Goring, who had just been defeated at Langport. Rupert agreed to that, but added the significant proviso that he was not to be held responsible for the consequences. This was utterly unlike Rupert. It shows him in a new frame of mind. And it suggests that this conversation at Blackrock may have struck the first jarring note in the long friendship between uncle and nephew. They had always been utterly dissimilar in temperament. Perhaps that was the secret of their friendship. Rupert, at any rate, had whole-heartedly admired this cultured, sensitive, obstinate, heroic little king; but what he could never understand in any man was a refusal to face facts, especially military facts. Charles seemed to him to be living in another world. To Rupert this was a war like any other war; to Charles it was a crusade.

And then there was Digby. That active intriguer, as Rupert well knew, had been working for years to undermine his influence with the King. To Digby the loss of the war seemed a small matter if he could, at the same time, bring Rupert down. Naseby was his opportunity. He worked day and night against the Prince, while publicly professing undying friendship. Warburton has produced a long letter which Digby wrote to Will Legge, who was the friend of both men—as, indeed, everybody. It is a nauseating document. While appearing to defend the Prince and praise him Digby ingeniously saddles him with the whole blame for the defeat. "Honest Will" replies bluntly:

I am extremely afflicted to understand from you that Prince Rupert and yourself should be upon so unkindly terms, and I protest I have cordially endeavoured, with all my interest in his Highness, to incline him to a friendship with your Lordship, conceiving it a matter of advantage to my master's service to have a good intelligence between persons so eminently employed in his affairs, and likewise the great obligation and inclination I had to either of you. But truly, my Lord, I often found this a hard matter to hold between you; and your last letter gives me cause to think that your Lordship is not altogether free from what he accused you of as the reason of his jealousies. Which was that you both say and do things to his prejudice, contrary to your confessions, and not in an open and direct line, but obscurely and obliquely; and this, under your Lordship's pardon, I find your letter very full of.

After this Will Legge was known in Digby's circle as "Prince Rupert's creature." On July 28 Rupert addressed to his friend the Duke of Richmond a letter which he intended should be shown to the King—as it was. In it he frankly advised the opening of peace negotiations with the Parliament, on the ground that there was no longer any hope of victory, and that it was "a more prudent way to retain something than to lose all." Charles read this letter quietly and graciously, but his reply was uncompromising. He admitted that "speaking as a mere soldier or statesman" Rupert might have some reason on his side. But:

As a Christian I must tell you that God will not suffer rebe and traitors to prosper, nor this cause to be overthrown; an whatever personal punishment it shall please Him to inflict c me must not make me repine, much less give over this quarre . . . For I know my obligation to be, both in conscience ar honour, neither to abandon God's cause, injure my successor nor forsake my friends. Indeed, I cannot flatter myself wi expectation of good success more than this, to end my da with honour and a good conscience; which obliges me continue my endeavours as not despairing that God may y in good time avenge His own cause.

He ended by forbidding Rupert to mention treaties him again.

GEORGE DIGBY
From an engraving after Van Dyck

In August it became known that Fairfax was advancing to the siege of Bristol. There was no Royalist army in the field that could prevent him. Rupert hurried to the threatened city, of which he was still the nominal governor, and gave his attention to the improvement of the defences, which had been somewhat strengthened since he had carried the place by assault twelve months before. Windmill Fort had been rebuilt and rearmed, and the "dead ground" through which Colonel Washington had crawled with his men on that September night in 1643 had, no doubt, been levelled up to bring it within sight of the Fort's gunners. Priors Hill Fort had also been strengthened. But the curtain wall was still too low and the ditch too wide and shallow. Worst of all, the people of Bristol, who had been ruthlessly taxed for the upkeep of the Royal armies, were now more definitely hostile than before.

When Fairfax arrived he acted in strict accordance with the new spirit which inspired the Parliamentary forces. By the end of August he had completed the investment of the place. On September 4 he summoned Rupert to surrender, and when he was refused delivered a general assault. On the south and south-east his storming parties were repulsed with slaughter, as the Cavaliers had been repulsed a year before. But on the west he made several lodgments within the curtain walls. The forts were more difficult. Priors Hill, in particular, held out for hours; but the Roundheads at last broke in and put its defenders to the sword. Rupert's men fell back through the streets, as those of Fiennes had done, but with far less support from the populace. And then—again like Fiennes—Rupert opened negotiations for surrender. What made his position hopeless was that the Roundhead infantry had got in between the castle and the forts that still held out. In self-defence he had set fire to the town in three places, and Fairfax was not unwilling to avoid unnecessary damage to property. Rupert was given easy terms, and his garrison marched out on September 11 with all the honours of war. They were even supplied with muskets and ammunition, wherewith to defend themselves against Roundhead attacks on the march to Oxford.

It must have been a curious scene—almost the last of its kind in the Civil War. Rupert had taken a position near the rear of the column, for the better protection of his men. He was determined to have no repetition of the massacres at Reading and at this same Bristol two years before. Part of his horse and foot went first, then his wagons and the remaining regiments, then his red-coated life guards on foot, carrying at the ready the muskets with which Fairfax had provided them. Then came Rupert himself, resplendent in scarlet "very richly laid in silver lace" and mounted on a black Barbary horse. He was followed by his mounted life guards and a group of senior officers of both sides apparently riding amicably together. Thomas Fairfax was in personal attendance upon the Prince, always giving him the right-hand side of the road and behaving with elaborate courtesy. There was a good deal in common between them. At the outskirts of Bristol Rupert parted from Fairfax and Cromwell, with many compliments and a sweeping of plumed hats.

But one of the Parliamentary chroniclers recalls that as the Royalist cavalry passed out through the gates the Ironsides of the New Model, looking on, could not restrain their laughter at the miserable appearance of these once formidable opponents, the sorry nags they rode, the wretched equipment, and their half-starved, despairing looks. To such a pass had Rupert's horsemen come!

CHAPTER XIV: LATER YEARS—A SUMMARY

WHEN King Charles heard the news of the surrender of Bristol he felt it like a stab to the heart. In his short, tragic life nothing can have hurt him more, except the murder of Buckingham. Rupert, his tall, splendid, dashing young nephew, whom he had loved from their first meeting—Rupert had deserted the cause, and deserted it in the hour of its adversity. That was the overwhelming fact, excluding all others from his consciousness. He tried to listen while Rupert's military friends explained earnestly that the Prince, by his timely surrender, had saved the garrison, which might otherwise have been massacred like the defenders of Priors Hill. He even roused himself to hear the testimony of the Parliamentary generals, who chivalrously hastened to bear witness that Rupert could have done nothing else.[1] If I have succeeded at all in indicating the fundamental difference between uncle and nephew in these matters it will be understood that all this soldiers' talk was a foreign language to the King. Indeed, it was worse than foreign: it was blasphemous. To Rupert the soldier the moment when he found himself faced by inevitable defeat seemed the best moment to hoist the white flag. To King Charles the Martyr it seemed precisely the worst. t was the moment to nail the original flag to the mast. Charles wrote to Rupert:

> Though the loss of Bristol be a great blow to me, yet your surrendering it as you did is of so much affliction to me that it makes me not only forget the consideration of that place, but is likewise the greatest trial of my constancy that hath yet befallen me. For what is to be done after one that is so near me

---

[1] *E.g.*, Carte's *Letters*, vol. i, p. 134; Miss Eva Scott, *Rupert, Prince latine*, p. 183.

as you are, both in blood and friendship, submits himself to so
mean an action? . . . I have so much to say that I shall say
no more of it . . . my conclusion is to desire you to seek your
subsistence, until it shall please God to determine of my condition, somewhere beyond seas: to which end I send you here-
with a pass; and I pray God to make you sensible of your
present condition, and give you means to recover what you have
lost.

The King refers, of course, to the loss of Rupert's soul.
But Rupert was furious. Faced by an enemy in over-
powering numbers and bloodthirsty mood, he had safely
brought off his 800 horse and near 1000 foot and led them
into Oxford. This was his reward! While he was still
fuming he learned that Will Legge was dismissed from
the governorship of the city and placed under arrest, for
no other reason than that he was Rupert's friend. Secretary Nicholas transmitted these orders with reluctance.
It was Digby's doing from beginning to end. Rupert
controlled himself to write a calm letter of protest to his
uncle. Charles had removed from Oxford at his approach.
He had wanted to go to Worcester, partly for military
reasons, but partly, no doubt, because Prince Maurice was
governor there, and his heart was now yearning towards
his younger nephew (who had been ill), and he was writing him pathetic letters, not condescending to argue
about Rupert's conduct, but appealing for his affection
and loyalty—just such letters as any man might write in
similar circumstances. Digby was aware of all this, and
by using his whole influence induced Charles to go to
Newark instead. It was at Newark that he received
Rupert's letter, protesting his innocence and asking for
an interview.

Rupert remained at Oxford, waiting for an answer and
striving to curb his temper. Everybody in Oxford was on
his side.[1] Walsingham, Digby's chief spy, wrote that h

[1] The Queen had fled to France.

had been disgusted to see Rupert walking with Will Legge
—just before his arrest[1]—in the gardens of Christ Church,
attended by one or two leading peers, while "the nobility
and gentry stand there bare at a distance, as if his
Majesty had been present." This is the old, silly suggestion of Rupert's enemies that he was aiming at the crown.
But no answer came from Newark, no invitation to plead
his case before the King.

It was a dangerous game to play with Rupert, as Digby
ought to have known. It was, in fact, the same mistake that
the Roundheads had made at Chalgrove Field. Rupert
had reached Oxford in the third week in September.
On October 8 he suddenly left the city and rode for
the north. He had no following of his own, but about
a hundred mounted Cavaliers voluntarily accompanied
him, and Maurice met him at Banbury with a score or so
more. They pushed on towards Newark, and Digby, at
their approach, announced that he would take the field
to assist the Scottish Royalists, and left conveniently for
the North. But the Parliamentary commanders also had
heard of it, and they sent out their cavalry to cover every
road by which the Prince could approach Newark. All
the latter part of the journey was through hostile country,
garrisoned and occupied by the enemy. It was a ride
after Rupert's own heart, and it seems curiously appropriate that it should have been his last taste of the English
Civil War. He evidently enjoyed it, for he has left a
full account of the adventure in his so-called 'diary,'
from which Warburton has quoted it, as he assures us,
"verbatim." [2]

Passing through Northamptonshire, Rupert approached
Burghley House, where there was a strong Parliamentary

[1] There is a confusion about dates here. Walsingham's letter is dated
September 14, but Rupert only reached Oxford on the 16th and Legge's
arrest took place after his arrival.
[2] Vol. iii, p. 194.

garrison. The Governor, who was a renegade Royalist and had served in Rupert's own regiment of horse, came out to intercept him. He brought nearly his whole garrison with him, and when the cavalry skirmish began, "knowing the Prince, he came up with his pistol and missed fire, and then cried for quarter, but the Prince shot him dead." It was the third of such occasions in Rupert's career. He never missed fire himself. The little party rode on, and at Belvoir Bridge found three hundred horsemen waiting for them. Rupert executed a feigned retreat, turned suddenly on the enemy and repulsed them. He did it again. Then "says the Prince to his people, 'We have beaten them twice, we must beat them once more, and then over the pass and away.'" Which accordingly they did, breaking right through the enemy and riding on towards Belvoir Castle, where the Prince's luggage and private papers were to be left. He himself, with a small party, branched off through some byways. He knew every inch of the country, for it seems from the 'diary' that he had shot rabbits there "in the last King's reign"—an obvious mistake, but the date of this diary is uncertain, and the reference may be to Charles I. Forty mounted Roundheads pursued him and, as they came near, cried out to know if he wanted quarter. By way of reply the Prince, who had kept his men close together turned and scattered the pursuers with a sudden charge Lord Molyneux, who was with him, killed a Roundhead who was mounted on a particularly good mare, and the Prince, whose horse was almost finished, thereupon changed mounts and rode "fair and softly" to Belvoir He was at Newark next day.

The King had sent his express command forbiddin this visit. He did not want to see Rupert. In the latter present mood he had said, "you are no fit company fo me." But now, as he sat waiting for his supper to b announced, the Princes Rupert and Maurice walked calmly in upon him. Their behaviour was unceremonious. Rupert briefly stated that he had come to defend himself in the matter of the surrender of Bristol. The King looked at him, but said little, and he presently allowed them to accompany him to the supper-table, where they stood beside his chair. During the meal he addressed a few remarks to Maurice, but none to Rupert, and as soon as it was finished he went to bed.

He must have relented during the night watches, for on the following morning Rupert was granted a court martial (very fairly composed of friends and enemies), before which he produced "a narrative of the matter-of-fact during the siege" and stated his case generally. There were two sessions, at the second of which the King presided ; and the result was a unanimous verdict, signed by the King, and declaring that "Our said right dear nephew is not guilty of any the least want of courage or fidelity to us or our service in that action." It was a personal triumph for Rupert (for Ashburnham and Bellasys, Digby's friends, were among his judges), and the matter should have rested there. But it happened that the Governor of Newark, Sir Richard Willis, was a staunch friend of his, and had made himself rather conspicuous by riding out to meet the Prince on his arrival with an escort of cavalry. At this unfortunate juncture it was announced that Willis was to be commander of the King's life guards (which meant leaving Newark) and that Bellasys was appointed governor in his place. In a sense it was promotion for Willis, but he took it badly, as did all Rupert's friends. It was another civilian intrigue against the military, with the marks of Digby's trail all over it.

The King was just sitting down to dinner on a Sunday afternoon when the two princes, Sir Richard Willis,

Charles Gerard, and about twenty discontented Cavalier officers appeared before him. Willis at once began to proclaim his wrongs, demanding satisfaction. The King rose from table, had his dinner taken away, ordered all the junior officers to leave the room, and then stepped over to a window, beckoning the leading malcontents to follow him. Rupert walked "discontentedly, with his hands at this sides"—which means that he was deliberately disrespectful. As Willis was speaking he interrupted loudly: "By God, this is done in malice to me, because Sir Richard hath always been my faithful friend!" And again: "The cause of all this is Digby!" Gerard said Digby was a traitor, and he could prove it. The King began to lose his temper, and when Rupert repeated his charge that Digby was the man "that hath caused all this distraction between us" he answered angrily that they were "rogues and rascals" who said so. Rupert then stalked out, "showing no reverence." Gerard and the others bowed and followed him. It was a disgraceful and ridiculous scene, and the memory of it must have haunted Rupert in later years. It was his last formal interview with Charles I. That same evening he and his friends sent in a petition demanding a counsel of war to consider their grievances, or, alternatively, their passports to go into foreign parts. The King sent them their passports.

But it could not rest there. As between the King and Rupert it was not humanly possible that they should part in this way. When two men like each other as well as these two did it is always possible to patch up the most passionate quarrel with a little outside help. Rupert had promptly obtained Parliamentary passports from London, and might have left the country at any moment he chose. But Will Legge gave him no peace. The King had just come to Oxford and released poor Will from his un-

COLONEL WILLIAM LEGGE
After J. Huysmans
National Portrait Gallery

deserved imprisonment, and the first use he made of his
liberty was to bombard Rupert with appeals to his better
nature. "I am of opinion you should write to your uncle
—you ought to do it!" "He is a King, and in effect a
parent to you." The King, of course, was demanding an
apology for the scene at Newark, and Legge writes again:
"'Tis your uncle you shall submit to, and a King not in
the condition he merits. . . . So may I speak my opinion
as a person that values you above all the world besides."
And another friend, Lord Dorset, wrote: "If my prayers
can prevail, you shall not have the heart to leave us all in
our saddest times . . . resolve, princely Sir, to sink or
swim with the King." This was more than Rupert could
bear, and when the King sent him a carefully worded
apology, for his signature, he tore it up and returned a
blank paper with his name at the bottom, thus indicating
that Charles might have any form of apology he desired.
The King saw it with tears in his eyes.

They met at Oxford, and the King reached up to
Rupert's shoulders and gave him a hearty embrace
according to the custom of those times.[1] He does not
appear to have restored him to his military commands,
but that was a matter of small moment. The war was
nearly finished. Every one knew that Oxford would
presently be besieged for the last time. Charles had
already conceived the fatal idea of taking refuge with the
Scots; he told Rupert of it, and the latter offered him a
last piece of good advice—that he should do nothing of
the kind. But the King was obdurate, and Rupert—it is
significant of his whole-hearted return to the old loyalty

[1] From a marginal note in Rupert's diary it would appear that the
charming Duchess of Richmond, whom Charles had always petted and
Rupert had perhaps loved, was in some way connected with this reconciliation. For the marginal note takes the form of a memo in which
Rupert reminds himself to ask the Duchess for her version of what
occurred. If she supplied any such narrative it is lost.

—at once offered to accompany him. The King said, however, and not without reason, that Rupert's great height would betray the party—and, indeed, there were few men in England more difficult to disguise!

So he stayed behind at Oxford with Maurice, and when Fairfax duly arrived and sat down before the place the Princes found entertainment in the alarums and excursions incidental to every siege. On one of these occasions Rupert was engaged with some hostile cavalry when a Roundhead lieutenant fired a pistol at him at close range, and achieved the unique distinction of wounding him in the shoulder. Rupert's pistol fell from his hand, but as it did so it exploded and killed his opponent's horse. The injury, evidently, was a slight one. About a fortnight later Oxford surrendered (June 1646), and Rupert and Maurice, after some bickering with the Parliament about the renewal of their passports, were allowed to proceed overseas.

After Rupert took ship for Calais he never commanded another cavalry charge on English soil. But he and Cromwell between them made the English cavalry the finest in all Europe and probably in the world. It was the one great military reform of the Civil War. And Rupert's early efforts at Leicester and Edgehill were its beginning and its inspiration.

Maurice, who was in poor health, went to his mother at The Hague; but Rupert, who was fighting fit, made arrangements to join the French army in the impending war with Spain. The French received him cordially. They gave him the rank of Mareschal de Camp—which pleased him—a regiment of foot, and a troop of horse, and the command of all the English volunteers that could be raised in France. The country was, of course, full of Cavalier refugees from England. Rupert threw himself enthusiastically into the congenial task of collecting these old comrades-in-arms and giving them remunerative employment—for many of them were half-starving by now, and the French pay was good. All through the winter of 1646-47 the number of English volunteers increased steadily, and Rupert, as a French Marshal, did his best to find places for them. Goring, however, was refused—and promptly took service with Spain.

By the spring of 1647 all was ready, and there began a curiously futile, theatrical campaign, as devoid of military or historic interest as it was prolific of personal adventure. A more striking contrast with the grim business in England it would be difficult to imagine. Technically it was, in many respects, on a higher plane. The French artillery, for instance, was, as usual, excellent—thoroughly effective and up to date. And the two French Marshals, Rantzau and Gassion, undoubtedly knew something about the art of war. But they did not seem over-anxious to win, and they quarrelled between themselves as fiercely as any English Cavaliers. Moreover, Gassion was bitterly jealous of the new Marshal, young Prince Rupert. Some curious incidents are worth recording—since Warburton found them among Rupert's own papers.

The first occurred when Gassion was attempting to relieve Armentières. He rode forward with Rupert to look at the enemy's positions. While Rupert crouched behind the hedge Gassion went forward to the river-bank, where he was startled to find a boat-load of Spaniards just landing. Pulling his hat over his eyes, he addressed them in their own language, and then, while they hesitated, turned and bolted for the hedge. "Mort Dieu!" he exclaimed, as Rupert pulled him into safety, "ça m'arrive toujours." "Je n'en doute point si vous faites souvent comme ça," answered Rupert drily. The French army fell back on Arras, and there was a fierce dispute when

Gassion ordered Rupert to halt and stand his ground against an overwhelming number of pursuers. Near La Bassée Gassion again invited the Prince to accompany him on a reconnoitring expedition; but they fell into an ambush, and one of Rupert's followers, Sir Robert Holmes, was wounded, and would have been left behind if the Prince had not lifted him upon his own horse and brought him off with great difficulty and danger. He complains that not a Frenchman moved to assist him. And when, a few days later, he again rode out with Gassion, and again they were ambushed, he became angry and suspicious. As they were hastily retreating Gassion made as though to dismount, and Rupert and several other officers immediately sprang to the ground; whereupon (according to Rupert) the French Marshal set spurs to his horse and left them. They fought their way to safety, but Rupert got a slight wound in the head. When Gassion said politely that he regretted this injury Rupert answered—more drily than before—"Et moi aussi!"

But he won the only French success in the campaign by his rapid descent upon La Bassée, which he invested with his cavalry before the reliefs could get in and captured it after a three weeks' siege. Moreover, he had the satisfaction of defeating Goring, who was commanding some of the horse on the other side. Otherwise the only importance of the campaign to Rupert's biographer is that it illustrates his bitter mood in those days.

An opportunity was presently to be offered him to work off some of his spleen. He had returned to Henrietta Maria's court at Saint-Germains, and had been there only two days when Digby arrived! Rupert, who knew that the Queen was determined to prevent a duel if she could, sent Digby a challenge while he was still in bed. We have an account of the affair written by O'Neill, Digby's friend, in the Carte Papers. Digby, who never lacked courage, accepted Rupert's challenge, and quarrelled fiercely with Jermyn, who came early next morning (sent by the Queen) to dissuade him. But in the meantime the young Prince of Wales had ridden out to the trysting place and arrested Rupert and his seconds, among whom was Charles Gerard. This gave time for negotiations, and Digby presently offered the Prince such an explanation and apology that he felt bound to accept it. Moreover—and this is the unexpected fact—the reconciliation was a real one. The two former enemies became firm friends. And when Wilmot, who was also at Saint-Germains, offered some unpleasant remarks on the subject it was Digby, not Rupert, who fought and wounded him. There remained Henry Percy. He had been less prominent than Digby, but equally venomous. Rupert, not to be baulked this time, confronted Percy at a hunting party, made him get down from his horse, and fought him then and there, running him through the side. After which, no doubt, he felt better!

We have done with Rupert the Cavalier. There remains only to glance briefly at the careers of those considerably less interesting personages, Rupert the Admiral and Rupert the Courtier.

Rupert the Admiral began his naval career in extraordinarily difficult circumstances. He hardly knew one end of a ship from the other when he was suddenly called from Saint-Germains in the summer of 1648 to take charge of a part of the English fleet which had just broken away from the Parliament. The defection of the fleet in the first few weeks of the war had been one of the principal causes of the Royalist defeat. Now, when it was too late, the sailors discovered a strong preference for their former allegiance. They mutinied, and the Royalist ships parted company from the rest. But they had no kind of plan: they were, in fact, mere mutineers, seeking to refund themselves by plundering for the pay of which Parliament had cheated them. Cowardly turncoats like Batten (who was one of the leaders) were quite incapable of controlling such men. Hence the appeal to Rupert. He came to the sea-coast and looked them over. Naturally his first idea was to use them to save the King. Charles was at that time a prisoner on the Isle of Wight, planning his unsuccessful attempt to escape. When he asked for help Rupert at once sent a small Dutch vessel, which dutifully hung about in the offing until it was certain that the attempt must have failed. Then the fleet, on the demand of some of the sailors, made an attack on Deal, which was repulsed with loss. In September they were in Helvoetsluys Harbour, with Lord Warwick, the Parliamentary admiral, anchored close beside them, the English ships growling at each other like muzzled dogs, and the Dutch authorities at their wits' ends to prevent a conflict in neutral waters. The Parliamentarians, adepts at propaganda, smuggled smooth-spoken orators on to the Royalist ships, who harangued the men while their officers were ashore. There were one or two mutinies and some free fights on the quay.

Rupert was rigging and refitting his little fleet for a long voyage. He had many adventurous schemes in his head, and never doubted his ability to dodge past Warwick. One day he sent over to H.M.S. *Antelope* with an order for a party of men to assist in rigging his own ship, the admiral. The boat returned with a message that the men would not come. There had been trouble with the *Antelope* before. Rupert himself now went on board, and, seeing the mutineers collected together in a body, he advanced fiercely upon them, sprang at the man who appeared to be their ringleader, and, lifting him by the waist, held him over the ship's side, and swore to drop him if the mutiny did not immediately cease. "The suddenness of this action," says Rupert's own 'diary,' "wrought such a terror upon the rest that they returned forthwith to their duty."

On January 11, 1649, Rupert set sail on a voyage that was to take him to the West Indies and back. It is important to note that in the eyes of every exiled Royalist except himself the voyage was more a financial than a naval venture. The exiled court at Saint-Germains was bankrupt. To the Queen and the Prince of Wales and every one else who knew the facts the chief importance of this little fleet—of seven sail—was that it might be expected to replenish the treasury with prize-money. Rupert, though eager for prizes, took a somewhat different view. It happened that he sailed first to Ireland, and he was in the harbour of Kinsale when the news reached him of the beheading of King Charles I. Dispatches from Ormonde confirmed it. Rupert was horror-stricken. He issued a proclamation to his fleet, announcing his determination to exact retribution. A Parliamentarian who was his prisoner about this time afterwards declared that

> Prince Rupert is not ashamed openly to profess that, provided he may ruin and destroy the English interest, especially the estates of the merchants and mariners of London, he cares not whether he gets a farthing more while he lives than what will maintain himself, his confederates, and his fleet.[1]

In fact, he cared not where the prize money went—he had never cared for money. His object was revenge. And since almost every European state except Portugal had acknowledged the new Parliamentary Government, he was legally entitled to treat their ships as prize. It was a pleasant prospect for his reckless crews, who already possessed something of the mentality of buccaneers.

[1] See Scott, p. 238, for this, and other contemporary authorities.

From Ireland he went to Lisbon and sheltered in the Tagus, while Blake and the Parliamentarian fleet waited for him outside. He had taken prizes on the way, and now sold their cargoes for money. But it was a difficult situation; there were frequent affrays on shore between his men and Blake's; and when foggy weather permitted him to slip out into the Bay of Biscay he found all the European coast so constantly patrolled by the Parliamentary fleet that he presently decided to strike out for Africa and the West Indies. He was in the Mediterranean when he came to this resolution, and had only got to the Canary Islands when he found most of his officers in revolt against the plan. With a tameness which Rupert the Cavalier would hardly have shown he consented to put in at the Azores. But there was no suitable harbour, and a storm sank his admiral, the *Constant Reformation*, with all his treasure, and though he himself got to safety in a small boat, the blow to his pride was such that he was prostrate for many days.[1]

Warburton has reproduced the journal of this voyage, and it is not my intention to follow it in detail. Rupert did not reach the West Indies till the summer of 1652. There he captured a number of English ships and not a few of other nationalities; but he suffered a terrible loss in the wreck of the *Honest Seaman*, which went down in a storm with all hands, including his brother Maurice, who had taken naturally to this sea service and proved an admirable lieutenant. In the spring of 1653 he was back in European waters, and was cordially received by the young King Charles II when he put into a French port with his prizes. The prize money, however, was disappointing, and this, combined with the efforts of his enemies at court, resulted in his first and only quarrel

[1] Warburton, vol. iii, p. 349.

HEAD OF AN OLD MAN
Mezzotint by Prince Rupert
British Museum

with the young King. It was a disappointing end to what had been, after all, a gallant adventure.

But Rupert may have found some compensation in the sudden tenderness of his mother, Queen Elizabeth, whom he had always adored. Elizabeth was mortally offended with Charles Louis, who had just been restored to the Palatinate, but was not allowing her enough money to support even her modest household. In her unhappiness she turned to Rupert—that dark, silent boy whom she had never tried to understand—and found at once more sympathy and affection than Charles Louis could ever give. Rupert also quarrelled with the restored Elector, whose wife seems to have shown too open a partiality for her distinguished brother-in-law. When not engaged in these family bickerings he lived very quietly and on a humble scale at Mainz, where his father had died of a broken heart twenty-five years before. Rupert was made of harder stuff. He does not seem to have repined. On the contrary, he returned to his youthful interest in the arts, learning from a German soldier the art of mezzotint engraving (which he later introduced into England) and inventing the glass bubbles, known as "Rupert's drops," which so delighted his contemporaries, and in these days of Patent Acts and expert advertising might have brought him in a comfortable income. You could hit them quite hard on their sides with a hammer, but the gentlest tap on the tail produced instant dissolution. It was the sort of scientific toy that 'curious' people liked in the seventeenth century.

It is characteristic of Rupert that he waited for eighteen months after the Restoration of Charles II to the throne of England before he came over from Germany and presented himself at the English Court. His reception was cordial in the extreme; Charles II could never quite forget that hero-worship of his youth (though he presently came to think Rupert a little mad). The tall, swarthy Palatine, with his "hawk-like" countenance and Wellington nose, staring disdainfully over the heads of the giggling courtiers, became a familiar feature of the daily life at Whitehall. "Son visage," says de Grammont, "était dur et sec." Pépys (a political opponent) and Evelyn (a friend) observed him reverently, de Grammont with a slight sneer. He lived spaciously, his rooms overlooking the Privy Garden, in a building on the site of the present Montague House.

He may have witnessed from the roof, on September 2, 1666, that advancing line of smoke and flames far away in the east which marked the beginning of the Great Fire of London. He would remember how his Cavalier colleagues, after the battle of Edgehill, had opposed his plan for a dash at Westminster. "If Rupert once gets into the City," old Bristol had urged upon the King, "he will set the place alight, he will massacre the citizens." And the King gave way! Yet it might have won the war. That was twenty-four years ago. Now, in a few short months, this rebellious city had lost twenty times as many lives by the Plague as it could ever have lost by the sword; and to-day it seemed well on the way to lose twenty times as much property by fire. Rupert, the middle-aged courtier, who had recently become almost embarrassingly popular with the City apprentices, may have allowed himself one of his short, dry laughs.

Yet he was no hoary old veteran, living in the past. On the contrary, he was essentially a man of his times. If he lacked most of the graces of a courtier, that was a small point. We have little evidence of his personal activities between his return to England in 1661 and the outbreak of the Dutch War in 1665; but we know that he was occupied with scientific experiments and with the practice of mezzotint engraving. He liked explaining these matters to his friends—as, in later years, at his house in Beech Street, Barbican, he explained them to John Evelyn. He was interested in exploration—though the age of the great discoveries was past—and was one of the patentees of the Royal African Company in 1663. Later he gave his name to Rupert's Land in Canada. He kept himself fit with his falcons and his tennis. About four years after the time we are dealing with (on September 2, 1667) Samuel Pepys was so fortunate as to witness "a great match at tennis" between Rupert and a certain Captain Cook on the one side and "Bab May and the elder Chichly" on the other. The King and the Court came to see it, for these were "the best players at tennis in the nation." Rupert was then forty-eight years of age! When the match was finished—we are not told its result—the King came out and played a 'friendly,' and immediately afterwards had himself weighed. There was something strangely modern about Charles II. Rupert and he were frequent opponents on the tennis-court.

Yet Rupert the Courtier, though physically young for his years, showed no perceptible itch for active service, whether by land or sea. It might even be argued that his character had changed. Never a great talker—though a hard thinker and swift to translate thought into action—he was now apparently relapsing into the character of a grave and peaceful citizen. When he was presently called upon to command the King's fleet against the Dutch all traces of the dashing cavalry leader seemed to have disappeared. He had lost his zest for battle—or, at any rate, for the charge. From being the most reckless of cavalry leaders he had become the most cautious of admirals. A Nelson on land, he was a mere Essex at sea.

So much so that we are driven back upon the old

suspicion that his cavalry tactics were forced upon him by circumstances—by the shortage of small arms among the Royalist horse, and by his quick appreciation of the technical value of 'shock'—rather than by any temperamental preference for such methods. His famous forays may be explained in the same way. But though the suspicion is there, it will surely be discarded by all who have tried to understand the character of Rupert the Cavalier. It is born of his later career, when he spent so much of his time at sea. He was never handy with ships. Since he first started out with the Royalist fleet he had handled this new and unfamiliar weapon in a manner a little too gingerly to be inspiring. It was the misfortune of his later years that he never again commanded a band of mounted men.

The Dutch Wars may be briefly touched upon. In January 1665 Rupert was seriously ill. He himself lost hope, and Pepys, commenting ill-naturedly upon his illness, remarks that "courage is not what men take it to be, a contempt of death," since no less a person than Prince Rupert was "chagrined the other day when he thought he should die, having no more mind to it than another man." But now that he is assured of recovery, adds the diarist, "he is as merry and swears and laughs and curses, and do all the things of a man in health, as ever he did in his life." [1] Which is only another version of a well-known jingle about the devil being sick, which applies equally to soldiers, sailors, and civilians.

The patient recovered, but another admiral took the fleet to sea, and Rupert was indignant. In April 1666 he was given the joint command with Monk—his old regimental commander at that brisk little affair on the hornwork at Breda thirty years before. Their new association was not an unmixed success. While Rupert

[1] *Diary*, January 15, 1665.

was looking for the French the Dutch attacked Monk, and Rupert, with the wind against him, only just got back in time to prevent a *débâcle*. He was blamed for this in some quarters, but when he reached London he turned the tables on the Admiralty with a long list of complaints about delayed supplies and so forth. From Pepys's *Diary* we get a glimpse of Rupert at a council meeting, glowering in his chair, with the King sitting near him, while the Clerk of the Acts nervously explains the inevitable delays. There was no love lost between them.

The head wound which Rupert had received in France began to give trouble, and kept him off the active list for some time. But on the outbreak of the Third Dutch War the Duke of York, who had proved himself a competent commander, was dismissed from the fleet, under the terms of the Test Act (he being an avowed Roman Catholic), and Rupert was appointed in his place. There was a howl of delight from the London mob, and loud cheers for the "Protestant Prince." No one remembered the "Prince Robber" of 1642! Rupert found a worthy opponent in the Dutch admiral, de Ruyter, and an unworthy ally in the Frenchman d'Estrées. He knew d'Estrées of old, and in two indecisive engagements off the Schooneveldt he carefully placed the French in the centre of the battle-line, where they were compelled to fight. At the Texel, however, the decisive engagement of the year, d'Estrées managed to slip away, and Rupert lost his chance of victory. We can see him raging up and down the deck, hurling curses at the Frenchmen, whom he had recently come to hate. He also blamed the gallant Spragge, who had engaged in a duel with Tromp, instead of keeping his place in the line—and had been killed for his pains. Spragge had commanded the English left wing, and Rupert was beginning to hate these

247

impetuous commanders who carried their squadrons away in pursuit without regard to the fate of the main body! The Texel was Rupert's last battle at sea.

Rupert the Courtier, though never a courtier in the strict sense of the word, was a man accustomed to courts, and neither better nor worse in his morals than the average frequenter of them. He lived and died a bachelor; but he never thought himself dedicated to bachelordom. On the contrary, he was well aware that he was, in the modern slang, a very eligible *parti*, and he more than once seriously contemplated matrimony. In 1653 rumour linked his name with that of his cousin Mary, the Princess Royal (Charles I's daughter), Rupert being then at the marriageable age of thirty-four—but an exile—and the young Princess already a widow, for she had been married to the late Prince of Orange. Nothing came of it. In 1664, when Rupert was already forty-five, he himself made proposals for a royal lady of France,[1] but this royal lady, whoever she was, objected that he had been "too long and too deeply attached to a certain Duchess."

The reference was obviously to the beautiful "Butterfly," but there is no evidence that Rupert ever made serious love to his friend Richmond's wife. When the charming Duchess married, in 1664, the French lady's objections should, of course, have been removed. But she evidently did not want Rupert, for nothing more was heard of his proposals. Then he met Francesca Bard, and never thought of marriage again. There seems to have been no legal union, but there was a child, young Dudley Rupert, as he was commonly called. He was killed in 1686 at the siege of Buda, serving with the Imperialists against the Turks, and desperately assailing the walls in his father's old reckless style, though not,

[1] *Bromley Letters* (March 22, 1664), p. 252.

unfortunately, with his father's strange immunity from hostile bullets. He was only nineteen at the time, and a very popular and promising young soldier.[1]

Rupert, it is safe to say, was but a lukewarm supporter of the Restoration drama. He would attend the play-house occasionally—almost every one did that—but we cannot imagine that he was moved to laughter or tears by a stage play, nor picture him leading the applause. Yet in 1668, only four years after his meeting with Francesca, he suddenly fell a victim to the charms of the beautiful actress Mrs Hughes. She was an actress of real distinction, and as popular in her way as Nell Gwynn. But Rupert was now a man of nearly fifty, and the affair caused considerable merriment at Court.

It was the last thing anyone had expected him to do. They had thought that he was fully occupied with his experiments in science and mathematics. He had no appearance of a ladies' man, no taste for the green-room. "He was polite," says de Grammont, "even to excess, unseasonably; but haughty and even brutal, when he ought to have been gentle and courteous: he was tall and his manners were ungracious: he had a dry, hard-favoured visage, and a stern look, even when he wished to please; but when he was out of humour he was the true picture of reproof." The Frenchman goes on to describe this strange love affair. The Court was at Tunbridge Wells:

> The Queen had sent for the players, either that there might be no intermission in the diversions of the place, or, perhaps, to retort upon Miss Stewart, by the presence of Nell Gwyn, part of the uneasiness she felt from hers. Prince Rupert found charms in the person of another player called Hughes, who brought down and greatly subdued his natural fierceness.

[1] Francesca's subsequent adventures as a Jacobite exile after 1688 have been carefully traced by Miss Eva Scott.

From this time, adieu alembics, crucibles, furnaces, and all the black furniture of the forges: a complete farewell to all mathematical instruments and chemical speculations: sweet powder and essences were now the only ingredients that occupied any share of his attention. The impertinent gipsy chose to be attacked in form; and proudly refusing money, that, in the end, she might sell her favours at a dearer rate, she caused the poor prince to act a part so unnatural that he no longer appeared like the same person. The King was greatly pleased with this event, for which great rejoicings were made at Tunbridge; but nobody was bold enough to make it the subject of satire, though the same constraint was not observed with other ridiculous personages.

We may reject de Grammont's sneers. It was a thing that might have happened to any man. The chief difference was that in Rupert's case no one laughed. He adored the pretty actress. She bore him a daughter, who was named Ruperta, and upon whom he lavished his love and his care, for the girl had much of her mother's charm. He was anxious that she should be given in marriage to Charles II's natural son by Nell Gwynn; but this apparently appropriate match was never arranged, and Ruperta eventually married a soldier, General Howe, a person of no special distinction, and lived with him very happily.

The concluding years of Rupert's life were passed in peace and contentment, mostly at Windsor. He shared the general prosperity of King Charles's golden reign, and appreciated as well as any man the all-round improvement in the standard of living—in food, and in drink, and especially in dress and manners. But for a brief friendship with that brilliant but disreputable Whig Lord Shaftesbury, he kept clear of politics: indeed, such political instincts as he possessed were entirely Tory. His real interests—his only interests in peace-time— were in science and the arts. He lived quietly but richly, moving towards the end with stately, dignified step—a strange contrast with his tempestuous earlier career. He had a "great black dog" (Boy's successor) which was his constant companion.

Unfortunately Rupert's health was not good. He suffered from pains in the head, a result of the old wound, and also from "a malady of the leg," which seems to have been the result of another injury. His last illness came upon him suddenly, in November 1682, when he was at his London residence in Spring Gardens. He caught a fever on top of his other troubles; pleurisy supervened; and he was dead in four or five days. The English people, with whom he had so often been at cross-purposes, mourned him unfeignedly. And his cousin, the King, who had admired him in his youth but had never quite understood him, gave orders that he should be buried in the Chapel of Henry VII at Westminster Abbey. So it was done. It was an honour that Rupert had well and truly earned.

INDEX